The Freshwater Angler™

THE BIG BOOK OF
BASS

Steve Hauge

Creative Publishing
international

www.creativepub.com

CONTENTS

Creative Publishing
international

Copyright © 2008
Creative Publishing international, Inc.
400 First Avenue North, Suite 300
Minneapolis, MN 55401
1-800-328-3895
www.creativepub.com
All rights reserved

President/CEO: Ken Fund
VP for Sales & Marketing: Kevin Hamric
Publisher: Bryan Trandem

Acquisitions Editor: Barbara Harold
Editor: Jennifer Gehlhar
Authors: Steve Hauge, Jim Moynagh, Don Oster, Dick Sternberg
Production Managers: Laura Hokkanen, Linda Halls
Creative Director: Michele Lanci-Altomare
Senior Design Managers: Jon Simpson, Brad Springer
Design Manager: James Kegley
Cover Design: Greg Nettles
Book Design: Emily Brackett
Page Layout: Greg Nettles

Printed in Singapore
10 9 8 7 6 5 4 3 2

Library of Congress Cataloging-in-Publication Data

Hauge, Steven.
  The big book of bass : strategies for catching largemouth and smallmouth / Steve Hauge.
    p. cm. -- (Freshwater angler series)
  Includes index.
  Summary: "Comprehensive strategies for catching both largemouth bass and smallmouth bass. Also discusses habitat and fish behavior. Detailed how-to photography shows how to put the information into practice.
Index"--Provided by publisher.
  ISBN-13: 978-1-58923-407-9 (soft cover)
  ISBN-10: 1-58923-407-3 (soft cover)
  1. Bass fishing. I. Title. II. Series.

SH681.H34 2008
799.17'73--dc22
                 2008007058

INTRODUCTION

American anglers pursue largemouth and smallmouth bass more than any other freshwater gamefish. The main reason: bass fishing is exciting. Once you experience the head-shaking leap of a largemouth or bulldogging run of a smallmouth, chances are you will come back for more.

One measure of the bass' appeal is the huge number of anglers that belong to tournament bass-fishing organizations, such as the Bass Anglers Sportsman Society and FLW outdoors.

Most of these fishermen can find bass within a short drive from home. Both species are found in waters from central Canada to Mexico. They live in muddy rivers and crystal-clear lakes, tiny golf courses, ponds and 100-mile-long reservoirs, knee-deep sloughs, and even brackish coastal estuaries alongside saltwater fish.

The purpose of *The Big Book of Bass* is to make you a better bass fisherman. It leads you through the world of the largemouth and smallmouth bass fishing with clear, concise text and spectacular color photographs.

The first requirement for catching bass is understanding the fish themselves. This book explains every important aspect of largemouth and smallmouth behavior based on input from prominent bass anglers and biologists throughout the country. The first section will focus on the largemouth bass, followed by an equally informative section on the smallmouth bass. You will discover how bass detect food, what they eat, when they are likely to feed, and how to use this knowledge to catch fish.

In most waters, only a small fraction of the acreage contains bass. To catch bass consistently, you must know where to look at different times of the day and year and under different weather conditions. The equipment sections will help you select everything from boats and motors to rods and reels. Not everyone needs a high-powered bass boat; sometimes a small, portable boat or float tube works better. But a serious bass fisherman should own a locator and know how to use it in conjunction with a mapping GPS unit. We'll show you how to do that.

Many bass fishermen know how to catch bass in their favorite lake when conditions are right. But if the weather changes or if they try a different lake, they fail to make the necessary adjustments. The last section of the book, *Advanced Bass Fishing*, will teach you how to use numerous proven techniques for catching largemouth and smallmouth bass, plus it includes little-known secrets used by the country's bass experts.

Whether you do most of your fishing in tiny farm ponds or sprawling reservoirs, whether you are a beginner or a veteran, this book is sure to improve your bass-fishing skills.

LARGEMOUTH BASS

Chapter 1

THE LARGEMOUTH BASS

Renowned for its explosive strikes and spectacular leaps, the largemouth bass is a favorite among millions of freshwater fishermen.

Largemouth were originally found only east of the Mississippi River and south of the Great Lakes. But as bass fishing grew in popularity, so did stocking programs in many states. Largemouth are now caught in waters throughout the continental United States and Hawaii, in addition to Canada and most of Mexico. Bass have been introduced in Europe, Asia, Africa, and South America.

The largemouth bass is the largest member of a group of closely related fishes called black bass. Others include the smallmouth, spotted, redeye, Suwannee, and Guadalupe. The largemouth is distinguished from all of these species by a jaw that extends beyond the eye. All black bass belong to the sunfish family, but differ from sunfish because of their longer bodies.

Biologists have identified two subspecies of largemouth bass: the Florida largemouth and the northern largemouth. Originally, Florida bass lived only in Florida waters. Stocking efforts have expanded their range to include much of the South, particularly Texas and California.

Although they look alike, the Florida largemouth grows considerably larger than the northern subspecies. A trophy Florida bass weighs from 10 to 20 pounds (4.5 to 9 kg), compared to 6 to 8 pounds (2.7 to 3.6 kg) for a northern largemouth bass.

Some biologists believe that the world record largemouth bass was a cross between the northern and Florida subspecies. The 22-pound, 4-ounce (10 kg) largemouth was caught in June, 1932, at Montgomery Lake in Georgia. This lake is one of many waters in Georgia and Alabama where largemouth crosses have been found.

LARGEMOUTH BIOLOGY

Largemouth bass vary in color, depending upon the type of water. Bass from murky waters are pale, while those from clear waters are darker. Largemouth range from deep green to pale olive across the back, with bellies that are a shade of white or yellow. All bass have a black lateral band that runs from the head to tail. The band becomes more distinct when a fish is exposed to sunlight, but may disappear when a largemouth is in deep or murky water.

SENSES. Largemouth bass have the five major senses common to most animals: hearing, sight, smell, taste, and touch. They have another sense, the lateral line, which is a series of sensitive nerve endings that extends from just behind the gill to the tail on each side of the fish.

The lateral line can pick up underwater vibrations as subtle as a swimming baitfish. In one experiment, researchers placed small cups over the eyes of several bass, then dropped minnows into a tank with them. Eventually the largemouth ate each minnow, using their lateral lines to locate the baitfish. This experiment suggests that bass can detect a lure in the murkiest water.

Largemouth bass do hear with internal ears located within the skull. They may be attracted by the ticking or rattling of some artificial lures. But when they hear loud, unfamiliar sounds, they usually swim to deeper water or cover. Many bass fishermen carpet the bottoms of their boats to reduce noise that spook the fish.

Bass can see in all directions, except directly below or behind. In clear water, they can see 30 feet (9 m) or more. But in most bass waters, visibility is limited to 5 to 10 feet (1.5 to 3 m). Largemouth bass can also see objects that are above water. To avoid spooking fish, many fishermen wear neutral-colored clothing that blends with the background.

Bass in shallow water can detect colors, especially red. In one study, red and white lures caught three times as many largemouth as any other color. This may explain why many top bass pros use red hooks on many of their lures. Color selection is less important in deep water because most colors appear as shades of gray.

Most experts are reluctant to say that one color is always better than another. The best colors vary, depending on light conditions and water color. Most believe that a lure's action is more important than its color.

The eye of a largemouth absorbs more light than the human eye does, enabling the fish to see its food in dim light or darkness. Bass will feed at any time of the day or night, but are less inclined to leave cover and search for food under bright conditions. Like most fish, they prefer shade. They find better ambush camouflage in shady spots or under lowlight conditions.

Largemouth smell through nostrils, or nares, on the snout. The nares are short passageways through which water is drawn and expelled without entering the throat. Like most fish, bass can detect minute amounts of scent in the water. However, bass rely on scent less than other species such as catfish, salmon, or trout.

Bass use their sense of touch to determine whether to reject or swallow an object. They will usually hold on to a soft-bodied, artificial worm longer than a metal lure.

Sense of taste is not as important to largemouth bass as it is to some fish species, because bass have few taste cells in their mouths.

FEEDING. Newly hatched largemouth feed heavily on tiny crustaceans and other zooplankton until the bass reach 2 inches (5 cm) in length. Young largemouth eat insects and small fish, including smaller bass. Adult largemouth prey mostly on fish, but crayfish, frogs, and insects are important foods in some waters.

Wherever they live, bass rank high in the aquatic food chain. A bass 10 inches (25 cm) or longer has few enemies and will eat almost anything it can swallow. Because of its large mouth and flexible stomach, a bass can eat prey nearly half its own length.

Largemouth bass inhale small foods. The bass opens its mouth quickly to suck in water and the food. It then forces the water out the gills while it either swallows or rejects the object. Bass can expel food as quickly as they inhale it, so anglers must set the hook immediately when using small lures or baits.

Bass usually grab large prey, then turn the food to swallow it headfirst. This explains why anglers who use large golden shiners, frogs, or salamanders wait a minute or two before setting the hook.

As the water warms, the metabolism of bass increases and they feed more often. Largemouth seldom eat at water temperatures below 50°F (10°C). From 50 to 68°F (10 to 20°C), feeding increases and from 68 to 80°F (20°C to 27°C), they feed heavily. However, at temperatures above 80°F, feeding declines.

Bass foods reflect a varied diet. Adult largemouth feed heavily on crayfish where they are available. In most waters, they feed mainly on fish, including gizzard and threadfin shad, golden shiners, young sunfish, and small rough fish. Bass also eat frogs, large insects, shrimp, salamanders, and even small mammals and ducklings.

No one is certain what causes bass to strike artificial lures or bait. Experts point to hunger as the main reason. However, many of these same experts believe that reflex, aggressiveness, curiosity, and competitiveness may play a part.

Reflex, or a sudden instinctive reaction, may explain why a bass with a full stomach strikes an artificial lure the instant it hits the water. The fish has little time to judge what it is grabbing, yet some cue triggers it to strike.

Male bass display aggressiveness when they attack lures or chase other fish that invade their nest sites. Although this behavior is common during nesting season, bass are not as aggressive at other times of the year.

Curiosity may be the reason that bass rush up to inspect new objects or sounds. However, it is doubtful they take food solely out of curiosity. Competitiveness probably explains why fishermen occasionally catch two bass on the same lure at the same time. Often several bass race to devour a single food item, particularly in waters where food is in short supply.

Bass growth is faster in southern waters than in northern waters, primarily because the growing season is longer. For example, in four years, the average Louisiana largemouth (top) reaches about 18 inches (46 cm); an Illinois bass (middle) is about 13 inches (33 cm), while a Wisconsin bass (bottom) averages about 11 inches (28 cm).

GROWTH. The best trophy bass waters are those where the fish grow rapidly as a result of proper temperatures and abundant food. Largemouth seldom reach large sizes in waters where they have become too abundant.

The amount bass grow in a year depends on the length of their growing season or the number of days suitable for growth. The growing season in the South may last twice as long as it does in the North. Largemouth gain weight most quickly in water from 75 to 80°F (24 to 27°C). They do not grow in water colder than 50°F (10°C).

Although bass in the South grow and mature faster, they rarely live as long as largemouth in colder northern lakes. In southern waters, bass occasionally reach 10 years of age; in northern waters, bass may live as long as 15 years.

Female bass live longer than males, so they are more apt to reach a trophy size. In one study, 30 percent of the females were 5 years or older, while only 9 percent of the male bass were 5 years or more.

SPAWNING BEHAVIOR

In spring, when inshore waters reach about 60°F (16°C), largemouth bass swim onto spawning grounds in shallow bays, backwaters, channels, and other areas protected from prevailing winds. Spawning grounds usually have firm bottoms of sand, gravel, mud, or rock. Bass seldom nest on a thick layer of silt. Some spawning areas are in open water; others have sparse weeds, boulders, or logs.

Male bass may spend several days selecting their nest sites. The beds are usually in 1 to 4 feet (0.3 to 1.2 m) of water, but may be deeper in clear water. Most largemouth nest in pockets in bulrushes, hydrilla, or other weeds. Bass in open areas often select a site on the sunny side of a submerged log or large rock. The males seldom nest where they can see another nesting male. For this reason, beds are generally at least 30 feet (9 m) apart, but may be closer if weeds, boulders, sunken logs, or stumps prevent the males from seeing each other.

Largemouth spawn when the water reaches 63 to 68°F (17 to 20°C) and temperatures remain within this range for several days. Cold fronts may cause water temperatures to drop, which interrupts and delays spawning.

A female bass lays from 2,000 to 7,000 eggs per pound (0.5 kg) of body weight. She may deposit all of her eggs in one nest or drop them at several different sites before leaving the spawning grounds. After spawning, the female recuperates in deep water, where she does not eat (or feeds very minimally) for two to three weeks.

Alone on the nest, the male hovers above the eggs, slowly fanning them to keep off silt and debris. He does not eat while guarding the eggs, but will attack other fish that swim near the nest. The male will not attack slow-moving objects, such as a crayfish or even a plastic worm. Instead, he gently picks up the object and drops it outside the nest.

Sunfish often prey on bass eggs or newly hatched fry. In waters with large sunfish populations, the panfish can seriously hamper bass reproduction. A school of sunfish surrounds a nest and while the male chases some away, others invade the nest and devour the eggs or fry.

Bass eggs hatch in only two days at 72°F (22°C), but take five days at 67°F (19°C). Cold weather following spawning will delay hatching. If the shallows drop to 50°F (10°C), the fry will not emerge for 13 days. At lower temperatures, the eggs fail to develop. A severe cold front sometimes causes males to abandon the nest, resulting in a complete loss of eggs or fry. From 2,000 to 12,000 eggs hatch from the typical nest. Of these, only five to ten are likely to survive to reach 10 inches (25 cm) in length.

Preparing the nest, the male largemouth shakes its head and tail to sweep away bottom debris. The typical nest is a saucer-shaped depression about 2 to 3 feet (0.6 to 0.9 m) in diameter, or twice the length of the male.

Spawning occurs as the male and female move over the nest with their vents close together. The male bumps and nips the female, stimulating her to deposit the eggs. Then the male covers the eggs with his sperm, or milt.

Nest-guarding is left to the male bass. After hatching, the tiny fry lie in the nest for eight to ten days. Once they are able to swim, the fry remain in a compact school, cowering beneath weeds or other overhead cover. As the fry grow larger, they spread over a wider area, but the male still protects them. The male abandons the fry when they reach about 1 inch (2.5 cm) in length. After that, he may eat any fry he encounters.

HABITAT REQUIREMENTS

Overhead cover in shallow water provides shade and cooler temperatures, allowing bass to remain all summer. Weedy edges provide points of ambush where bass can dart out to capture smaller fish.

Largemouth bass have certain habitat requirements that are important to their survival.

TEMPERATURE. Many studies of bass behavior have concluded that largemouth prefer temperatures of 77 to 86°F (25 to 30°C). But fishermen know that bass often bite better in water at lower temperatures, even when water in their preferred temperature range is available. This is explained by the fact that bass will abandon an area with ideal temperature to escape bright sunlight or to find food or cover. Bass cannot survive at temperatures above 98°F (37°C).

OXYGEN. Bass require more oxygen than most other gamefish. All lakes have sufficient oxygen in the shallows. But in fertile lakes, those with a high level of nutrients, the depths may lack oxygen. Fertile lakes produce large amounts of plankton. These tiny plants and animals eventually die and sink to bottom where they decompose. The decomposition process consumes huge amounts of oxygen, making the depths unsuitable for fish. Heavy algae blooms are a symptom of high water fertility.

In the North, fertile lakes may winter-kill. Thick ice and snow cover block out sunlight, so plants can no longer produce oxygen. Decomposition continues, drawing all oxygen from even the shallowest water. Bass are one of the first to die in winter-kill lakes.

In deep, clear waters such as canyon reservoirs and strip pits, water fertility is usually low. The water contains ample oxygen from top to bottom, so bass can move wherever they want.

FEATURES. A feature is any difference in the underwater world, including cover, structure, and less obvious differences like current or shadows. Features are more important to bass than to most other gamefish.

Largemouth bass require cover from the moment they hatch. Bass fry crowd into dense weedbeds to escape predatory fish. Later in their lives, bass use weeds, rocks, flooded timber and brush, sunken logs, and other objects for shade, shelter, and ambush points.

Structure is the geologic makeup of the bottom. It may be a reef, point, ledge, or any other place where the depth changes. It can also be a rock patch or any other place where the bottom material changes from one type to another. Largemouth use structure as a reference point to guide their daily movements. They also locate near structure simply because it is unique from the rest of the area.

In general, after the spawn fish will use structure leading toward deeper water. Look for fish in the 4- to 10- foot-range right after spawn, 10 to 20 feet in early summer and most summer largemouth structure is deeper than 15 feet. These seasonal movements, along with changing daily conditions may move the fish to different locations on a given piece of structure.

HOW BASS RELATE TO FEATURES IN A CONTROLLED LOCATION EXPERIMENT

In a controlled location experiment, researchers discovered that bass will relate to anything different in their surroundings. This same thing happens in nature where bass will always hold onto anything that is different than their surroundings. In some cases the difference can be very subtle such as a shade line, a dark spot a sand area, or a single twig in the water.

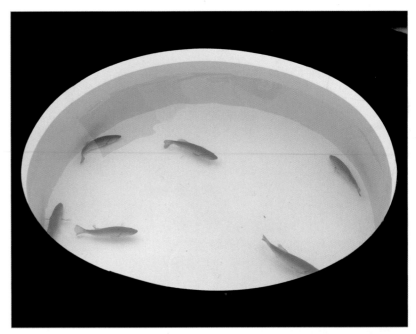

A plain white tank lacks features. Lighting is evenly distributed and sounds carefully controlled. These 2-pound (0.9 kg) bass swim about aimlessly.

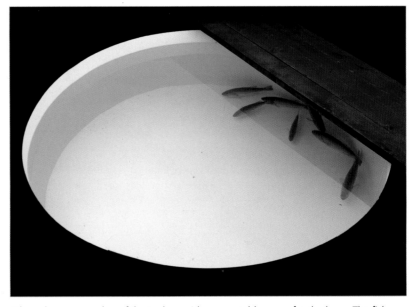

A board over one edge of the tank provides acceptable cover for the bass. The fish station themselves in the shade under the board.

Rocks piled in one area of the tank attract the bass immediately. They form a closely packed school along the edge of the rock pile.

A black stripe painted on the wall provides something to which bass can relate. They hover near the stripe, even though it offers no cover.

TYPICAL BASS WATERS

Largemouth bass can tolerate a wider range of water clarity, fertility, and temperature than any other gamefish. They thrive in waters ranging from desert reservoirs to northern glacial lakes. You're likely to find largemouth in any of the following waters:

RESERVOIRS. Most man-made lakes are created to control downstream flooding or to provide a reliable source of water for municipalities, farming, power generation, and river navigation. As a rule, shallow, warm reservoirs with plenty of submerged trees, brush, and aquatic plants for cover offer better fishing than deep, cold reservoirs with little cover. Because they were created for human needs, the water levels often fluctuate greatly throughout the year. These fluctuations determine where the fish will be located and sometimes determine at what times of the day they will bite, which is the case in reservoirs that pull water daily for power generation.

PONDS AND PITS. Millions of farm ponds have been stocked with largemouth bass, usually in combination with sunfish. Landowners often obtain the fish from state or federal conservation agencies. Bass and sunfish are also planted in pits and quarries, once sand-gravel or mining operations cease and the basins fill with water. Many pits and ponds are full of aquatic life and baitfish that provide and abundance of food for bass, which often leads to these type of waters producing very large bass in relation to their size.

NATURAL LAKES. Warm, shallow, weedy lakes usually hold more largemouth than deep, cold, clear lakes with little vegetation. However, shallow, weedy bays of deep, cold lakes may hold good largemouth bass populations. Natural lakes are commonplace in the northern half of the United States and are where most largemouth are found.

RIVERS, STREAMS, AND ESTUARIES. Slow-moving rivers and streams with weeds, brush, or fallen trees for cover often have excellent largemouth populations. Bass also thrive in the brackish water of estuaries, where fresh water from rivers mixes with salt water. Current is the main factor that affects largemouth location on these bodies of water. Knowing how and when the fish related to current is the key to locating bass.

Flatland reservoirs (shown) produce bigger and more largemouth bass than other reservoir types. Sometimes called flowages in the North, these waters are normally shallow and fertile with low to moderate clarity. Most have short creek arms, abundant weeds and flooded timber, and sand or mud bottoms.

Farm ponds (shown) are shallow and fertile. They have mud or clay bottoms and some submerged weeds. Brush piles are occasionally added to provide cover for bass and other gamefish. Runoff keeps most ponds murky.

Canyon reservoirs, found mainly in the West, are formed by damming large river gorges. Most are very deep and clear with steep walls, sharp-breaking points, and long creek arms. Bottoms consist of rock or sand with few plants. Creek arms may have some timber and brush.

Cove reservoirs, also called hill-land, highland, or mountain reservoirs, are intermediate in depth, fertility, and clarity between canyon and flatland types. Creek arms are also intermediate in length. Most have some weeds and timber with sand, rock, or clay bottoms.

Strip pits usually have sheer walls, jagged bottoms, sharp-breaking points, and rock slides. Most have rock or sand bottoms, with clear, infertile water. Strip pits are generally deep with few weeds.

Eutrophic lakes have shallow, fertile water of low to medium clarity. There are extensive stands of submerged and emergent weeds, commonly extending into mid-lake. The bottom is mainly mud, often with patches of sand or gravel. In the North, these lakes may winter-kill.

Mesotrophic lakes have moderate depth, fertility, and clarity. The shallows are often rimmed with emergent weeds and submerged weeds and may grow to depths of 25 feet (7.6 m). The bottom, which usually consists of sand, gravel, rock, and muck, normally has sandy humps or rocky reefs.

Big rivers with weedy backwaters, cuts, or bays off the main channel make ideal bass water. Few largemouth are found in the main channel itself because of the swift current.

Streams with warm water and deep pools make good bass habitat, particularly when there is an abundance of cover such as weeds and submerged logs, brush, or boulders.

Estuaries, with connecting marshes and canals and an abundance of weeds and water-dwelling trees, are well-suited to large-mouth. Fish location is greatly affected by the tides.

Chapter 2

WHERE TO FIND LARGEMOUTH BASS

To catch largemouth bass you must have a solid understanding of where they are located on a particular body of water. Largemouth not only move with their seasonal migrations throughout the year, but may also move locations on a daily basis. Where they move depends on a number of factors that we will try to give you a better understanding of in this chapter. Using this knowledge will keep you in areas that largemouth are most likely to be and will increase your chances of success.

A prominent bass expert once estimated that "80 percent of the challenge in bass fishing is finding the fish." Locating bass may be difficult because seasonal movement patterns differ in almost every body of water. Temperature, oxygen level, food supply, and even the angle of the sun's rays have an effect on bass location in each season.

It is also said that "80 percent of the fish on a given body of water are located in only twenty percent of the lake." Meaning that in most lakes, no matter what their size, the majority of fish are located in a small portion. Knowing this will allow you to eliminate large sections of a body of water, making them much more manageable.

BASS MOVEMENTS THROUGH THE SEASONS

SPRING. Springtime movements of bass center around spawning. Weeks before spawning begins, bass start moving from deep water toward shallows that warm quickly. Males move in first. During this pre-spawn period, look for bass near their spawning grounds, but in slightly deeper water. On a warm day, bass will move into the spawning area, even though spawning is weeks away. They retreat to deeper water when the weather cools. They may repeat this pattern often during the pre-spawn period.

Bass begin to feed when the water temperature edges above 50°F (10°C), but catching them is difficult until the water reaches about 55°F (13°C). Then they begin a feeding binge that is unequaled at any other time of the year. Anglers catch bass in the shallows throughout the day. Baitfish are scarce, so bass spend most of their time cruising shallow water in search of food. And because the sun is at a low angle, light penetration does not force them into deeper water.

Spawning begins when the water reaches the mid-60s (about 18°C). After depositing their eggs, the females abandon the nests. They feed very little for the next two to three weeks while they recover from spawning. Males guarding their beds will strike lures that come too close.

Water temperatures in the low 70s (about 22°C) signal the beginning of the post-spawn period and the resumption of good fishing. Females have recovered and males have completed their nest-guarding duties. Both feed heavily in the shallows but spend most of the day in deeper water.

Springtime movements of bass extend from February to April in southern waters. But in the North, they are compressed into just a few weeks, usually from May to early June.

SUMMER. As summer progresses, strong sunlight or warm surface temperatures may force bass out of shallow water. Bass form loose schools along deep structure and cover during midday, but feed in the shallows in morning and evening. Food is easy to find, so feeding periods tend to be short. Some largemouth stay in the shallows all day if the cover is dense enough or the water murky enough to block out sunlight.

Water temperature above 80°F (27°C) will usually push bass deeper, regardless of water clarity. But in fertile lakes, low oxygen levels in the depths prevent bass from going deeper. They must remain in warm, shallow water, where they become listless and difficult to catch.

FALL AND WINTER. When the water begins to cool in fall, bass in deep water return to the shallows. Early fall is much like the pre-spawn period. In most waters, the summer's predation has reduced their food supply, so bass roam the shallows looking for a meal. And with the sun once again lower in the sky, they can stay shallow all day. But many anglers have quit fishing for the season by the time bass begin their fall feeding binge.

As the surface water continues to cool, it eventually reaches the same temperature as water in the depths. This starts the fall turnover. With water at the same temperature and density throughout, wind circulates the lake from top to bottom. Bass may be almost anywhere, so finding them is difficult. In most waters, fall turnover lasts from one to two weeks.

In late fall, the surface water becomes colder than water in the depths. Bass prefer the warmer water, so they move to deep areas of the lake. They remain in these deepwater haunts through winter, whether or not the lake freezes over.

Temperatures below 50°F (10°C) make bass sluggish and difficult to catch. But a few days of warm, sunny weather may draw them into the shallows. Fishermen aware of this late season movement can enjoy some of the year's best fishing, especially for big bass. However, if water temperatures fall below 40°F (4°C), bass are almost impossible to catch.

Largemouth bass not only move throughout the season, but often on a daily basis depending on conditions.

Ice fishermen sometimes enjoy a short flurry of action just after freeze-up, but very few largemouth are taken during the rest of winter.

RESERVOIRS & NATURAL LAKES

The majority of largemouth bass fishing takes place on reservoirs and natural lakes throughout their range. The best of these offer bass everything they need to feel comfortable in their environment. These include, cover in the form of vegetation or woody cover, spawning areas, access to deep water, and an adequate food supply. The more of these a particular body of water has the better the odds are that it has a strong largemouth bass population. Bass will relocate seasonally through the reservoir or lake based on the factors discussed in this section.

Spring

RESERVOIRS. Creek arms, or coves, provide the best spawning habitat in most reservoirs. Bass prefer wide, shallow coves with slightly murky water to those that are deep and clear. Good spawning coves usually have some inflowing water. Adult bass return to traditional spawning areas year after year. If you can find a good cove, chances are that bass will be there the next year.

Bass wintering in the main river channel of a reservoir may have to swim many miles to find a shallow creek arm suitable for spawning. However, some bass spawn in shallow bays, on mid-lake humps, and along brushy shorelines within the main body of the reservoir. These fish do not move as far.

Prior to spawning, bass hang just outside the cove or along the creek channel within the cove. On a warm day, they move into flooded brush or timber on flats adjacent to the creek channel.

Bass spawn in the shallowest part of the cove, usually among timber or brush. After spawning, they spend most of their time along the creek channel or near shoreline points before moving back to the main body of the reservoir. How soon they leave a cove after spawning depends on the depth. Some deep coves hold bass through the summer.

NATURAL LAKES. Springtime movements in natural lakes are generally not as dramatic as those in reservoirs. In a small lake, bass frequently spawn in shallow water bordering their deep wintering sites. But in a large lake, they may have to cross an expanse of open water to find a protected bay or a dead-end channel. In lakes that lack sheltered areas, bass will spawn in shoreline weeds.

Prior to spawning, bass hold on breaks adjacent to shoreline vegetation or near the mouths of sheltered bays or channels.

After spawning, bass return to the pre-spawn areas for one to two weeks before scattering to mid-depth structure throughout the lake.

SPRING LOCATIONS IN RESERVOIRS

 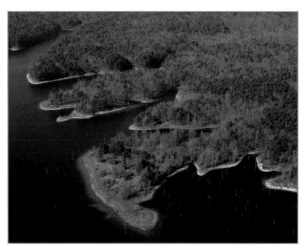

Back ends of coves (shown) have the shallowest, warmest water. Bass concentrate along the edge of the creek channel, then spawn in shoreline cover such as brush, timber, or weeds.

Fingers projecting off the main cove (shown), such as secondary creek arms or shallow bays, draw spawning bass. Fingers warm earlier than other parts of the cove; check them first for spawning activity.

Shoreline breaks within the main body of the reservoir hold pre-spawn bass. Flooded timber extending far out from shore indicates a wide shoal that warms quickly, attracting many spawners.

Sheltered bays warm faster than open areas. They provide good spawning habitat, especially in canyon reservoirs. The best bays are shallow and contain some cover such as flooded brush.

Shallow bays (shown) warm faster than the rest of the lake. Mud-bottomed bays warm first because the dark bottom absorbs the sun's rays.

Spawning areas for largemouth bass in natural lakes include shallow black-bottom bays, protected shorelines such as the lee side of a point, along the lee side of an island, weedy flats along protected shores, and channels connecting the main body of the lake with sheltered bays.

Dead-end channels are sheltered from wind. The best channels are lined with emergent vegetation and are shallower than 5 feet (1.5 m).

Bulrushes (shown) and other loosely spaced emergent vegetation attract spawning bass. Bass often build their nests in the middle of bulrush stands.

Floating vegetation, such as the roots of lily pads and drifting clumps of cattail or maidencane, provides overhead cover prior to spawning.

Lily pads begin to push toward the surface before bass start to spawn. The pads offer excellent cover for adult largemouth and their newly hatched fry.

Maidencane, or other emergent plants that grow in dense stands, provides good spawning cover. Look for nests in open pockets or along the edge of the weeds.

Summer

RESERVOIRS. Bass location can vary widely during summer, depending on the type of reservoir. In clear canyon reservoirs of the Southwest, anglers routinely catch bass in 40 to 50 feet (12 to 15 m) of water. But in murky flatland reservoirs, most bass are taken from water 15 feet (4.5 m) or shallower.

Some flatland reservoirs have wide expanses of shallow water that become too warm for bass during the hottest part of summer. Deep creek channels offer the only cool water. Bass sometimes move as deep as 25 feet (7.6 m) if the water is relatively clear.

Cove reservoirs offer a variety of bass habitat. Deep coves may hold as many bass as the main river channel. Bass also collect along shoreline points or rocky shelves with flooded brush and on humps just off the main channel. Look for bass in water less than 30 feet (9 m) deep. Despite warm surface temperatures, bass in cove and flatland reservoirs usually feed in the shallows early and late in the day.

Canyon reservoirs have little bass cover. Most lack flooded timber or brush. If you can find some, you are almost sure to catch fish. They also gather along points, in the shade of sheer walls, or where the cliff face has caved in, creating an underwater rock slide.

In reservoirs with large populations of shad, schools of small bass spend much of their time following the baitfish. The bass corner the shad against a line of brush or timber or push them toward the surface. Fishermen occasionally spot bass breaking the surface over open water far from cover or structure.

NATURAL LAKES. Finding bass in summer is easier in natural lakes than in most reservoirs. Largemouth seldom have the selection of structure and cover available to reservoir bass. And they inhabit a narrow range of depths during summer.

The type of lake makes a difference when searching for bass in summer. Shallow, murky lakes have weedlines in 3 to 8 feet (0.9 to 2.5 m) of water. Most bass will stay along these weedlines, but some may move to even shallower cover.

Deep, clear lakes have much deeper weedlines, usually from 15 to 30 feet (4.5 to 9 m). During midday, bass can be found along weedlines or on deep structure like sunken islands or points. They feed in the shallows in morning and evening.

Experts know that some bass stay in the shallows all day. There may be many more bass in deep water, but fish in shallow water are more likely to bite.

Southern marsh lakes generally have poor fishing once surface temperatures rise into the 80s (27° C). Bass cannot go deep because the depths lack oxygen or the basin is not deep enough to have any cooler water. Bass seek shade under the thickest overhead weed mass or on dense weedlines.

SUMMER LOCATIONS IN RESERVOIRS

Cliffs with uneven faces hold more bass than those with smooth, straight walls. Look for crevices, caves, ledges, or rock slides. Bass frequently hang near a tree or brush on the cliff face.

Points with large rocks, flooded timber, or brush draw more largemouth than those with little cover. In summer, bass feed on points near creek channels, then drop into deep water after feeding.

Green leaves on newly flooded vegetation provide excellent cover for bass. The leaves block out sunlight and attract many types of bass food.

Outside bends of creek channels or the main channel (dashed line) are usually deeper and hold more bass than inside turns or straight sections.

Brushy flats serve as feeding areas. Flats with deep holes and abundant cover are better than large flats with uniform depth and little cover.

Large docks with canopies and many posts provide shade and cool water for bass. The best docks are near deep water and have weeds nearby.

Slop, or thick overhead weeds, keeps the water cool and holds an abundant supply of food. Some bass can be found under slop all summer.

Rocky reefs attract more bass than reefs with clean sand bottoms. Largemouth bass find shade among large rocks and boulders.

Weedlines form where the water becomes too deep to allow enough light for weed growth. Look for bass along deep weedlines that have ragged edges.

Water-dwelling trees, such as cypress, grow in many southern lakes and swamps. Look for bass around extensive root systems of the largest trees.

Points with irregular edges and sharp drop-offs hold more largemouth than points with straight edges that drop off more gradually.

Fall & Winter

RESERVOIRS. In early fall, cool temperatures coax bass up from the depths to begin their fall feeding spree. In flatland and cove reservoirs, bass cruise over large, timbered flats along creek channels. They also roam shoals near shore and shallow points covered with brush and timber.

In canyon reservoirs, largemouth move into shallower arms where tributaries join the main body. Shallow points and gradually sloping rock slides will also hold fish.

After fall turnover, bass move much deeper and feed less frequently. The depth of bass in late fall varies from 25 feet (7.6 m) in flatland reservoirs to 40 feet (12 m) or deeper in cove and canyon reservoirs. Look for them along the steepest structure, in the bottoms of deep creek or river channels, or in deep timber. They stay in these spots through winter.

Power companies use some reservoirs for drawing water to cool their turbines, then return the heated water to the lake. Called cooling lakes, these waters generally provide better fishing in late fall and winter than nearby lakes. The discharge warms the lake enough for bass to remain active.

NATURAL LAKES. Early fall finds bass patrolling shoreline flats covered with emergent vegetation such as bulrushes or submerged plants like coontail or cabbage. Docks, channels between lakes, and shallow points also hold bass.

Like fish in reservoirs, bass in natural lakes seek the steepest drop-offs in late fall. In bowl-shaped lakes, they move to the deepest holes they can find. Typical late fall depth varies from 20 to 40 feet (6 to 12 m), depending on water clarity. Bass swim shallower to feed on warm days, but as winter approaches, they form tighter schools, stay deep, and feed very seldom.

In the southern U.S., bass move in and out of deep wintering areas as the weather changes. A few days of warm temperatures draw them into shallow weedbeds to feed. Fishing remains good until the next cold snap, when they retreat to deep water.

Shallow lakes provide the first good fishing in fall because they cool faster than deep lakes. But shallow lakes also turn over first and bass move into their deep wintering spots earlier. As a result, a deeper lake is a better choice in late fall.

FALL AND WINTER LOCATIONS IN RESERVOIRS

Deep water adjacent to cliff walls (shown) provides wintering habitat for bass in canyon reservoirs. Look for schools of bass along step-like ledges. Sheer rock faces hold fewer bass.

Deep junctions of creek channels are gathering points for bass filtering down both channels. Largemouth hang near points formed by the converging channels.

Cooling lakes in the South stay warm enough for anglers to catch bass anywhere in the lake. In the North, bass hang near the warm discharge because the rest of the lake is too cold.

FALL AND WINTER LOCATIONS IN NATURAL LAKES

Green weeds attract bass (shown) when most aquatic plants have died and turned brown. If you hook a piece of green vegetation, work the area thoroughly before moving.

Shallow flats draw bass, especially on warm, sunny days. Flats along protected shores warm faster and hold more largemouth than flats in mid-lake.

Edges of hydrilla beds hold bass in natural lakes of the Deep South, especially if the weedline is along a drop-off. Bass may also inhabit sparse areas in the weeds.

RIVERS & BACKWATERS

Many bass fishermen overlook the nation's large river systems. Yet warm-water rivers offer excellent fishing for anglers who know where to find bass at different times of the year.

Dams on many large rivers have created fertile backwaters with sloughs, connecting lakes, and side channels, or cuts. These quiet backwaters, with their flooded timber, brush, and extensive weedbeds, provide good habitat for bass.

Bass spawn in shallow backwaters, then move toward deeper areas in the backwaters or nearby cuts. However, some may remain in weedy or brushy shallows through summer.

Largemouth are highly sensitive to falling water levels. If the level drops only a few inches in the backwaters, bass will move toward deeper water to avoid being trapped.

In northern rivers, bass usually remain in the backwaters through freeze-up. But as oxygen levels drop, they move to deeper areas in or near the main river channel. In southern regions where rivers do not freeze, bass may live in the backwaters year-round.

In rivers without backwaters, bass spawn on shallow sandbars with little or no current. After spawning, they live near any features that break or deflect the current, such as logs, boulders, and bridge pilings. Many largemouth school in deep pools and eddies along the main channel or just below large islands, points, and sandbars. Undercut banks or rock ledges also attract bass.

From late fall to early spring, some bass linger in warm water discharges from power plants. The fish wedge together in tight schools, usually at the edge of the warm-water plume.

BASS LOCATIONS IN RIVERS

Riprap along the main channel or in backwaters (shown) attracts minnows and crayfish. Bass feed among the jagged rocks, sometimes within inches (cm) of shore.

Chutes between islands off the main river channel concentrate bass foods. Look for deepwater chutes that empty into large pools.

Bridges offer shade and cover. Largemouth hold along the edges of abutments near shore and just above or below pilings in mid-stream.

Points and the tips of islands draw feeding largemouth in morning and evening. Shaded points may hold bass throughout the day.

BASS LOCATIONS IN BACKWATERS

Stump fields (shown) are spawning grounds for bass. Some largemouth will stay through summer if the water level does not drop below 2 feet (60 cm).

Weedy shallows also attract spawning bass. The dense weeds shut out sunlight, keeping the water cool enough for bass through summer.

Fallen trees and submerged logs in narrow cuts offer cover for largemouth—cast along the shady side of these features.

SMALL STREAMS

To find bass in a small stream, you should know how to read the water. In clear streams, it is easy to see likely spots such as bars, boulders, and sunken logs. But in murkier water, you must learn to identify current patterns that reveal the location of underwater structures.

The best largemouth streams have slow to moderate current and warm water. Prime bass habitat includes eddies, deep pools, and undercut banks.

An eddy is indicated by current flowing the opposite direction from the main stream or debris floating in one spot, not with the current. Bass move into quiet areas of eddies to escape the current. Look for an eddy downstream from an obstruction such as a point, fallen tree, or boulder. A surface boil also reveals an eddy. A large underwater object will deflect the current upward, creating a boil several feet downstream from the eddy.

A deep pool appears as an area of calm, dark water. Good pools have ample cover such as rocks, downed trees, and sunken logs. Bass usually feed in shallow riffles or in the upstream part of a pool where current washes in food.

Undercut banks generally form along outside bends. Look for current flowing toward and disappearing under the stream bank. Tree roots, tall grasses, or other stream bank vegetation hold the surface soil in place, creating a large overhang. Several bass may hide in the root tangle or just below the drooping grass. Bass also hide under rock ledges gouged out by the current.

Bass often spend their entire lives in a small section of stream. In spring, they may swim only a few yards upstream to find shallow gravel bars suitable for spawning. In winter, bass hold in the deepest pools.

Riffles hold feeding largemouth in early morning and just before dark. Bass rest behind a rock or log, then dart into swift water to grab food.

ESTUARIES

Estuaries offer a variety of bass habitat including bays, islands, and deep channels. The lower end may be too salty, except for bays fed by freshwater tributaries.

Few anglers would ever dream of catching a saltwater fish one minute and a largemouth bass the next. But it happens in many coastal estuaries.

A coastal river flowing into the sea creates an estuary. The fresh and salt water mix to make brackish water. An estuary extends upstream to a point where higher land elevation prevents the sea water from advancing any farther. The salt water may penetrate 100 miles (160 km) inland where large rivers flow across flat terrain. On rivers that drop quickly from high elevation, the estuary is much shorter.

Estuaries are generally narrow at their upper end, but widen near the ocean. The lower end may be an intricate maze of deep channels cutting through a shallow flat. Or it may resemble a large lake or river backwater. Some estuaries have adjoining brackish marshes that are also connected to the sea.

Largemouth in brackish water may be found in the same vicinity as ocean fish such as redfish or flounder. The bass commonly feed on saltwater baitfish, like herring, and various kinds of shellfish, particularly shrimp and crabs.

Tidal currents dictate bass movement in estuaries. Tides change the current direction every 6 to 12 hours. Water levels normally fluctuate several feet (m), but fluctuations vary from only a few inches to more than 10 feet (3 m). Bass move to find slack-water areas and to feed on baitfish and shellfish that are also adjusting to the changing current and water level. During low tide, bass often concentrate in deeper pools and cuts.

One of the best times to fish is during high slack, the brief stable-water period following the peak of a high tide. Fishing is also good at low slack, the stable-water period following low tide. Check the tide table in a local newspaper for the times of high and low tides.

Locating bass in the narrow, upper part of an estuary is similar to locating bass in a slow-moving river. Look for them along steep banks, in eddies or where small tributaries enter the main channel. Bass in the lower portion are caught on large, weedy flats or in dense weedbeds bordering deep channels. The best cover is always under water, even at low tide.

PONDS

Many fishermen think that small ponds produce only small fish. But several state record bass, including a 14-pound, 4-ounce (6.41 kg) Alabama largemouth, have been caught in ponds.

Landowners build ponds either by damming a small creek or dry wash or by bulldozing a basin in a low-lying area. Most farm ponds are stocked with largemouth and sunfish.

The best ponds have light to moderate weed growth. If vegetation is too dense, bass populations decline. In light weeds, bass keep the number of sunfish in check. But if weeds are heavy, too many sunfish escape and their population skyrockets. The hungry sunfish quickly wipe out bass nests.

Fishing is best in spring. Ponds warm faster than nearby lakes, so angling may begin several weeks earlier. Look for bass in shallow, weedy areas or where shoreline grasses droop over the water.

Angling success usually tapers off in summer, especially in shallow ponds that offer no refuge from warm surface temperatures. Bass become lethargic and difficult to catch. Deeper ponds form thermoclines during summer so bass can retreat to the depths to find cooler water. However, they feed in weedy shallows in morning and evening.

Pond fishing improves in fall as bass return to the shallows. In late fall, bass edge toward the deepest areas of the pond where they find the warmest water. They remain deep through winter.

Ponds in the North can support bass if most of the water is 15 feet (4.5 m) or deeper. Shallow ponds winter-kill. In the South, ponds only a few feet (m) deep produce bass.

PITS & QUARRIES

Strip pits usually have crystal clear waters. Most are long and narrow with one steep edge and one gradually sloping shore. The ends are shallow.

Most people consider abandoned mine pits to be eyesores. But to a savvy bass angler, an abandoned pit offers a fishing opportunity often overlooked by the masses.

Coal strip mines, or strip pits, are found in many eastern states, but primarily in Ohio, Illinois, Indiana, and Kentucky. Old pits are seldom deeper than 20 feet (6 m); newer pits may be 100 feet (30 m) deep.

Pits with a maximum depth of about 40 feet (12 m) offer the best fishing. Deeper pits produce fewer bass because their waters are cold and infertile. In many old pits, the water is too acidic to support fish.

Recent reclamation laws are reducing the amount of acid runoff into pits, making it possible for newly stocked bass to survive. If you are unsure whether a strip pit has fish, check the shoreline for minnows or other small baitfish. If you fail to see any, the water is probably too acidic.

Fishermen also catch largemouth bass in gravel, iron-ore, and phosphate pits. Gravel pits throughout the country have been stocked with largemouth, especially in the Plains States. Minnesota has hundreds of abandoned iron-ore pits that offer excellent fishing. Phosphate pits in central Florida produce large numbers of trophy bass.

Most easy-to-reach pits offer fair fishing, while inaccessible basins often teem with bass. If the pit has infertile water, even moderate fishing pressure will quickly reduce its bass population.

WEATHER & BASS LOCATION

Weather plays a greater role in the daily activity of largemouth bass than any other factor. To improve your success, you should know how the following weather conditions affect bass fishing.

STABLE WEATHER. When weather conditions are stable or gradually changing, bass go through a routine of feeding and resting that is often predictable from one day to the next. For example, during an extended period of overcast weather, a school of bass may feed on a sharp-breaking point at midday, then drop back into deeper water. The school usually repeats this daily pattern, as long as weather conditions remain stable.

FRONTS. Largemouth bass, like most species, feed heavily just before a strong cold front, often providing spectacular fishing for several hours. But once the front arrives, they eat very little until one or two days after the system passes. Catching bass under these conditions is difficult and requires special techniques with lighter lines and smaller lures.

Warm fronts affect bass in different ways, depending on the season and water temperatures. A series of warm days in spring or fall will raise water temperatures in the shallows, causing bass to feed.

In winter, several unusually warm days may draw bass toward the surface to absorb the warmth of the sun. The fish become more accessible to fishermen and more likely to feed or take a lure. But a string of hot days in summer may warm a shallow lake or pond so much that largemouth become sluggish and difficult to catch.

WIND. Like warming trends, wind can either improve or ruin fishing. A steady wind will concentrate minute organisms near shore or along timber and brush lines. Baitfish feed in these areas, attracting bass and other predators. In spring, warm winds blowing from the same direction for several days can pile up warm water on the downwind shore. This warmer water holds more bass than other areas of the lake.

Waves washing into shore loosen soil and debris, creating a band of muddy water. Bass hang along the mudline, where they can avoid bright light, but still dart into clear water to grab food.

If the wind becomes too strong, it can impair fishing success in shallow areas. Turbulence caused by heavy waves pushes bass into deeper water, where they are harder to find. In shallow lakes, strong winds often churn the water enough to make the entire lake murky, slowing fishing for several days.

RAIN. Rainy weather usually improves bass fishing. The overcast skies reduce light penetration, so bass are more comfortable in shallow water. In reservoirs, runoff flows into the back ends of coves. The murky water causes bass to move in and feed. The same situation occurs near stream inlets on many natural lakes.

Fishing success may decline during and after heavy rains. Runoff from torrential rains can muddy an entire body of water, causing fish to stop biting. Angling remains slow until the water clears, which may take several days or weeks.

Lightning and thunder, which are often associated with rain, will drive bass to deeper water and may make them very tough to catch.

Experienced fishermen can identify certain clouds and other atmospheric conditions that indicate coming changes in the weather. They know how bass react to these changes and plan their angling strategy accordingly. Keeping a weather radio on board your boat can give you advanced warning of changing weather patterns.

HOW A COLD FRONT AFFECTS BASS FISHING

Cirrus clouds usually precede a major cold front. These clouds may be 100 miles (160 km) ahead of an approaching front. They indicate that largemouth will soon be feeding heavily.

Thunderheads build as a front approaches. Lightning and strong winds often accompany these towering clouds. The feeding frenzy may peak just before these clouds arrive.

Stalled fronts may leave skies overcast for several days. Look for bass feeding in the shallows during this low-light condition.

Clear sky following a cold front filters out few of the sun's rays. Light penetrates deeper into the water, forcing bass to move out of the shallows.

Cumulus clouds promise better fishing. The white, fluffy clouds signal that the front has passed. Bass will soon resume their normal activity.

Waves breaking against shore (shown) dislodge food items. Winds also push plankton toward shore, attracting minnows. Bass move in to feed.

Calm conditions enable bass in clear water to see objects above them. Fishermen and boaters easily spook bass in shallow water.

Wave action bends or refracts light rays, making it more difficult for largemouth to see movements on or above the surface.

Heavy runoff into clear lakes creates patches of muddy water. Bass congregate wherever turbid water enters the lake, such as the inlets of streams and drainage ditches or near storm sewer pipes.

Lightning and thunder drive largemouth into the depths. If the weather looks threatening, head for shore immediately. Your boat may be the highest point on the lake, making you vulnerable to a lightning strike.

Chapter 3
EQUIPMENT

If you look on the front deck in the boat of a top bass angler, you will often see as many as a dozen rods rigged. Be assured, this is not for show. Each rod is a tool to allow that angler to catch more fish. Most will have lures tied on that run from the surface to water over 20-feet deep. The style of reel, action and length of the rod, and size of the line is often different on every set-up.

While you do not have to have a high-powered, fancy bass boat, having the proper equipment is a key element to being a successful bass angler. Having the correct gear allows you to find fish and then properly present a lure or bait to them in the most effective manner.

Choosing the proper gear is often the difference between catching fish and just fishing. Taking the basics from this chapter should allow you to make informed equipment purchases.

BASS BOATS

The evolution of the bass boat can be traced to the sprawling reservoirs of the South. Bass fishermen wanted a boat that could be operated at high speeds, so they could travel to distant fishing spots in a hurry. They needed a boat that could be maneuvered through thick weedbeds and stump fields in shallow water. They also wanted a stable, comfortable craft with a raised casting deck to enable them to see and cast to specific targets. Large storage compartments and oversized rod lockers were a must for carrying the large amounts of tackle and gear that tournament fishermen often bring when fishing.

Today, fiberglass bass boats are the number one choice of bass anglers across the country. These rigs, which often cost from $15,000 to well over $50,000, give anglers a comfortable, dry ride even in rough water. These boats, with their high-performance hulls are powered by 150- to 300-hp engines. Some can exceed 75 mph (120 kph).

Aluminum bass boats are lighter in weight and less expensive than most fiberglass models. They can be launched easily, even at shallow, unimproved sites. Most aluminum boats have 50- to 150-hp outboard motors. They are becoming more popular because they are less expensive to buy and operate than fiberglass models. Aluminum bass boats come with either a traditional riveted hull or more modern welded hull, which gives them a faster ride and a design closer to that of a fiberglass boat.

An ignition kill switch is an important safety feature on high-speed boats. The switch is attached to the boat operator and the engine's ignition. If the angler is thrown from his seat, the engine shuts off.

The trailers these expensive rigs are carried on are also important. Modern trailers are equipped for long-distance travel and many years of use. Features on modern trailers include a detachable tongue (to fit longer rigs into small garage areas), dual axles, surge breaks, and LED lights.

Bass Boat Features

A modern, fully equipped bass boat is the ultimate fishing machine, offering many features intended to help you find and catch more fish, and enabling you to fish in comfort.

Most top-of-the-line bass boats come equipped with the following features: multiple depth finders, high-thrust trolling motors, water temperature gauge, volt meter, speedometer, automatic bilge pump, marine radio, GPS (Global Positioning System), high resolution LCRs (Liquid Crystal Recorders), special lights for night fishing, and a large-capacity gas tank. They also have air-ride pedestal "bike seats" on elevated casting decks, a built-in cooler, a live well with a timer, recirculating pumps, and plenty of dry storage compartments for rods, batteries, and other gear. Many have a built-in charging system, so you can charge batteries easily, without having to hook up a charger each time.

But many veteran bass fishermen prefer to keep their boat rigging very simple, using only a depth finder and an electric trolling motor. They maintain that the more equipment you have, the more time you spend in the repair shop, which keeps you off the water.

Control panels are located on the steering console of large bass boats. Features on this panel include a depth finder, 12-volt power supply, fuel gauge, volt meter, speedometer, tachometer, trim gauge, and water pressure gauge. Switches control the internal lights, bilge pump, running lights, live well pump, and live well aerator.

SMALL BOATS & INFLATABLES

You do not need an expensive boat to catch bass. Fishermen pursue largemouth in float tubes, inflatable boats, canoes, jon boats, and a variety of small crafts designed for cartop racks or light trailers.

Small boats and float tubes are perfect for isolated lakes, small ponds, and other waters where launching a big boat would be impossible. And as many bass anglers know, these hard-to-reach waters frequently offer prime bass fishing, sometimes within minutes of heavily populated areas.

When fishing far from a road, some anglers strap on a float tube and walk to the water. Most tubes have an inside diameter of 16 to 20 inches (41 to 51 cm). The larger sizes provide more stability. Fishermen can attach kick fins to their waders for propelling the tube forward. Some anglers wear swimming trunks, then use standard swim fins and push the tube backwards. Tubes should not be used in heavy waves or strong current. For safety, anglers often work in pairs.

The best inflatable boats are made from puncture-resistant heavy-gauge vinyl with nylon backing. They have several air compartments, so if one is punctured, the boat will still float. But you can make do with an inexpensive, Army-surplus rubber raft. Transport an inflated boat on a cartop carrier. A deflated or partially inflated boat can be hauled in a minivan. Controlling an inflatable can be difficult in wind, so bring along an anchor.

Small molded plastic boats can also be loaded into a station wagon. They range from 70 to about 100 pounds (31.5 to 45 kg) and 7 to 10 feet (2 to 3 m) in length. They should be used only on quiet waters.

Canoes are lightweight but they tip easily, especially when the angler is fighting and landing a fish. For extra stability, lash a long board or pole across the canoe, then attach a large styrofoam float.

Flat-bottom jon boats draw only a few inches (cm) of water. They work well in stump fields or shallow, rocky rivers. The blunt bow and low sides of a jon boat make it a poor choice in rough water.

Some anglers rig small boats with gas or electric motors, depth finders, swivel seats, and many of the accessories used on larger craft. Most tube fishermen carry only a pocket-sized lure box and a rod or two.

Types of Small Boats & Inflatables

Canoes work best on small lakes and ponds and on small streams. They are ideal for portaging from one body of water to another. They can be outfitted with many features available in larger boats, such as seats with back rests, electric motors, and depth finders. Canoes allow you to fish comfortably and quietly.

Float tubes have a canvas seat to keep the angler high enough in the tube to cast properly. Kick fins are used to move the angler through the water.

Kick boats offer more mobility than traditional float tubes and help anglers stay warm in cold water by keeping their body above the water.

Jon boats have good side-to-side stability because of their flat bottoms. Jon boats with a semi-V bow work best for cutting through waves.

DEPTH FINDERS/GPS UNITS & MAPS

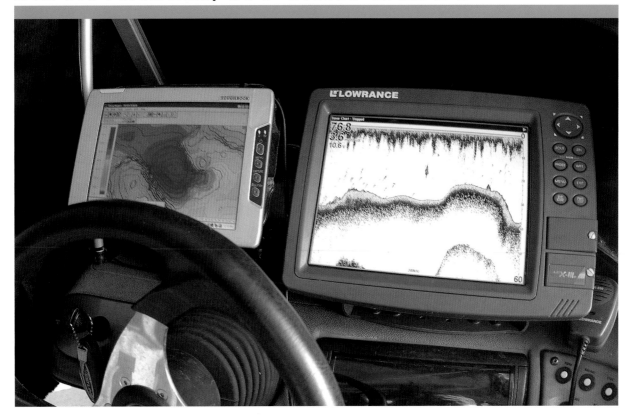

A depth finder/GPS may well be your most important fishing tool because it enables you to locate likely bass habitat in minutes and keep productive areas stored forever.

The ability to read and interpret what a depth finder is telling you can greatly improve your chances of finding and catching bass, particularly in deep water. Combine this with a working knowledge of a mapping GPS unit and you are light-years ahead of anglers in the past.

All depth finders have a transducer that emits a sonar signal and a receiver that converts the returning signal to a display of the bottom, fish, weeds, or other objects.

Common types of depth finders include liquid-crystal recorders (LCR), videos, and flashers.

LIQUID-CRYSTALS. The most popular style of depth finder, LCRs are compact and are relatively inexpensive. A good unit should have at least 160 vertical pixels to provide adequate detail. Many units will also provide a digital depth readout, water temperature, and "zoom" capability. Some have a 3-D readout; others, called "sidefinders," enable you to see what's off to the side of the boat.

VIDEOS. These are available in 8-color or monochrome models. Videos display signals on a cathode-ray tube, similar to that in a television set. They're bulkier and more expensive than most other types of depth finders, but provide excellent detail. They are most common for saltwater applications.

FLASHERS. These units display the bottom, fish, and other objects as lines or blips on a circular, calibrated dial. Some flashers even display different-sized objects in different colors. A flasher with a 0- to 30-foot (0 to 9 m) scale is the best choice for bass fishing. Units with greater depth scales show less detail. Because of the enormous popularity of LCRs, some anglers forget that a flasher is a valuable fishing tool.

MAPS & MAP CHIPS. Only a small fraction of the water in any lake contains largemouth bass. A good hydrographic contour map or map chip used with your depth finder can save hours of random searching. Most modern locators have the ability for you to load a *map chip*. A map chip is a data storage card that loads into the LCR and contains maps of most of the major lakes and reservoirs in your state. Once loaded, you will be able to view a chosen map on your screen and add and save GPS points directly onto the map.

Hydrographic maps, whether they are made of paper or on the screen of your locator, indicate water depth by contour lines. Maps usually show a contour line at every 5- or 10-foot (1.5 to 3 m) depth change. Lines that are close together reveal abrupt bottom changes; lines far apart mean a gradually sloping bottom.

Maps show the locations of good bass-holding structures such as sunken islands, creek channels, and submerged points. Maps of reservoirs sometimes pinpoint man-made features that have been flooded, including roads and houses. Most maps show various shoreline features, while some identify bottom types and the locations of weedbeds, flooded timber, and brush.

After studying your contour map, look for a landmark such as a point to help you find the right vicinity. Then use your depth finder/GPS to locate the exact spot. If you catch fish, mark the spot in your GPS. Before leaving, list some notes of interest, such as what the fish were caught with, for the next time you visit the spot.

Contour maps seldom show every detail on the bottom. Mapmakers often miss humps and reefs and other smaller structure. These small structure may lie between survey lines used by crews when charting lake depths.

It pays to do some extra scouting with your locator to look for any features that the map does not show. Few fishermen discover these areas, so they sometimes offer prime fishing.

RODS, REELS & LINE

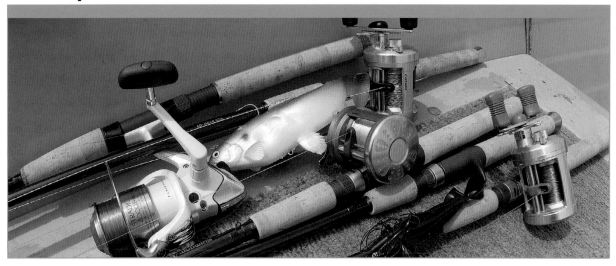

Anglers need to carry several different rod/reel/line combinations to properly present a variety of lures to bass.

When selecting rods, reels, and line for bass fishing, check manufacturer's recommendations. Don't try to pair a rod recommended for 6- to 8-pound (2.7 to 3.6 kg) line with a reel recommended for 10- to 15-pound (4.5 to 6.75 kg). A heavy reel would impair the outfit's balance and sensitivity. The following are important considerations in rod, reel, and line selection:

RODS. Most bass rods are relatively stiff for strong hook sets and good sensitivity. And the stiffness comes in handy for horsing fish out of heavy cover.

Baitcasting rods generally range from 5½ to 7½ feet in length, with power designations from medium-light to extra-heavy. Most spinning rods are 5 to 7 feet (1.5 to 2.3 m) long and range from light to medium-heavy. Fly rods vary from 8 to 9½ feet (2.4 to 2.6 m) and carry line-weight designations from 8 to 10.

Top bass anglers often carry specialty rods:

Flippin' rods are about 7½ feet (2.3 m) long, usually heavy power, and have a telescopic design for easy storage. The extra length enables you to flip lures into hard-to-reach spots and comes in handy for other uses, such as casting big crankbaits and buzz baits.

Pitchin' rods, usually 6½ feet (2 m) long, are medium-heavy in power with a fast action. Pitchin' means tossing lures under low cover, such as branches or docks, and using an underhand, low-trajectory, swing cast. When pitched properly, the lure travels only a few inches above the water.

Crankin' rods are 6½ to 7 feet (2 to 2.3 m) long with a slow-medium power rating. They have a slower action because they are often made of fiberglass. They're intended to hold hooked fish better than stiffer graphite rods; when the fish thrashes, the rod bends instead of the hooks tearing out. Crankin' rods work best with crankbaits and some topwater plugs, because little sensitivity is needed to detect strikes.

With the exception of crankin' rods and some specialty rods, most quality bass rods are made of high-modulus graphite. The higher the modulus (stiffness), the better the rod telegraphs subtle strikes.

REELS. Most bait-casting reels have a thumb bar that switches the reel to free spool. This eliminates resistance that would result from a turning reel handle, allowing longer casts. All top-quality reels have a magnetic anti-backlash device that places slight pressure on the spool to prevent overruns. This device is superior to mechanisms that operate by friction. But fishermen must still thumb the spool to prevent backlashes. A narrow-spool reel is less likely to backlash because the light spool does not have as much momentum as it slows. This type of reel is recommended for nearly all applications.

Spinning reels should have interchangeable spools so you can change line quickly. A longer-than-normal spool adds distance to your casts and, because it holds more line, allows you to cast well even when a fair amount of line has been lost.

Consider the gear ratio when choosing any reel. A high-speed reel has a ratio of 7:1, enabling faster retrieves for rapid-fire casting. In general, reels with high ball-bearing counts (6 or more) operate more smoothly and last longer than those with low bearing numbers. For crankbait fishing or in situations where you want a slow retrieve, a gear ratio of 5:1 is a good choice.

Practically any fly reel will work for bass fishing. Fly reels are mainly for line storage, so there's no need to buy an expensive model.

LINE. Almost all bass fishermen use a variety of lines. Use the lightest line practical for the conditions. Light line casts better, allows more lure action, and is less visible to fish. The options pretty much come down to nylon monofilament, fluorocarbon, co-polymer lines that blend mono and fluorocarbon, and braided lines.

Use abrasion-resistant line such as co-polymers or fluorocarbon when fishing around rocks, weeds, timber, or brush. Soft, limp mono casts better and is a good choice when fishing in unobstructed water and on spinning reels. In situations when water clarity is poor or you are horsing fish from very heavy cover, braid may be the best option.

Most fly fishermen use weight-forward line to overcome the weight and wind resistance of large bugs and poppers and for punching into a wind.

SOFT PLASTICS

When asked to choose their favorite lure, many top pros will choose soft plastics. Plastics are effective because of their tantalizing lifelike action. And when inhaled by a bass, the soft body feels like natural food.

Worms and other soft plastics tend to work best in warm water, and when rigged Texas-style, you can retrieve them through thick weeds or brush without snagging. You can also float them over shallow cover or jig them along deep structure. Soft plastics most often resemble baitfish, lizards, or crayfish. Others look like nothing a bass has ever seen.

Plastics range from 3 to 10 inches (7.6 to 25 cm) in length and 6- to 8-inch (15 to 20 cm) sizes work best in most situations. Use smaller plastics in clear water or when bass are biting light, such as after a cold front. Some anglers drag giant 10-inch (25 cm) worms on a Carolina rig through heavy cover to catch trophy bass.

Experiment to find the best color. Green pumpkin and black plastics will catch bass in almost any type of water. In murky water, solid, bright colors such as chartreuse or red may work better. Some plastics have bright or fluorescent tails, called firetails, and metal flakes molded into the body for extra attraction in the murky water. In clearer water, translucent plastics in shades of green or brown work best.

When fishing in heavy cover, rig a soft plastic Texas-style. Most fishermen use bullet-shaped slip sinkers. For better feel when fishing in brush or weeds, some anglers use self-pegging sinkers that keep the sinker from riding up the line. Use a ¹⁄₁₆- or ⅛-ounce (1.8 or 3.2 g) sinker in water less than 6 feet (1.8 m) deep, ⅛- or ¼-ounce (3.2 or 7 g) in 6 to 12 feet (1.8 to 3.6 m), ¼- or ⅜-ounce (7 or 10.6 g) in 13 to 18 feet (4 to 5.5 m), and ⅜- or ½-ounce (10.6 or 14 g) in water deeper than 18 feet.

To rig soft plastics for surface fishing, use a plain hook and no sinker. Some manufacturers offer worms with extra flotation.

Where snags are not a problem, some anglers thread plastics onto a *shakey* head jig with the hook exposed or use a Carolina rig. A "shakey" head is a generic term for a plain exposed-hook finesse jig where small soft plastics are threaded on and fished on a light-line spinning outfit.

For best results, rig plastics on large, long-shank worm hooks. Many worm hooks have a bend near the eye of the hook to keep the plastic from sliding down the shank. Hook size depends mainly on the size of the bait. Use a 1/0 or 2/0 hook with a 4-inch bait (10 cm), a 3/0 with a 6-inch bait (15 cm), a 4/0 or 5/0 with an 8-inch (20 cm) bait, and a 5/0 or 6/0 for large baits.

Fishing with soft plastics demands a delicate touch. A strike, or pick-up, usually feels like a light tap. But sometimes the line moves off to one side or the lure suddenly feels weightless. Bass take plastics with a quick gulp. If you feel anything unusual, set the hook.

Use a rod heavy enough to drive the hook into the tough jaw of a bass, yet sensitive enough to detect a subtle strike. Powerful hook-sets place considerable stress on the knots, so retie often.

Fishing a soft plastic, rigged Texas-style is often the number-one way to catch bass. On the following pages we will show you how to rig a soft plastic bait Texas-style. You can use this same method to rig any type of soft plastic bait you choose. Then, we will take you through a basic sequence on how to fish this setup correctly. The key to this technique is to "feel" what the lure is doing. With practice you will be able to distinguish between whether you are feeling weeds, brush, rocks, or bass at the end of your line.

Thread the line through a sliding bullet sinker and tie on a plastic worm hook. Insert the point about ½ inch (13 mm) into the worm's head.

Push the point through and slide the worm up the shank to cover the eye. Rotate the hook one-half turn and bury the point in the worm.

Avoid twisting the plastic worm before inserting the hook. If it does not hang straight, the worm will revolve and twist the line as it is retrieved.

Cast, then hold the rod tip high as the worm settles. Allow enough slack so the lure can sink, but keep enough tension so you can detect a strike.

Retrieve slowly with a lifting and dropping motion. Keep a tight line as you lower the rod, because bass often take a worm as it sinks.

Drop the rod tip when you detect a pickup. Lean forward and point the rod at the fish. The bass should not feel any resistance at this crucial point.

Set the hook immediately with a powerful upward sweep of the rod. Jerk hard enough so the hook penetrates the worm and the bass's jaw. If the first hook-set does not feel solid, set the hook again.

Keep the rod tip high and the line tight. The bass will lunge for cover the moment it feels the hook. Maintain steady pressure so the fish cannot wrap the line around weeds or brush.

SPINNERBAITS

The outstanding success of the spinnerbait proves that a lure does not have to imitate natural bass food. A spinnerbait attracts bass with its flash, action, and color. These qualities, combined with its semi-snagless design, make it a favorite among anglers who fish weedy or brushy waters.

The spinnerbait combines two excellent lures: the spinner and the jig. The wire shaft resembles an open safety pin. It has a lead-head jig on the lower arm and one or two spinners on the upper arm. Models with one blade are called single-spins; those with a pair of blades are called tandem-spin spinnerbaits. The best spinnerbaits have ball-bearing swivels so the blades can turn rapidly. Most models have a silicone or rubber skirt that adds color and action and conceals the hook.

Many anglers customize their spinnerbaits to change the action or color. Carry a variety of skirts and blades and keep switching until you find the combination that works best. The best skirts are typically those that flare the rubber or silicone strands.

Spinnerbaits can be retrieved many different ways. Experiment to find the best retrieve for the situation at hand. Most fishermen use a steady retrieve. But you can also buzz a spinnerbait across the surface or slow-roll it along the bottom. The lift-and-drop technique will sometimes trigger a strike when bass ignore other retrieves.

Be sure to run a spinnerbait against submerged brush, stumps, or timber to give it an erratic action. Some anglers cast the lure past a visible obstruction such as a bridge piling or dock post, then retrieve to intentionally hit the object. The sudden change in the lure's speed and direction may trigger an immediate strike.

Many anglers add a stinger hook to their spinnerbait when bass are short-striking the bait. You can buy these at most good retail shops. It involves sliding plastic tubing over the eye of the trailer hook, then threading the main hook of the spinnerbait through the tubing on the eye of the stinger.

There are three basic retrieves for spinnerbaits:

STEADY RETRIEVE. Reel a spinnerbait through weeds or brush, varying the speed and depth on successive retrieves. The hook lies directly behind the wire arms, which keep the hook from fouling in weeds.

BUZZ RETRIEVE. Begin reeling a tandem-blade spinnerbait as soon as it hits the water. Keep the rod tip high and reel rapidly so the top blade barely breaks the surface. Try this retrieve in warm shallows over heavy cover.

LIFT-AND-DROP RETRIEVE. Cast a spinnerbait, then let it slowly helicopter to the bottom. Raise your rod to lift the lure, reel in slack, and lower your rod so the lure helicopters back to the bottom, then repeat.

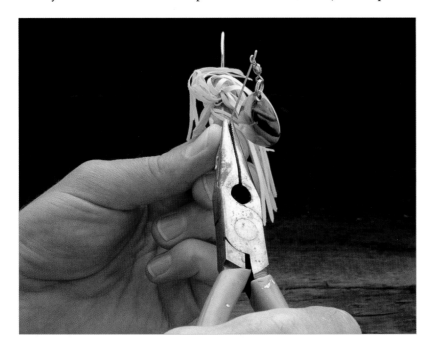

Make sure your spinnerbait is tuned. To tune a standard wire spinnerbait, use a pliers to bend the upper arm so it aligns directly with the hook. A properly tuned spinnerbait runs with its blades turning directly over the top of the hook, not tilted to the left or right.

CRANKBAITS

Even the most stubborn largemouth finds it difficult to resist a crankbait wiggling enticingly past its nose. Crankbaits work well for locating bass because you can cover a lot of water quickly.

Bass anglers use three basic styles of crankbaits: standard lipped crankbaits, minnow baits (jerkbaits), and lipless crankbaits. Most are made of plastic, either hard or foamed, or wood, usually balsa or cedar. Some have rattle chambers filled with metal beads that create extra noise and vibration.

Although color selection changes from day to day, bright-colored plugs tend to work best in murky water and dull or natural-colored plugs in clear water. Most anglers prefer crankbaits from 2 to 4 inches (5 to 10 cm) long for largemouth.

Standard crankbaits have a lip that has the line attachment on it, a comparatively short, wide body, and a violent wobble. The length, width, and angle of the lip determine the running depth. Some models with long, wide lips that extend straight off the nose can reach depths of 20 feet (6 m). Most standard crankbaits float at rest, but some are neutrally buoyant or even sink, so you can count them down.

Minnow baits are longer and slimmer than crankbaits and generally have a smaller lip, resulting in a gentler but more lifelike swimming action. They come in floating, sinking, and neutrally buoyant models, as well as jointed and straight models. Floaters can be worked on the surface with a twitch-and-pause retrieve or reeled steadily to run at depths of 1 to 5 feet (0.3 to 1.5 m). Some long-lipped floaters dive to a depth of 12 feet (3.7 m). Sinking models can be counted down to any depth. The most common method of retrieve, as the name "jerkbait" would suggest, is to use a jerk-and-pause retrieve. Try different cadences until you get a fish to strike, then stick with that rhythm.

Lipless crankbaits have a deep, narrow body, an attachment eye on the back, and no lip. They have a tight wiggle and are filled with rattles of some type that give off high-frequency sound waves, detectable by fish even in murky water. Most lipless crankbaits sink, so you can fish them at any depth.

In general, crankbaits should be fished with the lightest line practical for the conditions. You'll cast farther and the plug will run deeper because there is less water resistance on the line.

For maximum wobble, make sure to attach a plug to your line with a split-ring or snap, not a heavy snap-swivel. Tying the knot directly to the attachment eye may restrict the lure's action, particularly when you're using heavy line.

Always experiment with different retrieve speeds. As a rule, the warmer the water, the faster the retrieve you should use. Often, an erratic stop-and-go retrieve will catch more bass than a steady retrieve. Another trick: give the crankbait an occasional twitch as you reel. The change in action sometimes triggers fish that aren't feeding.

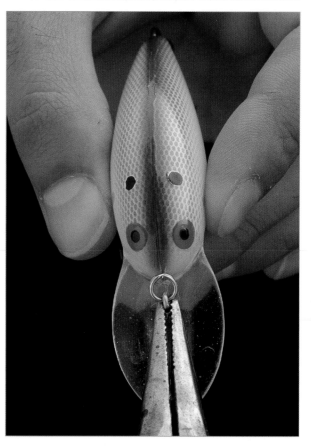

Test a crankbait to see if it is running straight. The lure at left is working properly; the other is running on its side and tracking to the right.

Tune the lure by adjusting the angle of the eye. If the crankbait is tracking to the right, turn or bend the eye to the left.

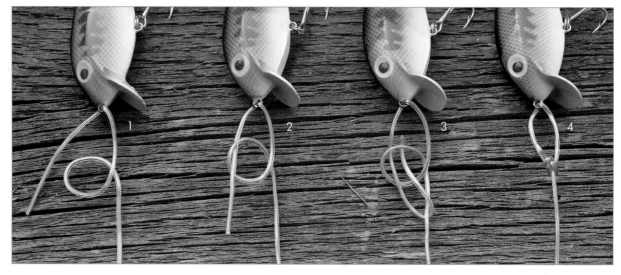

A bowline knot allows a crankbait to swing freely on a loop. (1) Thread the line through the eye and form a loop about 1 inch away. (2) Push the free end through the loop. (3) Wrap the free end around the standing line and push it through the loop again. (4) Snug up the knot by pulling on the free end.

SURFACE LURES

One of the most exciting moments in fishing is just after your surface lure hits the water. As the ripples die, you can almost sense the bass eyeing your lure. You know that the surface may erupt at any second.

Surface, or topwater, lures work best on calm summer mornings and evenings when bass are feeding in the shallows. They are not as effective in water below 60°F (15.5°C) or when the surface is rough.

Topwater lures may be the only solution for catching bass nestled under thick mats of vegetation. The commotion often attracts bass even though they cannot see the lure. In this type of cover, anglers sometimes catch bass during midday.

Surface lures also work well for night fishing. Bass may not be able to see a deep-running lure. But they can detect the noise and vibration of a topwater lure. And when they move closer, they can see its silhouette against the moonlit sky.

Bass anglers use six basic types of topwater lures:

PROP BAITS have a long, thin body with a small propeller at one or both ends. Retrieve them by reeling slowly and steadily or in short twitches followed by pauses. Before buying a propeller-type bait, blow on the blades to make sure they turn freely.

CHUGGER/POPPERS have a concave face that creates a popping or gurgling sound when retrieved. Most models have a feathered treble hook on the rear of the bait. A twitch-and-pause retrieve usually works best, but there are times when bass prefer continuous twitching.

BUZZ BAITS resemble spinnerbaits, but the blade revolves around a shaft rather than spinning on a swivel. The large aluminum blade generates turbulence as the lure churns across the surface. Some models have tandem blades.

CRAWLERS have a metal lip or arms that cause the lure to wobble widely from side to side. Most crawlers make a loud gurgling sound when retrieved.

STICKBAITS resemble propeller-type plugs, but they lack propellers. A bait called the Heddon® Zara Spook is the main bait in this category and they come in several sizes. Walk a spook across the surface by reeling slowly while steadily twitching the rod tip in a rhythmic motion to get the lure to run left to right or "walk-the-dog," as it is commonly called. This type of retrieve is widely used by fishermen on clear water lakes and reservoirs to bring bass up from deep water.

HOLLOW FROGS AND RATS have a weedless design with upturned hooks and can be retrieved over thick slop without fouling. Crawl a plastic frog through lily pads or other floating-leaved weeds. Pull the lure onto a pad, hop it into the water, then twitch it frequently so the legs kick. Bass usually strike when the lure moves into a pocket.

Bass will sometimes follow surface lures repeatedly without striking. You may be able to see the wake just behind the lure. To coax a strike, stop reeling, let the lure rest for several seconds, then twitch it. Not every bass strikes with an explosive smash. Sometimes a strike is merely a gentle slurp. Set the hook when you feel the weight of the fish.

Jerk a topwater crawler (top) across the surface by twitching the rod tip as you reel steadily. Or reel a short distance, then stop while you twitch the lure. Topwater lures are often used at night.

Walk a stickbait across the surface. Reel slowly while twitching the rod tip. This type of retrieve is widely used by fishermen on southern reservoirs to bring largemouth up from deep water.

Skim a lightweight plastic weedless spoon across the surface by keeping your rod tip high as you reel. Or, retrieve with a twitching motion. You can draw these lures over dense weeds and brush without snagging or fouling.

Crawl a plastic frog through lily pads or other floating-leaved weeds. Pull the lure onto a pad, hop it into the water, then twitch it frequently so the legs kick. Bass usually strike when the lure moves into a pocket.

Wait for ripples to subside after casting a floating topwater lure (bottom). Sometimes bass will strike as the lure lays motionless.

JIGS & JIGGING LURES

Bass that ignore fast-running plugs will often strike lures jigged vertically near their hiding spots. Jigging lures include brushguard jigs, jigging spoons, vibrating blades, and tailspins, all of which are good choices when fishing in deep water.

Detecting strikes may be difficult with jigging spoons, vibrating blades, and tailspins because bass commonly strike a jigging lure on the fall. Try to keep the line tight to feel the light tap and set the hook immediately if you feel any weight on the line.

Jigs, particularly brushguard versions, are considered the best big bass bait available. They became a staple of every top bass angler's arsenal with the advent of the *flipping* technique in the 1970s. Flipping allows you to get a brushguard jig into hard-to-reach heavy-cover areas where bass live.

Brushguard jigs typically have silicone or rubber skirts with a soft plastic craw or "chunk" added on the hook. Some anglers tip jigs with live bait. They are retrieved with a slow, steady, lift-and-drop motion, bounced along the bottom, or most commonly are flipped or pitched to specific cover where a bass may be holding.

Jigging spoons are made of heavy metal. Most have a hammered unpainted finish. They work well during coldwater periods when bass hold tight in deep timber, along deep cliff walls, or when fish are feeding on suspended baitfish. Most spoons are heavy enough to be jigged vertically in water up to 50 feet (15 m) deep.

Vibrating blades are made of thin metal. Tie a snap to your line, then attach it to a hole in the lure's back. Jig these lures vertically or retrieve by reeling rapidly. The action is much like a lipless crankbait.

Tailspins have a heavy lead body and a spinner on the tail. They work best for vertical jigging in deep water, but can be hopped along the bottom or retrieved steadily when needed.

Flipping a brushguard jig is one of the best ways to catch bass that are holding tight to cover.

CAROLINA RIGS

Originating in South Carolina, the aptly named Carolina rig is one of the most effective ways to cover large amounts of water using soft plastic baits. The system came into the national spotlight in the early 1990s with a string of bass tournament wins that have continued ever since.

The ability to change the weight size, leader length, and type of soft plastic makes this a great presentation under a variety of conditions from early spring through fall. Carolina rigs work best in areas with sparse vegetation and little or no woody structure. Ideal places to fish a Carolina rig are inside weedlines, hard-bottom areas outside of weedlines, main and secondary points, and clean mid-lake humps.

The depth of water being fished determines how much weight is used. In shallow water (less than 10 feet [3 m]), sinkers as light as ¼ ounce (7 g) are preferred. In deeper water, most choose a ¾-ounce (21 g) or 1-ounce (28 g) sinker. Leader length is a function of water clarity and lengths up to 6 feet (1.8 m) are used in clear water, as short as 12 inches (30 cm) in dirty water. Weed height can also affect leader length, as the lure should ride above any weeds that are in the area.

The technique for fishing a Carolina rig is simple: make a long cast, wait for the rig to sink to the bottom, then slowly reel it back in with a series of short pulls or "drags." Make sure the weight stays in contact with the bottom. As a rule, start with a faster retrieve and slow it down or pause longer as the fish dictate.

Lure choices are virtually any type of soft plastic, depending on the time of year, weather conditions, and water color. Larger baits and more visible colors are used in darker water. Smaller baits and more natural colors are used in clear water or during cold front conditions. Hook size is determined by the size of the bait being used and is most often in the 1/0 to 4/0 range. Anglers should change bait styles often when looking for fish or when the fish have stopped biting on a certain spot.

Carolina rigs consist of a weight and a bead placed in front of a swivel, a section of leader with a hook attached, and a soft plastic rigged on the hook. The bead is placed between the weight and the swivel to protect the knot from the sinker and it creates a clicking sound when the rig is worked across the bottom.

LIVE BAIT

The overwhelming majority of bass fishermen use artificial lures, but there is no doubt that live bait may work better in many bass-fishing situations.

Trophy bass hunters swear by live bait. A glance at the record book shows that a 21-pound, 12-ounce (9.8 kg) largemouth was taken on a crayfish and a 20-pound, 15-ounce (9.4 kg) fish was caught on a nightcrawler.

Largemouth bass are more apt to strike live bait after a cold front or when the water temperature is above or below their active feeding range. Sluggish bass grab only slow-moving food. But some artificial lures lose their action at slow speeds. Live bait, however, can be inched along the bottom or dangled from a bobber. Lethargic bass take more time to examine their food, so they are more likely to spot an imitation.

Bass in extremely clear water can recognize an artificial lure quickly. To catch these wary fish, some fishermen switch to live bait. They use the lightest line possible and keep their boats well away from the fishing zone to avoid spooking bass.

When fishing is slow, anglers often tip their lures with live bait such as worms or minnows. This adds scent appeal to the lure. A lively bait can also add action to a jig or spinnerbait, although it will ruin the action of a crankbait so it is not a real option with those baits.

Largemouth bass eat a wider variety of natural foods than most game-fish. They will strike almost any live bait, from an inch-long (2.5 cm) grasshopper to a foot-long (0.3 m) shiner. The best baits have a lot of action and will stay lively despite repeated casting.

The type and size of bait must suit the fishing conditions. For example, some anglers use a technique called freelining to catch bass in thick weeds. They allow the bait to swim into dense cover. This method requires a large-sized bait with enough power to pull the line through the tangle. Big baits generally work best for big bass, especially when the fish are feeding actively. Smaller baits are better when bass are sluggish.

Nationwide, the most popular bass baits include minnows, frogs, cray-fish, and nightcrawlers.

Some fishermen still rank frogs as the top bait for largemouth bass, but frog populations have plummeted as a result of disease and wetland drainage. Many anglers regard crayfish as the best bait for smallmouth bass, yet these crustaceans work equally well for largemouth. And while they rarely see earthworms in their environment, hungry bass will seldom ignore a gob of wiggling nightcrawlers.

Other live baits have gained popularity in certain regions. Bass in most estuary situations often prefer live shrimp or crabs to any other bait. In weedy lakes of Florida and Georgia, 8- to 12-inch (20 to 30 cm) golden shiners account for most trophy largemouth. Californians choose crayfish.

Hooking & Rigging Live Bait

Even the most irresistible bass bait is worthless if not hooked and rigged properly. Choose the hook, sinker, and line that best suits the conditions at hand.

When selecting a hook, consider the size of the bait and the type of cover. With a small hook and large bait, the bass is likely to steal your offering without getting hooked. If the hook is too large, the bait appears unnatural. Always use a weedless hook when fishing in heavy cover.

The size and type of sinker depends on water depth, cover, and bottom material. A ⅛- or ¼-ounce (3.2 or 7 g) sinker works well in water shallower than 15 feet (4.5 m), but deeper water requires more weight to keep the bait near the bottom. A bullet sinker is best for snaking baits through weeds and brush. A snag-resistant sinker such as a bottom-walker helps you to avoid constant hang-ups when fishing a rocky bottom.

When choosing line, keep in mind the water clarity, the potential for snagging, and the abrasiveness of the cover or bottom. Bass in clear water are most likely to strike live bait presented with clear, thin-diameter monofilament. Use heavier line in murky water or when snags are a problem. Hard-finish, abrasion-resistant co-polymer lines work best in tough weeds or in brush, timber, or rocks.

Almost all of the baits and rigs shown on these pages are interchangeable. Anglers should experiment to discover the rigging methods and fishing techniques that work best in their favorite bass waters.

Bobber-fishing works best where casting or trolling would be impossible, such as dense weeds. It is especially effective for sluggish bass in cold or warm water.

HOW TO RIG MINNOWS

Hair jigs tipped with minnows (shown) work well when casting or vertical jigging for largemouth along deep structure. Use a ½-ounce (14 g) or heavier jig in water deeper than 15 feet (4.5 m).

Spin-rigs are designed for tipping with a minnow or night-crawler. Similar to a spinnerbait, a spin-rig can be retrieved through thick weeds or brush without fouling.

Stinger hooks increase your chances of hooking bass, especially when using large baitfish. Insert a 4/0 weedless hook through the lips and a #4 treble hook just ahead of the tail.

MORE TIPS

Weedless hooks (shown) enable you to retrieve live bait through weeds, brush, or other dense cover. Most have a springy wire weedguard that seats under the hook point.

Floating jig heads keep bait above the bottom where it is less likely to snag and easier for fish to see. Use a slip-sinker rig with a 2- to 3-foot (0.6 to 0.9 m) leader.

Bottom-walker rigs resist snagging and fouling because of their safety-pin design. Use ¼- to ⅜-ounce (7 to 10.6 g) sizes, along with an 18- to 24-inch (46 to 61 cm) leader and a single hook.

Pyramid-head jigs work well for fishing in dense weeds or along weed-lines. The tapered head slides easily through the vegetation and weeds seldom catch on the attachment eye.

Bait-saver tabs prevent your bait from wiggling off the hook. Punch tabs out of a plastic lid. Push on a tab, hook the bait through the lips, then add another tab.

Many fishermen choose their lures by trial and error. They keep changing until they find one that catches bass. But choosing a lure is not a random choice for expert bass fishermen. They select a lure only after considering the following factors.

DEPTH. This is the prime concern in lure selection. For example, bass in deep water will seldom chase a lure retrieved just below the surface. Try to estimate the most probable depth based on the season, time of day, weather, water clarity, and past experience on the body of water.

In water shallower than 10 feet (3 m), bass anglers use surface lures, spinnerbaits, spinners, or shallow-running crankbaits. Lightly weighted soft plastics will also work. In deeper water, use deep-running crankbaits, jigging lures, heavily weighted soft plastics, or spinnerbaits helicoptered to the bottom. Live bait can be used in both shallow and deep water.

COVER. When fishing in thick weeds or brush, use a hollow frog, Texas-rigged plastic, spinnerbait, brushguard jig, or any lure with a design that prevents snagging. When fishing with live bait, use a bullet sinker and a weedless hook.

ACTIVITY LEVEL. The activity level of bass determines the size and action of the lure and the speed of the retrieve. Water temperature affects bass activity more than any other factor. However, weather conditions, especially cold fronts, can also play a role.

Bass in their optimum feeding range of 68 to 80°F (20 to 26.6°C) are more likely to strike a larger, faster-moving lure or bait than bass in warmer or colder water. An 8-inch (20 cm) plastic worm may be a good choice at 75°F (24°C), but a 4-inch (10 cm) worm would probably work better at 83°F (28°C). In 55°F (13°C) water, bass will respond better to a smaller lure retrieved slowly. But lures like buzz baits would not work properly if retrieved slowly.

Live bait works well in cold water because it can be crawled along bottom or suspended from a bobber. Lures such as jigging spoons and small jigs are also good coldwater choices. Constantly lifting and dropping the lure through a tight school of bass will eventually pay off with a strike.

WATER CLARITY AND LIGHT LEVELS. Bass fishermen have different theories for selecting lure color. However, most agree that water clarity affects their choice of colors.

Many anglers insist that light-colored lures are better for fishing in clear water. But that does not explain the success of black or green pumpkin worms in clear waters. Fluorescent lures in yellow, chartreuse, or orange seem to work best in murky water. Dark colors usually out-produce light colors on overcast days or at night.

When fishing at night or in a murky lake, use a noisy lure or bait. Good choices include a surface popper or chugger, a spinnerbait with large blades, a buzz bait with a blade that ticks the shaft, or a lipless crankbait with beads that rattle. Some anglers hook on a lively frog that will kick across the surface.

Beginning fishermen are often overwhelmed by the huge selection of bass lures at their local tackle shop. Many buy a large tackle box and fill each tray with a different lure. They never stick with one lure long enough to learn to use it properly.

Some beginners go to the opposite extreme. They catch a few fish on a particular lure and refuse to change. The lure may work well at times, but too often it catches nothing.

Top bass fishermen contend that you cannot catch the maximum number of fish in an area unless you have confidence in your presentation, meaning your choice of lure and how you retrieve it. When buying lures, select a few of each basic type and learn how and when to use them. Catching fish is the quickest way to gain confidence in a lure.

Bass anglers need to carry a variety of lure styles and several different colors and sizes of these lures to be successful.

Chapter 4

HOW TO CATCH LARGEMOUTH BASS

Once you have learned the basics of largemouth bass biology, location, and movements, there is an equally important set of rules on how to catch them. One of the most basic concepts for catching bass is establishing a "pattern." Being able to pattern largemouth is the basis for consistent success. Once you establish a pattern, catching them becomes a very easy task.

A pattern consists of figuring out a particular technique and location of bass that you can repeat virtually anywhere on the lake where these same variables exist. An example would be the following: Say you are fishing down a shoreline on a given lake and you catch a bass that is under a willow tree that has fallen into the water. That is the only fish you catch on that stretch or it is the biggest fish. Then you go to another shore and catch a fish on a similar willow tree that is in the water there. You may be onto a "pattern." To test this, you would drive directly to any willow trees that are in the water and see if they are holding fish. If you catch them on most willows, you have established a pattern.

This is only one specific example. The predominant pattern could be anything from fish on deep rock piles, to fish under docks with wooden posts, a particular type of weed they are using, or a specific depth that most of the fish are located. Catching a single fish does not create a pattern; you have to able to be able to consistently catch fish with the same method on different locations to have a solid pattern.

Also remember that on a given day there may be multiple patterns that exist at the same time on a lake. You may be able to catch fish on shallow willow trees, but there may also be a group of fish using offshore ledges in 15-feet of water, for example.

FINDING THE PATTERN

Establishing a pattern is the basis for top bass anglers success.

An observer at a professional bass tournament would hear a great deal of talk about finding the best *pattern*. When bass pros use this term, they are not referring to lure design. Instead, a pattern involves an elusive combination of two factors: bass location and the presentation needed to make fish bite. The pattern often changes from day to day and may even change several times a day.

The first step in unraveling a pattern is to locate the right type of fishing spot. Take into account the season, time of day, and the weather. For example, on an overcast fall day, bass will most likely stay in the shallows. On a bright day in summer, bass may feed in open shallows in early morning. But as the sun moves higher, they will move deeper or into shaded areas of the shallows.

When scouting for bass, most anglers use some type of fast-moving lure like a crankbait or spinnerbait. Hungry bass will strike almost anything, so this technique is the quickest way to locate an active school.

Concentrate on features within the most likely depth range, but occasionally move to shallower or deeper water. If you catch a bass, carefully note the exact depth and the type of cover and structure. Work the area thoroughly, but continue moving if you fail to catch another fish.

If you find an active school, try to avoid spooking the fish. Keep the boat at a distance and noise to a minimum. Without changing lures, work the school until the bass quit biting.

Presentation becomes more important after you have skimmed the active fish from the school. Switching to a lure with a different action, color, or size often triggers a strike immediately. Try to select a different lure based on the situation and continue casting toward the fish. Experiment with various lures and retrieves to find the right combination.

Before you leave a good spot, mark its exact location in your GPS so you can return later to see if the fish have resumed feeding. When a spot no longer produces, try to duplicate the pattern by looking for a similar location nearby. If you found bass on a sharp-breaking point with bulrushes on top, chances are you will find bass on similar points elsewhere. If these areas fail to produce, the pattern has probably changed.

If the weather remains stable, the patterns you find one day will probably be repeated about the same time on the next day. But a change in weather will probably result in a new set of patterns.

In some instances, several patterns exist at the same time. Bass sometimes bite equally well in deep and shallow water and the type of lure makes little difference. On these rare days, almost anyone can catch fish.

Finding a pattern for deepwater bass can be difficult and time-consuming. These fish often ignore fast-moving lures, so you may have to use a slower presentation. When you hook a fish in deep water, try to land it quickly. Otherwise, its frantic struggling may spook other bass in the school.

At times, there is no definite pattern. You may catch a bass here and there, but seldom more than one in any spot. Keep moving and cover as many areas as possible, including those places where you caught fish earlier in the day.

FISHING ON STRUCTURE

Finding structure is the key to finding largemouth bass. Experts estimate that only 10 percent of a typical lake holds bass and that 10 percent is usually around some type of structure. Fishermen who do not know how to find and fish structure have little chance for consistent success.

Structure simply means a change in the lake bottom. It could be a change in the depth or just a difference in the type of bottom material. Points, sunken islands, rock or gravel reefs, creek channels, and shoreline breaks are typical structure in many waters.

Largemouth bass use structure as underwater highways. It provides easy access for bass moving from deep to shallow water. Structure also supplies bass with something to which they can relate. Given a choice, a bass will select a location near some type of recognizable feature.

The best bass structure has natural cover like weeds, flooded brush, or timber, or man-made cover like riprap or brush shelters.

The quickest way to locate structure is to use an accurate mapping GPS unit with a good quality locator. With a little practice, you will learn to identify landmarks on shore for finding the general location of a good area. Then, by crisscrossing the area with your depth finder and marking spots on your GPS, you can pinpoint specific structure shown on the map. When you locate fish, note the exact depth. Chances are, bass on other structure throughout the lake may be at a similar depth.

Fishermen who spend a lot of time fishing one lake usually discover certain pieces of structure that routinely produce bass. In many cases, other pieces of structure that seem identical produce nothing. Some anglers have even hired divers to inspect their secret spots, thinking there must be some difference that attracts bass. Often the diver finds nothing that could not be found in dozens of other areas. Bass sometimes choose spots for reasons we do not understand. The only solution for fishermen is to work many pieces of structure. Keep moving, trying different depths and presentations until you find the right combination.

Where to Find Bass on Shallow Structure

Locating bass on shallow structure can be challenging, even for the best anglers. Most lakes have an abundance of structure in shallow water, providing bass with an endless selection of feeding areas.

All types of structure can be found in either shallow or deep water. The term shallow structure generally refers to any structure in water 10 feet (3 m) deep or less.

Begin your search for bass by working the most likely areas based on local reports, the season, and your knowledge of the lake. Spend only a few minutes in each spot and keep moving until you find some active fish.

To reduce your scouting time, concentrate on a small section of the lake. Many anglers find it more productive to thoroughly fish one creek arm rather than spending the day roaming the lake.

In clear lakes, you can see shallow structure. Wear polarized glasses to find areas like the sharp break off the side of a weedy point or a creek channel meandering through a flat. Bass in these areas can feed in shallow cover, then quickly retreat to deeper water. You may need a depth finder to spot structure in murky water.

When fishing on shallow structure, look for something slightly different from the surrounding area. Examples include a small section of reef that drops faster than the rest of the structure, a slight projection along the side of a point, or a shallow depression on top of a flat. Clumps of weeds, timber, or brush attract largemouth on flats. Look for bass in the thickest clumps or in those isolated from other cover. These subtle variations frequently hold schools of bass.

LOCATION TIPS

Small creek channels provide bass with an easy-to-follow migration route leading from deep water into the shallows. They feed on the flats along both sides of the creek. The channels themselves hold bass just before and after spawning or after a front.

Flowing streams may wash bass foods into the back of a creek arm. Streams provide warmer water in spring and cooler water in summer. These areas need to be checked after any substantial rainfall.

Shallow flats are also prime feeding areas for largemouth bass. Flats are large expanses of water that have a uniform depth. Look for flats that border deep-water ledges. Bass fishermen also work flats that rise gradually from bottom in mid-lake or those that extend from shore.

How to Catch Bass on Shallow Structure

Fishermen stand a much better chance of catching bass in shallow water than in deep water. Bass in the shallows are usually feeding and more likely to strike a lure. But bass in the shallows pose two problems for anglers. The fish are often scattered and they tend to spook easily, especially if the water is clear. To find bass on shallow structure, keep moving and use lures that can be cast and retrieved quickly so you can cover a lot of water. When you catch a fish, remember the exact location. You may want to return later for a few more casts.

When fishing in the shallows, avoid making unnecessary noises. Be especially careful not to drop anything on the bottom of the boat and do not run your outboard. Keep the boat as far away as possible and make long casts. If the water is very clear, watch the angle of the sun to avoid casting your shadow over the fish.

Almost any lure will work for fishing on shallow structure. The lure does not have to bump the bottom to catch fish. A hungry bass in 6 feet (1.8 m) of water will not hesitate to chase a buzzbait ripped across the surface, especially in warm water.

Cast a spinnerbait or some other type of weedless lure onto shallow structure that has trees, brush, or heavy weeds. Horse the bass away from cover to keep it from wrapping your line around weeds or limbs.

Most anglers prefer spinnerbaits or shallow-running crankbaits so they can cover a large area in a hurry. You may need a weedless lure if the structure has heavy weeds or brush. Carry a rod rigged with a brush-guard jig or Texas-rigged soft plastic so you can work a brush clump or an isolated weedbed slowly and thoroughly.

Casting is the best technique for working most types of shallow structure. Approach quietly and cut the outboard long before you reach the fishing area. Follow the edge of the structure while casting into the shallow water. Cast a spinnerbait or some other type of weedless lure onto shallow structure that has trees, brush, or heavy weeds. Horse the bass away from cover to keep it from wrapping your line around weeds or limbs. Cover the shallows first, but if you do not catch fish, try deeper water along the structure's edge.

Drifting sometimes works well for fishing on shallow flats if the fish are scattered and there is wind. Start at the upwind side and let the wind push the boat slowly across the structure. Use your electric trolling motor to adjust the boat's direction. Always cast with the wind. This enables you to cover water the boat has not crossed and you can cast farther with the wind at your back.

TECHNIQUES FOR FISHING ON SHALLOW STRUCTURE

Position your boat over the middle of a creek channel (shown). Cast to the shallows on either side of the channel, then retrieve the lure down the drop-off. Continue casting as you move down the channel.

Spot-cast to any unusual cover on top of a flat, sunken island, or point. A lone tree or bush or an isolated clump of thick weeds is likely to hold bass. Cast beyond the feature and retrieve the lure along the shaded side.

Move slowly along a gradually sloping shoreline, keeping the boat within casting distance of emergent weeds, flooded brush, or submerged logs. Angle some casts toward shore, others toward deeper water.

Where to Find Bass on Deep Structure

Before the advent of the modern depth finder, finding bass on deep structure was largely guesswork. Most fishermen worked shoreline structure because they could find it easily. Much of the deep, mid-lake structure was left unexplored.

The first anglers to buy depth finders enjoyed a fishing bonanza. Some schools of deepwater bass had never seen a lure. Fishing is not that easy today, but the angler who knows how to use a depth finder in conjunction with a GPS can consistently find bass on deep structure.

LOCATION TIPS

Roads that once crossed creek channels (shown) may reveal the location of submerged bridge pilings. Bridge decks are usually removed before the reservoir is filled. Intersections of two creek channels often concentrate largemouth, especially if there is ample flooded timber and brush bordering the creeks. If the junction has deep water, bass will generally stay in the area through winter.

Points that extend from shore to meet a creek channel provide ideal bass habitat. Largemouth bass that rest in the deep water of the creek channel must swim only a short distance to feed in heavy timber and brush on top of the point.

Steep drop-offs hold bass in summer, late fall, and winter. Largemouth often hang near large boulders or piles of rocks. To find largemouth bass near a cliff wall, cruise slowly along the edge while watching the depth finder for any type of projection different from the rest of the cliff.

Other options include rock reefs 12 to 20 feet (3.6 to 6 m) below the surface, especially if surrounded by deep water. In clear lakes and reservoirs, bass may inhabit reefs 25 to 50 feet (7.6 to 15 m) deep.

Prior to fishing any deep structure, explore the area thoroughly with your depth finder. Look for any variations on the structure, because these areas are most likely to hold bass. Make sure you understand the bottom configuration.

When scouting a deep sunken island or flat, crisscross the area several times. Toss a marker buoy onto the shallowest part of the sunken island or into the middle of the flat. The marker will serve as a reference point. On the top of your GPS, mark the location of any projections or indentations along the edge of the structure or any deep pockets.

To determine the shape of a submerged point, zigzag across it while edging farther into the lake. When you locate the tip of the point, throw out a marker. Then run the boat along each edge to find any irregularities and mark them in your GPS.

Creek channels bordered by flooded timber are easy to follow. But channels without timber or brush can be difficult to trace. Watch your depth finder as you follow the edge. It often helps to drop enough markers to provide a picture of the channel configuration.

How to Catch Bass on Deep Structure

In general, you can locate bass along deep structure by using a fast presentation. Even though deepwater bass may not be feeding, chances are one or two fish out of the school will chase a fast-moving crankbait. Maneuver your boat along a drop-off as you cast toward shallow and deep water. When you catch a bass, stick with the crankbait and work the area until the fish quit biting. Then switch to a slower-moving lure and cover the area thoroughly. In cold water, fast-moving lures seldom catch bass. Use slower retrieves or try vertical jigging.

Vertical jigging is also ideal for fishing along a steep ledge or any type of structure where bass school tightly. Drop the lure straight below the boat and jig it at different depths until you locate the fish.

To fish irregular structure, such as a breakline with many sharp turns or the tip of a point, anchor your boat or hover above the spot. If you fish from a moving boat, it is difficult to keep your lure in the strike zone.

When fishing a long breakline with few twists and turns, try deep-running crankbaits or a lipless crankbait to cover water. To find the proper depth, make several passes along the breakline while using lures that run at different depths. Note the exact location of any strike on your GPS and continue to work the area until the fish stop biting. Then switch to a slower presentation, such as slow-hopping a brushguard jig.

Follow the contour of a shoreline point or other deep structure by using an electric trolling motor. Flooded timber or emergent weeds on top of a point provide a clue to the location of the drop-off.

Cast a sinking lure such as a Texas-rigged plastic worm into the shallows along the outside bend of a creek channel. Bump it along the bottom until it reaches the drop-off, then slow your retrieve as the lure drops down the slope.

Keep the line tight as the lure sinks (shown). Bass holding along the channel edge will grab a plastic worm or jigging lure as it drops. Set the hook immediately and pull the fish away from the cover as soon as possible.

Vertical jigging is ideal for fishing along a steep ledge or any type of structure where bass school tightly. Drop the lure straight below the boat and jig it at different depths until you locate the fish.

Parallel casting works well for covering any sharp drop-off with a straight edge. Position the boat so you can cast parallel to the ledge. Count the lure down to different depths to find bass.

FISHING ON MAN-MADE FEATURES

Nearly all bass fishing waters show signs of human activity. Docks and boat houses surround the shoreline. In some lakes, tires, cement blocks, and other debris litter the bottom. Some people consider these discarded items offensive, but you will not hear bass fishermen complaining. They know that many of these features provide excellent cover for bass.

Man-made features lie beneath the water in every reservoir. Occasionally, entire towns were flooded. Bass in reservoirs can be found near a wide array of features, from roadbeds and railroad tracks to the foundations of buildings and, most often, brush piles planted by anglers to attract fish.

Some waters, fisheries, agencies, and anglers place fish attractors to provide habitat for bass. Attractors vary from clumps of brush or trees, to stakebeds with rows of upright slats on a wooden platform, to crib shelters made of large logs.

Bass will relate to man-made features in any lake, especially if they provide cover within the right depth range. But these features are more important in waters that lack adequate natural cover or structure. For example, in a murky lake with uniform depth and few weeds, bass scatter throughout the lake and become difficult to find. Man-made features in this type of lake will concentrate bass, making the fish easier to find and catch.

To find man-made features, obtain an up-to-date hydrographic map or map chip for your mapping locator. Original reservoir maps often show the location of features like submerged buildings, roadbeds, and power line crossings. Some maps also pinpoint the location of fish attractors. River charts show dredged channels, wing dams, levees, and riprap shores.

Maps sometimes lack detail on man-made features, so fishermen must rely on local information and their depth finders. Modern mapping GPS locators can be especially valuable for reading man-made features. They provide more detail than old-style flashers, enabling you to distinguish between features like a man-made brush pile and a clump of weeds.

Where to Find Bass on Man-Made Features

Bass prefer man-made features near some type of structure. Without deepwater refuge, the cover is of little value to bass. For example, you would be more likely to find bass near a bridge over a deep channel than a bridge over a shallow expanse of water.

Man-made features connected to a natural movement path will also concentrate bass. Earthen dams are often built across dry washes to create farm ponds. After the reservoir is filled, bass moving along the dry wash channel encounter the dam and gather along both sides.

Features near heavy natural cover will not hold as many bass as those that are isolated. Bass pay little attention to a brush pile placed in the middle of a thick weedbed. But the same brush pile would definitely hold bass if placed on a weedless hump.

Finding submerged features can be difficult. Fishermen sometimes mark their favorite spots with plastic jugs, while some conservation agencies pinpoint fish attractors with buoys. But most underwater features lack visible signs. To find them, you must have reliable information.

Local anglers or bait shop operators may be able to help you find man-made features. If not, keep an eye on other fishermen, especially those anchored in unusual locations. When they leave, check out the spot. You may find a school of bass hanging around a brush or rock pile.

Shade is often the key to locating bass around man-made features. The fish often hold along the junction of shady and sunlit water. Note the angle of the sun and try to imagine where the shadow would fall under water.

Always make your cast to the shady portion of the feature and work those areas first. Also, keep an eye out for objects that protrude down into the water that the fish may locate next to. These are typically the prime spots on any man-made structure.

Good docks provide ample shade. They have some weeds nearby, but not a dense stand that covers the area. Look for docks in water at least 3 feet (0.9 m) deep and close to deeper water.

Shade is the key to locating bass around man-made features. The fish often hold along the junction of shady and sunlit water. Note the angle of the sun and try to imagine where the shadow would fall under water.

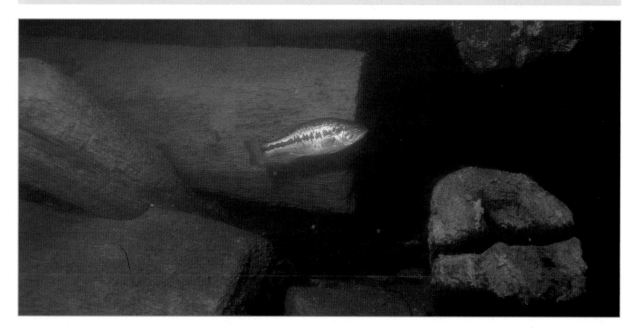

Cribs are constructed from logs or railroad ties (shown) weighted down with large concrete blocks. Look for bass resting along the shaded side or hovering above these large attractors.

Brush piles (shown) are made by sinking evergreen trees or bundles of large branches lashed together and weighted. They provide excellent cover for baitfish and aquatic insects, which in turn attract panfish and largemouth.

Bridges across narrow parts of a lake or reservoir funnel wind-blown foods into a small area. Look for bass hanging tight to the pilings or near the concrete abutments next to shore.

Channels dredged between two lakes or leading into a boat harbor may attract spawning largemouth. Watch for signs of nesting activity in the vegetation along both sides of the channel.

Riprap prevents waves from eroding channel edges or steep shorelines. Look for bass where the bank drops quickly into deep water. Largemouth often hang near rocks close to shore.

Where to Find Bass on Man-Made Features in Reservoirs

Bass fishermen can easily find old buildings or any man-made feature that protrudes above the surface. But locating submerged features in a reservoir is difficult, even for the fisherman with an accurate mapping locator.

If a good hydrographic map is not available or if the map chip does not show many man-made features, you still have other options. You can wait for a drawdown to expose man-made features. Irrigation systems draw water from many reservoirs, gradually lowering the water level through summer and fall. Some reservoirs are drawn down rapidly in fall or winter to make room for heavy spring runoff. The water level may drop 40 feet (12 m) below the normal summer stage. With the water this low, you can note the exact location of man-made features. Some fishermen take photographs of the lake bed during low water. When the basin fills, they know where to look for bass.

Maps made before the reservoir was filled can be helpful. U.S. Geological Survey maps, called quad maps, pinpoint the location of features such as houses, roads, railroad tracks, and ponds. Quad maps are available for almost all of the country. They also show land elevations, so if you know the surface elevation of the reservoir, you can easily calculate the depth of specific man-made features, then find them and mark them in your GPS.

To work a specific spot like a bridge piling, jig vertically around the perimeter while working different depths. Some anglers intentionally

mis-tune a crankbait by bending the eye to one side so it veers to the left or right, toward hard-to-reach locations like the spaces between dock posts.

Flippin' works well for placing a lure in spots that are difficult to reach by casting. It may be hard to cast into the area between two docked boats or to drop a lure next to the inside wall of a duck blind. But you can flip a jig easily into either spot.

How to Catch Bass on Man-Made Features

Fishing along man-made features like riprap banks and roadbeds is little different than working natural features such as shoreline breaks and weedlines. Bass may scatter over a long distance, so you must keep moving until you find them.

But when fishing around man-made features like docks and bridge pilings, you know exactly where to look. To catch bass holding tight to these features, cast beyond the spot where the fish are likely to be. Then retrieve the lure so it passes only inches (cm) away. When fishing a straight-edged feature like a

MAN-MADE FEATURES TO LOOK FOR IN RESERVOIRS

Power line clearings (shown) and boat roads were cut before the reservoir was flooded. Bass hold near the clearing rather than far back in the flooded timber.

Fence rows dividing open fields (shown) may provide the only cover in a large area. Look for bass near the largest trees or where fence rows cross.

House foundations in flooded towns appear as solid black squares on a reservoir map. The dashed lines trace old roads. The solid line is the shoreline.

Roadbeds, especially those with hard surfaces, attract largemouth. Work the ditches and any intersections with creek channels and other roads.

Railroad tracks are usually built on elevated grades. Bass relate to the edge of the embankment just as they would a natural breakline.

house foundation, chances are that bass will be lined up near the base of the wall along the shady side. Many fishermen make the mistake of casting at right angles to the wall, then pulling the lure away. With this technique, the lure is in the strike zone for only an instant, so it would take dozens of casts to cover the wall completely. Instead, position your boat so you can cast parallel to the edge. Your lure will stay in the strike zone for most of the retrieve, enabling you to cover the edge quickly and thoroughly. This method also works well for fishing around natural structure and cover.

To work a specific spot like a bridge piling, jig vertically around the perimeter while working different depths. Some anglers intentionally mis-tune a crankbait so it veers toward hard-to-reach locations like the spaces between dock posts.

Flippin' works well for placing a lure in spots that are difficult to reach by casting. It may be hard to cast into the area between two docked boats or to drop a lure next to the inside wall of a duck blind. But you can flip a jig easily into either spot.

HOW TO FISH MAN-MADE FEATURES

Cast a crankbait or spinnerbait parallel to a channel wall (shown). Retrieve the lure along the bottom, keeping it as close to the wall as possible. The noise and erratic action of the lure bumping the wall often trigger strikes. Some fishermen walk along the wall, then vertically jig over the edge.

Retrieve a Texas-rigged plastic worm or a brushguard jig through a brush shelter. Slowly work the lure among the branches.

Toss your lure into shade along a dock. Some fishermen prefer a 5½- or 6-foot (1.7 or 1.8 m) spinning rod to skip the lure under the dock.

Cast a deep-running or sinking crankbait parallel to a bridge pier. Some fishermen troll a figure-eight pattern around two adjacent bridge pilings. The lure will bump against each piling on the turns.

Suspend a lively bait to catch bass lurking inside a culvert. Lower the bait to the right depth on a jig head. Or use a split-shot or slip-bobber rig.

Flip a lure to the motor "washout" area when fishing a dock. The water is often free of weeds and deeper than the surrounding area.

FISHING IN THE WEEDS

A largemouth tail-walking above the weeds as it tries to shake an artificial lure is a sight familiar to bass fishermen.

Weeds are the most common type of bass cover and certainly the most important. Bass fry crowd into dense weedbeds to hide from predators. Adult bass hide in weeds to ambush prey. The weeds provide homes for small insects that attract baitfish and other bass foods. Heavy mats of floating weeds prevent the sun's heat from penetrating the surface. Bass move into cool water below the weeds when the rest of the shallows becomes too warm.

Weeds perform yet another important function. Through the process of photosynthesis, they produce oxygen that is vital to the survival of fish.

The aquatic plants used by bass fall into the following categories:

SUBMERGED WEEDS. These weeds grow below the water, although some have flowers that extend above the surface. Water clarity determines how deep these plants will grow. In extremely clear water, they may get enough sunlight to flourish in depths of 30 feet (9 m) or more. In murky lakes, they seldom grow in water deeper than 5 feet (1.5 m).

A distinct edge forms where the water becomes too deep for submerged weeds to grow. Called a weedline, this edge generally occurs at the same depth throughout a body of water. Weedlines are important bass-holding features.

You can call up bass through dense weeds by using a surface lure.

FLOATING LEAVED WEEDS. Some weeds, such as lily pads, have leaves that float on the surface. The broad leaves provide more shade than the leaves of most other plants. They offer excellent shallow-water cover for largemouth.

Many weeds will also grow to the surface and fold over forming mats, which offer the same shade and cover that floating leaved weeds do. They also provide cooler water temperatures for bass to be more comfortable in summer heat.

EMERGENT WEEDS. These plants protrude well above the surface. Often they form a band extending around much of a shoreline. Bass frequently spawn among emergent weeds in 2 to 3 feet (0.6 to 0.9 m) of water. Emergent weeds in deeper water may hold bass through the summer.

The best emergent weeds often have submerged weeds mixed in with them to offer fish more cover. Look for areas where a different weed species creates an edge that may give away bass location.

Water lilies include some 15 species in North America. Round or heart-shaped leaves, called pads, float or stand slightly above the surface. The showy, cup-shaped flowers may be white, pink, blue, or yellow, depending on the species. Lilies grow on muddy bottoms, usually in water shallower than 8 feet (2.5 m).

Water hyacinth was introduced into the United States in the late 1800s. It is considered a nuisance in several southern states and California, where large beds float on the surface, covering entire lakes and waterways. It has rounded, shiny-green leaves and blue, white, or violet flowers.

Pondweeds total over 50 species. These rooted plants grow in fresh or brackish water. Leaves may be thread-like or broad; broad-leaved types are called cabbage. Most species have submerged leaves, but some have floating leaves. Most pond-weeds have flowering heads, or spikes, that protrude above the surface.

Coontail forms dense blankets as much as 10 feet (3 m) thick. A stand is made up of plants anchored on the soft bottom along with pieces of coontail that have broken off, but continue to live. Each branch, with its thick cluster of narrow leaves, resembles a raccoon's tail. Color varies from olive to dark green among the six kinds.

Bulrushes include 55 types. Many grow in both fresh and brackish water. Most have round, leafless stems that taper to a slender point. Color varies from grayish-green to dark green. Small brownish flowers appear at the top of the stem. These rooted plants may grow to 5 feet (1.5 m) above the surface.

Cattails are named for the brownish, fur-like flower at the tip of the stem. All four species prefer soft bottoms and can live in fresh or brackish water. The leaves are long and flat, varying from yellowish-green to dark green. They sprout from large roots, or rhizomes. Cattails can grow as high as 8 feet (2.5 m) above the water.

Milfoil includes 13 types, some of which grow in brackish water. Sometimes confused with coontail, milfoil often has pinkish or reddish, rather than greenish, stems. It grows on soft bottoms and may form a dense layer up to 10 feet (3 m) thick. Eurasian water milfoil, though an unwelcome invader in much of the country, makes excellent bass cover.

Hydrilla, a fast-spreading exotic, was first discovered in Florida and has spread through much of the South. It requires little sunlight, so it grows to greater depths and in darker waters than most other aquatic plants. Although it causes serious navigation problems in shallow lakes, it has revitalized the fisheries in many old reservoirs.

Where & How to Catch Bass in Shallow Weeds

Bass fishermen in natural lakes catch more largemouth bass in shallow weeds than in any other type of cover. Shallow weeds include any type of emergent, floating-leaved, or submerged plant in water 10 feet (3 m) or less. The type of weed matters little to bass, as long as it provides adequate cover.

The best times to find bass in shallow vegetation are spring and early fall. In summer, weeds serve mainly as morning and evening feeding grounds. But some bass stay in the weeds all summer if the cover is dense enough to block out sunlight.

Shallow weeds near deep water usually hold the most bass. Given a choice, bass will choose a weedbed near a drop-off over one located in the middle of a large, shallow area. Avoid weedbeds so thick that bass would have difficulty moving about.

Bass prefer distinct edges to solid masses of weeds. Look for pockets and projections along weedy edges and open areas within weeds.

Fishing in shallow weeds requires special equipment. Most anglers prefer a powerful rod and a high-speed bait-casting reel. Once you hook a bass, pull as hard as your equipment allows; this will get the bass headed toward the surface and out of the weed. Hold the rod tip high as you reel, exerting strong pressure to keep its head up. If you allow the bass to dive into dense cover, it will probably tangle your line around the stems and break free. Strong pressure also reduces the chance of the bass throwing the hook when it jumps.

Abrasion-resistant line, generally 14- to 20-pound-test (6 to 9 kg) co-polymer works well for most weed-fishing situations. Some fishermen use braided line up to 80-pound-test (36 kg) when fishing in dense weedbeds. It cuts through weeds better and the heavy line does not seem to spook bass in thick cover.

Weedless lures are a must for fishing in most shallow weeds. You may be able to snake a standard lure through scattered weeds, but even moderately dense weeds will foul your hooks and ruin the lure's action. Brushguard jigs and hollow frogs are two good choices for dense weeds.

Although they lack weedless hooks, Texas-rigged plastic worms and spinnerbaits are among the most weed-resistant lures. Some fishermen bend their hook points slightly toward the hook shank. The point is less likely to pick up weeds but is exposed enough to hook a bass.

Angling in shallow weeds demands accurate casting. Bass in dense weeds may be reluctant to chase a lure. You must be able to hit small pockets by flipping or pitching or to cast parallel to a weed edge.

Fly-casting is an extremely effective method of presenting a lure into a small opening in shallow weeds. But horsing a big bass out of heavy cover will test the tackle of any fly fisherman.

Many bass fishermen swear by live bait rigged on a weedless hook. You can flip a frog, salamander, or minnow into holes in the weeds; you can let the bait swim through cover with a free line; or you can suspend it from a bobber. Some anglers gently lob the bait a short distance, then skitter it across weed-tops. Long casts will kill most live baits quickly.

Pockets in matted weeds or floating-leaved weeds such as lily pads serve as ambush points for feeding largemouth. When fishing pockets in deeper water, look for areas with harder bottom types.

Slop consists of various floating-leaved and submerged weeds (shown) mixed with filamentous, or moss-like algae. The water temperature may be 10 degrees cooler below the top.

Edges of emergent weeds such as bulrushes are top shallow-water locations. The inside edge of a weedbed may hold as many bass as the outside edge. Look for bass in any boat lanes or openings in the weeds.

Clumps of emergent weeds often break away from dense mats along shore. These clumps float about the lake, providing temporary cover for largemouth bass, usually in early spring.

Cast parallel to weed edges (top). Drop the lure within a few inches of the weeds, then retrieve it as close as possible to the margin.

Spot-cast into pockets (right). Let a sinking lure flutter downward into the opening, allowing it to rest a few moments before giving it a shake.

Wear polarized glasses to cut glare while fishing; they allow you to see bottom features, structure, and fish under the water surface.

Cut the leading hook from each of the trebles to make a surface lure more weedless. Some anglers replace the hooks with weedguard trebles.

Sharpen the edges of the prop on your trolling motor using a file. The sharp edges cut weed stems so they don't foul the prop.

Pull off about two rod-lengths of line. Let half of the line dangle from the rod tip; hold the other half in your free hand. Keeping the tip up, point the rod in the direction of the target. Swing the lure toward your body while lowering the rod tip and pulling on the line in your free hand.

Flip the lure with a short upward snap of the rod tip. At the same time, release the line in your free hand, propelling the lure toward the target.

Where & How to Catch Bass in Deep Weeds

The secret to catching bass in deep weeds is to find a weedline. You can catch some largemouth in a wide expanse of deep weeds, but to improve your odds, concentrate on the edges.

In a clear lake, weeds may grow to depths of 20 or 25 feet (6 or 7.6 m). But with a depth finder and a little practice, locating a deep weedline is not as difficult as you might expect. When you find a weedline, throw out one or more markers along the edge, keeping them just inside the weeds.

Use your trolling motor or move along the weedline while casting a deep-running crankbait or lipless crankbait along the edge. Variations along the weedline will hold the most fish. Bass recognize and use these specific spots as resting sites or ambush points. Look for a break in the weed or a slight indentation along the edge. Largemouth also school around points of weeds that project farther out than the rest of the weedline.

If you catch a bass while trolling or drifting, it is probably an active fish within a school. Mark the spot on your GPS, then work it thoroughly. You may have to switch to a slower presentation to catch more fish.

If you do not have a depth finder, you must rely on your sense of feel. When your lure tracks through weeds, it catches momentarily, pulls loose, then catches again. Veer toward deeper water until you no longer feel weeds and slowly angle back toward the weedline.

Most lure types used in shallow weeds will also work in deep weeds. But you may need a larger sinker with your soft plastic, a heavier spinnerbait brushguard jig, or a deeper-diving crankbait.

Bass along a deep weedline sometimes ignore artificial lures. If the fish are not feeding, live bait may be the only solution. Using a slip-sinker rig, cast parallel to the weedline, then inch the bait toward the boat. Or suspend the bait from a slip-bobber. Retrieve it slowly or let the wind push it along the edge of the weeds.

Tall weeds provide bass with shade. Some types of pondweeds may grow to the surface in water as deep as 15 feet (4.5 m).

TIPS FOR FISHING IN DEEP WEEDS

Flip a ¾- to 1-ounce (21 to 28 g) brushguard jig with a pork or soft-plastic trailer in dense weedbeds (shown). Make a short cast, shake your rod tip to get the lure down through the weeds, yo-yo it a few times, then reel up and cast again.

Locate a deep weedline with a flasher or graph. While over the weeds, you'll see a wide band of blips or marks above the bottom. The marks will disappear when you cross the weedline.

Rip a crankbait through brittle weeds, such as cabbage, by reeling rapidly. Use a stiff rod so you can jerk the lure free from weeds. The lure will dart erratically when it breaks loose, often coaxing a strike.

Substitute a self-pegging bullet sinker for an ordinary worm-sinker rig when fishing in dense weeds. These weights screw or peg into the worm, preventing the two from separating and eliminating the need to peg the sinker.

FISHING IN FLOODED TIMBER & BRUSH

When a bass feels the sting of a hook, its first reaction is to head for cover. And if that cover happens to be nearby trees or brush, the ensuing battle will test the skill of any angler.

Although it may be difficult to fight and land a bass in woody cover, fishermen who know how to work timber and brush rarely fail to catch bass.

Dams on large rivers have flooded vast expanses of timber and brush over the past few decades. After a reservoir fills, over 100 feet (30 m) of water may cover the trees. In some impoundments, the entire basin is flooded timber with the exception of farm fields, roads, and towns.

A low dam on a river will not cover an entire forest, but it will flood timber and brush in the backwaters. These trees also rot off in time. Waves pounding on stumps in shallow water wash soil away from the bases, exposing the root systems. The spaces between the roots make ideal bass cover. Stumps in shallow areas of reservoirs also have exposed roots underwater.

Submerged trees may last indefinitely. Timber that protrudes above water eventually rots off at the waterline, leaving only partially exposed trunks.

In some cases, the U.S. Army Corps of Engineers or other government agencies cut the trees as a reservoir is filling. Once filled, the reservoir appears to be void of timber, but it has a forest of tree trunks several feet below the surface. Occasionally, loggers clear-cut most of the trees before a reservoir is created, leaving only stumps. Although tall timber may be hard to find, the chances of it holding bass are better than if the reservoir was filled with trees.

Some reservoir maps show the location of timber; some do not. If your map chip lacks such information, obtain a quad map, which shows the location of woodlands before the reservoir was filled. Chances are, the trees will still be there.

Flooded brush decays much faster than timber. You may find brush in deep water in some new reservoirs, but in older ones, brush grows mainly in the shallows. During prolonged periods of low water, brush flourishes along shore. When the water level returns to normal, the brush is submerged, providing excellent bass habitat.

Bass in natural lakes and river backwaters seek cover in flooded brush, especially during spring and early summer when runoff raises water levels. The brush harbors foods such as minnows and insects.

Anglers who spend a lot of time fishing around timber know that certain types of trees are better than others. Generally, the largest trees or those with the most branches attract the most fish. Cedar trees, for example, with their dense network of branches, are consistent bass producers.

In southern lakes and sloughs, water-dwelling trees such as cypress provide homes for largemouth. Erosion along riverbanks often results in trees tumbling into the water. The branches offer cover and break the current.

In steep-walled reservoirs, rock-slides carry trees and brush down the slope and into the water. The trees may provide the only cover along a cliff wall. In lakes and ponds that lack good shoreline cover, fishermen sometimes fell trees into the water, then cable the tree to the stump.

Where it is legal, man-made brush piles or Christmas trees are often weighted and lowered onto key points or near docks to attract baitfish and bass in areas void of other structure. These key fish-holding spots can be found with the use of a depth finder.

Where & How to Catch Bass in Shallow Timber and Brush

When searching for feeding bass in a reservoir, most anglers head for a patch of shallow timber or brush.

Bass use shallow timber and brush the same way they use shallow weeds. They offer a protected spawning area in spring, a morning and evening feeding zone in summer, and an all-day feeding area in early fall. Bass abandon this cover in late fall and winter.

The best shallow timber and brush is near deep water. Look for bass around isolated patches, along a distinct tree line or brushline, and in deep pockets on brush- or timber-covered flats. Fishermen can sometimes see clues that reveal the location of submerged timber and brush. A small limb extending above the surface may be part of a large tree. Stickups, or the tips of small branches, pinpoint the location of submerged brush. A tilted log in open water probably means a tree has floated in and lodged along a drop-off. A clump of trees or brush standing higher than others nearby indicates an underwater hump.

Weedless lures are a must for fishing in brush and stumps. Spinnerbaits and brushguard jigs were developed specifically for this purpose. Other popular lures include buzzbaits and Texas-rigged plastics.

With a little practice, you can learn how to work a crankbait through openings in the brush and how to bounce it off stumps without snagging. Many tackle companies have special square-billed crankbaits designed specifically for this purpose.

Casting accuracy is important when fishing in shallow timber and brush. A bass holding tight under a log may refuse a lure that passes more than a foot or two away. But when bass begin to feed, they move out of their hiding spots to cruise about in openings between the trees or brush. Anglers often ignore these open areas, thinking that all bass are near cover. Largemouth in clear water generally hold tighter to cover than bass in murky water.

Use heavy abrasion-resistant line or braided line for fishing in timber or brush. The constant friction of line against limbs will soon cause fraying. Check your line and knot frequently after catching a bass. A rough spot on the line or a weak knot could result in a lost trophy. Cut off a few feet (m) of line and retie your knots several times a day.

Be sure to leave your lure in the cover and shake it a couple times to give the bass a chance to locate it.

Brushy flats near deep water (top) often hold feeding bass. If a flat is bordered with a distinct line of brush, the fish will congregate along this edge. Bass will also hold in the thickest clumps of brush on the flat.

Tree lines and brushlines (right) are similar to weedlines. Look for bass along the edge or several feet inside the cover. Sharp bends, pockets, or points along the edge hold more bass than straight portions.

Isolated trees or brush concentrate bass. A small stand of trees away from other cover is more likely to hold bass than a similar stand within a flooded forest or near a large weedbed.

Downed trees offer several types of cover for bass. The fish hang among the branches or under the main trunk. If the entire tree has toppled into the water, look for bass among the roots.

Buzz the lure across the surface by holding the rod tip high (left) and reeling rapidly. Stop reeling when the lure is next to the tree.

Float an unweighted plastic lizard or worm over shallow brush (right). Twitch the lure as you retrieve it slowly. Watch for a slurp that signals a strike.

Flip a jig-and-eel or plastic worm into openings between stumps, trees, or brush. Drop the lure into areas with the heaviest shade. Wait until the lure hits bottom. Hop the jig through the opening by lifting the rod tip, then lowering the rod to ease the lure back to bottom.

Bump a crankbait against the side of a log or bush. The erratic action may tempt a bass. A big-lipped crankbait will bounce off branches, reducing snags.

Where & How to Catch Bass in Deep Timber & Brush

If you ran a locator over a submerged forest, you would probably see a large number of fish scattered among the trees. And a good share of them would be bass.

A high quality LCR is valuable for locating bass in deep timber because it enables you to distinguish fish from tree limbs. On a flasher, bass look much like the branches and are hard to distinguish.

Finding bass in deep timber and brush may be difficult, especially in a reservoir that has a lot of trees. The secret is to locate edges or isolated clumps of woody cover.

Prime locations include tree lines along structure such as creek channels. Other good locations include farm fields, orchards, windbreaks, and power line clearings. Look for bass in brushlines along road ditches and fencelines. They also congregate in timber and brush on sunken islands, points, and deep flats.

In clearcut areas, stumps may provide the only bass cover. If your depth finder shows a jagged bottom, you may be over a submerged stump field.

In summer, look for bass in timber or brush from 20 to 45 feet (6 to 13.7 m) deep. Fish brushlines or timberlines much like you would a weedline. Use a deep-running crankbait to find the bass, then switch to a brushguard jig or Texas-rigged soft plastic. Vary the depth of your retrieve because bass may be suspended halfway up the trees.

During late fall and winter, many bass can be caught by vertical jigging in 30 to 40 feet (10 to 12 m) of water. Start jigging at 10 to 15 feet (3 to 4.5 m) and work your way down until you contact fish. After a few warm days in winter, bass often gather near the surface. Catch them by retrieving a surface lure above the deep treetops.

Some anglers prefer 50-pound-test (22 kg) braided line for fishing in deep timber and brush. Braid has almost no stretch, so it signals a bite better than mono. It also resists nicks and abrasions better than monofilament. If needed, tie on a 6-foot (1.8 m) fluorocarbon leader to reduce visibility.

Position your boat as close as possible to a large tree. Drop the lure down through the limbs, keeping it close to the trunk. Twitch the jig, then keep a tight line as it sinks. This lets you detect even the lightest tap. Jig around the tree at different depths.

Chapter 5

SPECIAL SITUATIONS

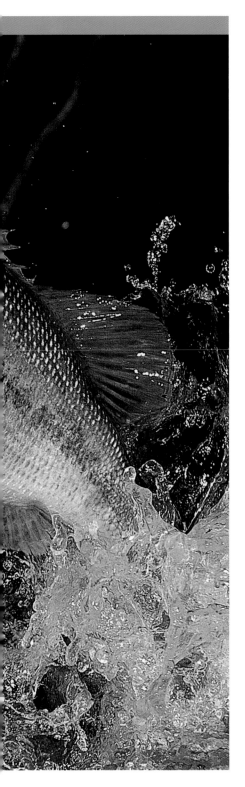

For consistent bass-fishing success, anglers should know how to deal with special situations. Included in this chapter are many of the most common challenges bass anglers will face and how to turn them into opportunities.

Tough fishing conditions are not unusual. They begin in spring when bass complete spawning and the females refuse to bite. Heavy spring rains cause drastic fluctuations in water levels and clarity, both of which can slow fishing. From late spring to summer, cold fronts often pass through only a few days apart, bringing fishing to a standstill. By mid-summer, abundant food makes bass less inclined to bite. In late fall and winter, bass spend much of their time suspended in deep water where catching them can be difficult.

The difference between a good bass fisherman and an expert is the ability to solve these tough fishing problems. For example, when reservoirs become muddy after a heavy rainfall, most anglers give up. But the expert fisherman finds a creek arm with a clear stream flowing in and enjoys some of the best fishing of the year.

Successful anglers have another important skill. They know how to recognize and take advantage of fishing opportunities. Rivers and streams, for example, can provide quality angling in summer when fishing on lakes and reservoirs is slow. And fishermen who master night-fishing techniques often catch bass when daytime anglers fail.

Sometimes these opportunities last only a moment. An inexperienced fisherman will motor past a flock of diving gulls, paying little attention to the noisy birds. But the expert knows that gulls wheeling over the water often reveal a school of largemouth feeding on shad near the surface. He races to the spot and boats several bass before the school disappears.

COLD FRONTS

Few anglers agree as to why bass fishing slows down after a cold front. But all agree that it does slow down. And if the cold front is severe, bass may not bite for several days.

Some fishermen blame the poor fishing on a rising barometer. But studies have failed to confirm that barometric pressure alone has any effect on fishing. Falling water temperature may have some impact, even though the air temperature may change drastically, the water temperature changes little.

The most logical explanation is a combination of these factors along with the extremely clear skies that follow a cold front, allowing more sunlight to reach the water. The strong light drives bass into deeper water or heavier cover. Divers have reported seeing bass buried in deep weeds with only their tails sticking out. The fish generally remain inactive for one to two days after the front passes. If bass do not have access to deep water, they bury in the thickest weeds in the shallows.

Catching bass holding tight to thick cover requires pinpoint casting. Most fishermen use small lures, slow retrieves, and light lines to tempt lethargic bass.

Flippin' into heavy cover enables you to present a lure within a few inches of a bass. Jig the lure slowly, but pause occasionally so it hangs motionless. Sometimes a bass will stare at a lure several seconds before striking.

If a bass does bite, it often takes only a half-hearted nip at the lure or bait. Keep a tight line and watch carefully for the slightest twitch. You may need a stinger hook to catch these short-striking fish.

TIPS FOR AFTER A COLD FRONT

Live bait such as a nightcrawler (shown) may be the best solution for catching largemouth after a cold front. Bass examine their food closely, often ignoring everything but the real thing.

Rivers and other murky waters continue to produce bass after a cold front. The turbid water allows little light penetration despite clear skies.

Avoid fishing in shallow bays following a cold front. These areas cool faster than the rest of the lake, making the effects of the front more noticeable to bass.

Deep cover holds bass after a cold front, often in a dense stand of timber.

SUSPENDED BASS

Bass suspended near some type of cover are easier to catch. Fishermen on reservoirs often catch suspended bass by vertically jigging along sheer cliffs or in flooded timber at depths up to 50 feet (15 m).

Bass also suspend below large schools of baitfish in open water. The small fish usually hang from 5 to 30 feet (1.5 to 9 m) below the surface with the bass several feet below them. On calm mornings and evenings, the baitfish may dimple the surface while feeding on tiny insects. Many anglers have seen the quiet water disturbed by the occasional swirls of bass grabbing small shad or other baitfish. If you see this happening, try drawing bass to the surface with a topwater lure. Some anglers use the countdown method if bass refuse surface lures. Cast a lipless crankbait into the vicinity of the bass, then count as the lure sinks. Begin your retrieve at different counts until you catch a bass. Then count the lure down to the same depth on succeeding casts.

Largemouth suspended in open water are more likely to strike if you use light line. A line weight of 8- or 10-pound-test (3.6 or 4.5 kg) is enough to land even the largest bass in water free of obstructions. Bass suspended in treetops or near other underwater obstructions may require heavier line to pull the fish away from the cover immediately after the hook set. Matching your lure choice to the baitfish type the fish are keying on will also increase your chances of catching suspended bass.

Largemouth suspended over shallower water are often feeding on baitfish and can be found by locating schooling baitfish "clouds" on your depth finder. Bass that are over deep water without baitfish present are often the hardest to catch because they are not actively feeding and may be roaming. Roaming fish are difficult to locate because of the amount of water they can cover on a day-to-day basis.

Be aware that in most cases bass will be located under the baitfish schools and respond best to lures fished above the depth at which they are suspended.

If you see fish on your locator and are unable to get them to bite, try fishing live bait on a slip bobber rig. Set the bait just above the depth you have seen the most bass.

Bass will also move up and down in the water column and feed at a certain depth range. Be sure to make a note of what depth you catch fish from in open water. Fish in other areas of the lake will often feed at this same depth. Also be aware that unless conditions change, bass may feed at the same depth for days in a row. Be aware that as the bait moves the fish will go with them, so the bass may be a great distance from where you first found them. In many cases, you can't find them at all.

When fishing for suspended bass, always look in the water behind a hooked fish. Often, other fish in the school will follow this fish up, hoping to get food that has been dropped by the struggling bass. These "followers" can be caught if another angler in the boat casts behind the hooked fish.

Some tournament anglers believe that releasing suspended bass back into a school will shut off the bite. To avoid this situation, they keep all of their bass in the live-well until they are done fishing that area.

HOT WEATHER

There are many reasons for poor bass fishing during hot weather. Most significant is the abundant food supply. Baitfish hatched in spring reach a size attractive to bass in mid-summer. With natural food so easy to find, artificial lures have less appeal.

Mid-summer also finds sunlight penetration at its highest. With the sun directly overhead, bass must move deeper or find thick cover. If the water temperature exceeds 80°F (26.6°C), bass look for cooler water in the depths, around springs, or near coldwater tributaries. Studies have shown that if they cannot find water cooler than 80°F, they become sluggish and eat very little.

Some anglers assume that largemouth do not feed during mid-summer because they cannot catch the fish shallow like they had in the spring. But with the exception of shallow lakes in the deep South, bass eat more in mid-summer than at any other time of the year. In one study of a northern lake, bass ate 222 percent more food per day during July and August than they ate in May and June. These figures prove you can catch bass in summer. But you must be in the right place at the right time. When food is plentiful, it takes only a few minutes for a bass to eat its fill for the day.

If the weather is hot, clear, and calm, these short feeding bursts take place at dusk, dawn, or at night. Bass feed on the same shallow flats used at other times of the year. But you can also find active schools in deep water. If you catch bass at a certain time one day, they will probably feed about the same time the next day, unless the weather changes. Bass sometimes bite throughout the day if the weather if overcast, rainy, or windy.

Unless the water temperature exceeds 80°F (26.6°C), hot weather fishing requires no special techniques. Use presentations appropriate for the situation. At temperatures above 80°F, small lures and slow retrieves work best. When fishing in slop, slowly retrieve a surface lure over the matted weeds. Or flip a 4-inch (10 cm) plastic worm into openings in the weeds. In deep water, try vertically jigging with a spoon, tailspin, or brushguard jig. If bass refuse these offerings, live bait may be the answer.

When casting, try to target shaded areas on hot, clear days. Bridges, docks, weeds, and other solid overhead cover may provide enough shade to keep the surface water several degrees cooler than the surrounding area.

If the bass still refuse to cooperate, wait for overcast or rainy days during a prolonged period of hot weather and clear skies. The low-light conditions and slightly cooler surface temperature cause bass to leave thick cover or to move shallower to feed. Night fishing is often the best method for catching bass during these periods.

Most people begin their summer vacations about the time bass fishing takes its hot weather nosedive. Even the best fishermen sometimes have trouble catching bass in mid-summer.

Check the water temperature by using a thermometer that traps a small volume of water from the desired depth or an electric thermometer. If the temperature is above 80°F (26.6°C), bass will be in deeper water.

Work dense overhead weeds to find bass in hot weather. Slop or other matted vegetation may offer the only cool water in shallow lakes that lack manmade cover such as docks.

CLEAR WATER

Ultra-clear water presents one of bass fishing's toughest challenges. In some canyon reservoirs, strip pits, and natural lakes, fishermen have observed bass cruising in water 20 feet (6 m) deep. And when you can see the bass, the bass can see you.

Finding bass in clear water may be more difficult than finding them in murky water because the fish may go very deep to escape sunlight and warm temperatures. In canyon reservoirs, bass have been found at depths exceeding 100 feet (30 m). In murky lakes with heavy algae blooms, bass are confined to the shallows because the depths lack oxygen.

Not all bass go deep on sunny days. If there is dense cover in the shallows, they may simply move into the shade. Thick vegetation such as brush and floating-leaved weeds provides shallow-water refuge for bass in ultra-clear lakes. Bass will hold extremely close to cover, so accurate casts are necessary. When fishing in clear, shallow water, wear neutral-colored clothing, keep a low profile, and avoid moving suddenly or

Overhanging cliffs, docks, bridges, and other overhead cover offer ample shade. Under this type of cover, bass will remain in the shallows all day.

casting your shadow over the fish. Although bass in shallow water tend to be spooky, they are still easier to catch than largemouth in deep water.

Low-light periods are best when fishing in clear water. Bass in the depths move into shallower water, while bass in shallow water move out of heavy cover. Because of this, largemouth in clear lakes bite best at dusk or dawn and on windy or overcast days when light penetration is at a minimum. Fishermen on some crystal-clear lakes catch the majority of their bass at night, especially in summer.

Long casts help you avoid spooking bass in clear water. To increase your casting distance, use spinning tackle with 4- to 10-pound (1.8 to 4.5 kg) fluorocarbon. Fast retrieves also work best in clear water. A slow retrieve gives bass too much time to inspect the lure. Avoid fluorescent or gaudy lures.

Clear water allows bass to go almost anywhere in the lake. Weeds growing at even 25 feet (7.6 m) provide ample cover in the depths. Because of low water fertility, the deep water has ample oxygen.

Low-light periods are best when fishing in clear water (top). Bass in the depths move into shallower water, while bass in shallow water move out of heavy cover.

Murky water from inflowing streams (bottom) or from waves washing against a shoreline allows bass to escape bright sunlight. Look for fish along the mudline where the murky and clear water meet.

Thick vegetation such as brush and floating-leaved weeds also provides shallow-water refuge for bass in gin-clear lakes. Bass hold extremely close to cover, so accurate casts are necessary.

Long casts help you avoid spooking bass in clear water. To increase your casting distance, use spinning tackle with 4- to 10-pound (1.8 to 4.5 kg) monofilament. Avoid high-visibility line.

MURKY WATER

Shallow cover such as fallen trees, weeds, and brush attracts largemouth bass, even though the water is murky. However, bass range farther from cover than they would in clear water.

The fisherman who finds a patch of murky water in a clear lake may salvage an otherwise wasted trip. But more often, murky water means trouble.

Fishing surveys show that anglers catch bass at a significantly slower rate in extremely turbid water. To check water clarity, tie a white lure to your line, lower it into the water, and note the depth at which it disappears. If you can see the lure at a depth of one foot or more, chances are you can catch bass.

Murky water confines bass to the shallows. If weed growth ends at about 6 feet (1.8 m), the water below 12 feet (3.7 m) lacks oxygen. Turbidity filters out enough sunlight so bass are comfortable at depths of 4 to 8 feet (1.2 to 2.5 m).

Stay in the shallows when fishing in murky water. Little sunlight penetrates the cloudy water, so bass remain shallow all day. Cast large, noise-making lures and those with a lot of flash. Some fishermen carry fine steel wool to polish their spinner blades and add glitter or reflective tape to their lures.

Shallow cover such as fallen trees, weeds, and brush attracts largemouth bass, even though the water is murky. However, bass may range farther from cover than they would in clear water so search lures like spinnerbaits and crankbaits are often good choices.

Murky water results from muddy runoff, heavy blooms of algae or plankton, rough fish that root up the bottom, or the roiling action of large waves and current. Many shallow, fertile bodies of water remain turbid year-round.

FLUCTUATING WATER LEVELS

Willows and other overhanging vegetation often become flooded when the water rises. Flip a jig-and-eel or plastic worm as close to the bank as possible and retrieve it through the branches.

When avid river fishermen meet to begin a day of fishing, the first question is: "What's the water doing?" They know that even a slight rise or fall can have a big impact on bass location.

Heavy rainfall or a lack of rain causes most water level fluctuations, but there may be other reasons. Irrigation pipes draw huge quantities of water from many rivers and reservoirs during summer. Flood-control reservoirs are drawn down in fall to make room for heavy spring runoff. The Corps of Engineers uses dams to control river levels for purposes of navigation.

A rise in water level causes any fish, including bass, to move shallower; a drop pushes them deeper. Fluctuations affect largemouth in shallow water more than bass in deep water. And a rapid rise or fall has a greater impact on fish movement than a gradual change.

Water levels change quickly in a river following a heavy rain. Bass often respond by moving into flooded vegetation near shore. But even a slight drop will send them scurrying to deep water, an instinctive response to avoid being trapped in an isolated pool.

It takes longer for the water level to change in lakes and reservoirs. A slow rise in water level will draw bass toward shore, although it may take several days. The fish remain shallow as long as the water is rising or stable, but they begin to filter into deeper water when the level starts to fall.

Changes in water level can be good or bad for fishing, depending on circumstances. A rise may draw inactive fish out of deeper water. They feed heavily because the flooded shallows offer a new food supply. But in some cases, rising water draws bass into shallow areas, where fishing is impossible.

Bass do not bite as well when falling water drives them deep. But falling water levels may concentrate fish in deep holes or other areas where they are easier to find. For example, if bass are scattered over a shallow flat near a creek channel, falling water would force all of the fish into the channel.

For up-to-date information on water levels, check water gauges, phone the Corps of Engineers, or check water stage data in a local newspaper. If this information is not available, establish your own reference point on a bridge piling, dock post, or other object where a change would be easy to detect.

Flooded brush will hold bass as long as the water is rising or stable. Move slowly just out from the deep edge and cast a spinnerbait into openings or flip a brushguard jig right into the brush.

Photographs taken at low water (shown) help you record the exact location of structure and cover that is normally underwater. Use a large tree or other object as a reference point when the level returns to normal.

Flooded brush will hold bass as long as the water is rising or stable. Move slowly just out from the edge and cast a spinnerbait into openings. Or cast parallel to the edge of the brush.

Water gauges can be found on many large rivers and reservoirs. Look for gauges on bridge pilings or around a dam.

Use a dock post or other object in the water at the boat access to mark the water level. When you return to the dock later in the day or the next time you come to the lake, you can judge the fluctuation up or down.

In low water levels, fish may hold on the first sharp drop in depth off the shoreline.

SPAWNING BASS

Fishermen continually debate the ethics of catching bass on their spawning beds. Most states allow fishing during the spawning period. But some anglers believe that catching spawners is detrimental to the long-term welfare of the bass population. Wherever such fishing is legal, many anglers voluntarily return their bass.

Both male and female bass will bite until spawning time arrives. But they refuse to strike lures while in the act of spawning. Afterward, fishermen catch mostly nest-guarding males. However, anglers in the southern U.S. report catching big females that appear to be guarding the nest along with the males.

Large bass generally spawn before small ones, so fishermen seeking a trophy should start early in the season. If you catch nothing but small males, it probably means the females have finished spawning and dropped back to deeper water.

To locate spawning areas, cruise slowly through the shallows in a sheltered bay or along a shoreline protected from the wind. Toss out a small marker when you see a nest. Approaching this close may spook the bass, but it enables you to sneak back later and find the spot.

While guarding the nest, largemouth bass may strike noisy, fast-moving lures that threaten the nest. Good choices include buzz baits, shallow-running crankbaits, and spinnerbaits. If the bass aren't aggressive, however, try crawling a small plastic worm or tube into the nest.

Polarized glasses are a must when fishing for spawners as they reduce glare on the water and allow you to spot nests and bass and to see when a fish grabs your lure.

Trophy largemouth bite best just before spawning. Look for them in slightly deeper water adjacent to their spring spawning grounds. More large bass are caught during the pre-spawn period than at any other time of the year. Releasing large females assures good spawning and helps keep bass populations strong.

SCHOOLING BASS

When largemouth rip into schools of shad in open water, you can often catch your limit in minutes.

Anglers often encounter schooling bass, or schoolies, in late summer or fall while crossing open water on reservoirs. The frenzied feeding is most common in reservoirs with large populations of threadfin or gizzard shad.

Huge schools of shad roam the reservoir to feed on plankton. Schoolies tend to run smaller (1 to 2 pounds [0.45 to 0.9 kg]) and will follow the baitfish schools, periodically herding them to the surface. Feeding bass sometimes boil the surface for several minutes before the shad escape. In this situation bass will often be schooled by size, so if you catch a fish, chances are that most of the fish in this school are that same size.

Reservoir fishermen frequently carry a spare rod rigged with a shad-imitating lure so when the bass suddenly appear, they can begin casting immediately without taking time to re-rig.

When you spot schooling bass, quickly motor toward the fish, then cut the engine so the boat's momentum carries you toward the school. Use your electric motor to follow the school, staying just within casting range. When the bass go back down, try vertical jigging a spoon, a deep-running, or lipless crankbait through the area where the bass were surfacing. If they are not biting, try to relocate the school by using your locator.

Look for swirls on the surface and shad skipping across the water. Some anglers carry binoculars so they can watch for diving gulls. The birds swoop toward the surface to pick up shad injured by the feeding bass.

STREAM FISHING

Stream fishermen contend that a bass living in current is a completely different animal than a bass in still water. It looks different, eats different foods, and fights better for its size.

Largemouth in streams have sleeker bodies than bass in lakes. They seldom grow as large because they must expend energy just to fight the current. Crayfish, minnows, adult insects, and insect larvae comprise a large part of their diet in most streams.

Fishing success on streams is more consistent than on most waters. Cold fronts have less effect on streams and bass continue to bite through summer. Flowing water does not become as warm as standing water and low oxygen levels are rarely a problem.

Fishermen who know how to read the water can easily spot likely holding areas. Bass rarely hold in fast current. They prefer slack water below some type of obstruction. Prime bass locations include eddies, log jams, deep pools, and undercut banks. They sometimes feed in a shallow riffle, but usually find a rock to break the current.

Experienced stream fishermen know of certain locations that routinely produce bass. A good example is a fallen tree in a deep pool. If a largemouth is removed, another fish about the same size will soon move in to take its place. Once you discover one of these spots, you will rarely fail to catch bass.

Remember to work an eddy from the downstream side. Cast into the slack water behind a log or boulder and retrieve the lure or bait along the current margin. Then cover the slack water close to shore.

Wading is the best method of fishing a small stream, because it enables you to cover specific areas thoroughly. Most anglers use light spinning gear for casting small jigs, spinners, or live bait rigs. Flyfishing gear works better for drifting insect larvae and other small baits or for dropping lures or baits into hard-to-reach places.

When wading, cast upstream or across the current. Bass seldom strike a lure or bait retrieved against the current, because they are not accustomed to seeing food move in that direction.

When fishing in large streams and rivers, use a shallow-draft boat and drift with the current. A trolling motor or outboard can be used to slow your drift, allowing more time to work good spots. Drop an anchor to hold the boat near deep pools that may hold several bass.

Work an eddy from the downstream side (shown). Cast into the slack water behind a log or boulder and retrieve the lure or bait along the current margin. Then cover the slack water close to shore.

Cast live bait upstream of an undercut bank. Take in line as the current washes the bait toward the overhang. Drift the bait as close to the bank as possible because bass seldom hang in the current.

Drift your bait through a riffle by standing downstream of the fast water, then casting above it. Let the current tumble the bait along bottom. Cover the fast water thoroughly, then work the bait through the slack water along both edges of the current.

NIGHT FISHING

Asked to recall their first night-fishing adventure, most fishermen would tell of tangled lines, snagged lures, and bass that got away. No doubt, fishing for largemouth at night poses some problems. But anglers who fish popular urban lakes, warm ponds, or ultra-clear waters know that night fishing is often the only way to catch bass.

Bass seldom move far from their daytime haunts to reach nighttime feeding areas. Look for shallow shoals adjacent to typical midday locations. To avoid spooking bass in these shallow areas, place markers during the day. Then sneak in to position your boat in the precise spot after dark.

Night fishing is generally best in summer, especially after a warm, still day with clear skies. On windy, overcast days, bass feed during the day so they may not feed at night.

Most night fishermen use dark-colored lures that create turbulence or vibration. But some anglers swear by plastic worms. Try surface lures first to catch the active feeders. Shallow-running lures work best for night fishing because bass can easily see the silhouette against the light background at the surface. Then switch to deeper-running lures and work a break leading to deep water. Some fishermen attach a snap to the line so they can change lures easily without retying. A slow, steady retrieve works best at night because bass use their lateral line to home in on the lure. If you use an erratic retrieve, the fish may miss.

Moon phase may also have some influence on night fishing success. Most experts prefer to fish two to three days on either side of a new moon or a full moon.

Prime areas for night fishing include distinct points along shoreline breaks, large, shallow flats extending from shore, and shallow mid-lake reefs. Bass often move into the shallows and begin to feed just before dark.

A headlamp is a must when night fishing to avoid tangled lines and for removing hooks from fish.

SMALLMOUTH BASS

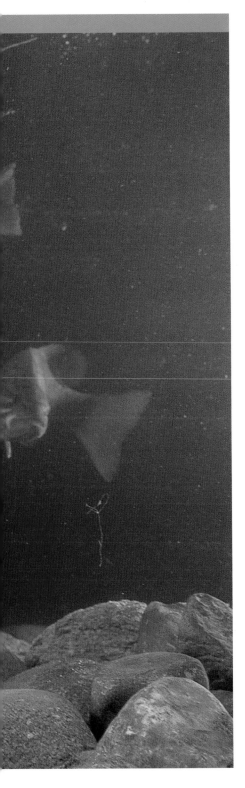

Known for its aerial acrobatics and never-give-up determination, the smallmouth bass has a well-deserved reputation as the fightingest freshwater gamefish. After a smallmouth strikes, it usually makes a sizzling run for the surface, does a cartwheel in an attempt to throw the hook, then wages a dogged battle in deep water.

The smallmouth bass, Micropterus dolomieui, was originally found mainly in the eastern United States. Its range extended from northern Minnesota to southern Quebec in the north and from northern Georgia to eastern Oklahoma on the south. It was not found east of the Appalachians. But owing to its tremendous popularity, the smallmouth has been widely stocked and is now found in every state with the exceptions of Florida, Louisiana, and Alaska. It has also been stocked in most Canadian provinces and in Asia, Africa, Europe, and South America.

The smallmouth is sometimes called bronzeback because of the bronze reflections from its scales. Other common names include brown bass, Oswego bass, redeye, and green trout.

Many angler consider the smallmouth to be the hardest fighting freshwater gamefish on the planet. This section will not only show you where smallmouth live, but also how and where to catch them under a variety of conditions throughout the year.

Like its close relatives, the largemouth and spotted bass, the small-mouth belongs to the sunfish family. Smallmouth have been known to hybridize naturally with spotted bass and biologists have created a smallmouth–largemouth hybrid nicknamed the meanmouth because of its aggressive nature.

The modern trend in smallmouth fishing is toward catch-and-release, especially in heavily fished waters. Where fishing pressure is heavy, the large smallmouth are quickly removed, leaving only the small ones. Catch-and-release fishing is the best solution to this problem.

On July 9, 1955, D.L. Hayes was trolling a pearl-colored Bomber around a shale point in Dale Hollow Lake, Kentucky. At about 10:00 a.m. he hooked a huge fish and after a 20-minute fight landed what turned out to be the world-record smallmouth. It weighed 11 pounds, 15 ounces (5.4 kg) and was 27 inches (68.5 cm) long.

Appearance of smallmouth (1) differs from that of spotted bass (2) and largemouth (3). Smallmouth have nine dark vertical bars that come and go and three bars radiating from the eye. Smallmouth lack the dark horizontal band present on large-mouth and spotted bass and normally have a darker belly. On spotted bass, the horizontal band consists of a row of dia-mond-shaped dark spots. They may have several rows of spots below the band. The band on largemouth lacks the diamond-shaped spots.

SENSES

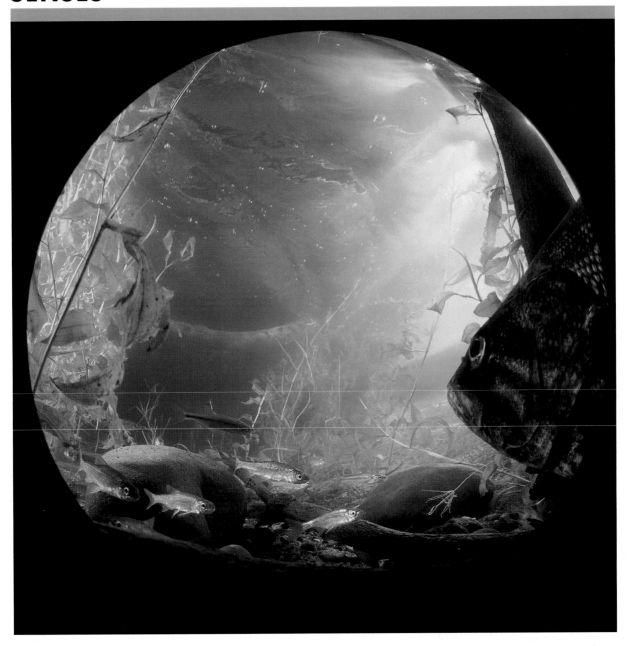

Little scientific research has been done on the smallmouth's sensory capabilities, but some conclusions can be drawn based on field observation. For instance, smallmouth evidently have a well-developed lateral-line sense because they can detect lures that produce vibration in water where the visibility is only a few inches. They also have good hearing as evidenced by the fact that they are easily spooked by noise, especially noise that is transmitted directly into the water. Experienced smallmouth fishermen are careful to avoid slamming the live-well lid or dropping the anchor on the floor of the boat.

To find food and escape danger, smallmouth rely on eyesight to a far greater degree than any of their other senses. As a result, good smallmouth anglers generally use lures with a natural look. And they take great pains to avoid being seen by the smallmouth, especially when fishing in clear water.

The sense of smell evidently plays some role in extremely turbid water, but in most other situations it appears to be less important than the other senses. Some smallmouth anglers believe that scent products, particularly crayfish scents, improve their success. But others who have tested scented lures alongside unscented ones have found no difference. Some scent manufacturers claim their products cover up foreign odors, like those of gasoline and human hands. But anglers who have deliberately soaked their lures in gasoline report that these lures catch smallmouth as well as any other lures, whether treated with scent or not.

Studies have shown that smallmouth bass are less line- and lure-wary than largemouth bass, thus easier to catch. But the degree of wariness varies greatly in different waters, depending mainly on the amount of competition.

In waters where the smallmouth population is low and food plentiful, smallmouth can be extremely wary. Any sudden movement by a fisherman will scare them into deeper water, where they refuse to bite. The best policy is to keep a low profile and avoid throwing your shadow over the fish.

But if the population is high and food relatively scarce, smallmouth are not as wary and spooking is not as much of a problem. In fact, scuba divers have attracted smallmouth to within a few feet (m) by tapping rocks on their air tanks.

Knowing how smallmouth use their senses will help you choose which techniques are best to catch them in a particular body of water.

HOW THE SENSES OF SMALLMOUTH BASS COMPARE TO THOSE OF OTHER GAMEFISH

Fish Species	Daytime Vision	Night Vision	Lateral Line	Smell	Hearing
Smallmouth Bass	Excellent	Fair	Good	Fair	Good
Spotted Bass	Excellent	Good	Good	Fair	Good
Largemouth Bass	Good	Fair	Good	Fair	Good
Walleye	Fair	Excellent	Good	Fair	Good
Sauger	Fair	Excellent	Excellent	Fair	Good
Yellow Perch	Good	Poor	Fair	Fair	Fair
Crappie	Good	Good	Fair	Fair	Fair
Bluegill	Excellent	Fair	Fair	Good	Fair
Northern Pike	Excellent	Poor	Good	Poor	Good
Catfish	Fair	Fair	Excellent	Excellent	Excellent

HABITAT PREFERENCES

Smallmouth bass are fish of clear, clean waters. They are equally at home in streams and lakes, but are rarely found in small ponds, lakes shallower than 25 feet (7.6 m), or any water that is continuously murky or polluted.

To locate smallmouth, you should become familiar with their preferences in regard to the following environmental conditions:

TEMPERATURE. During the summer months, smallmouth in northern lakes are usually found at water temperatures from 67 to 71°F (19 to 22°C) and seldom at temperatures above 80°F (27°C). But smallmouth in southern reservoirs are often found at temperatures of 78 to 84°F (26 to 29°C). This difference can be explained by the fact that the deeper, cooler water in the reservoirs lacks sufficient oxygen in summer.

Laboratory tests have shown that smallmouth prefer a temperature of about 82°F (28°C). But most of these tests were conducted using juvenile smallmouth, whose temperature preference is considerably higher than that of the adults.

These findings have great significance for smallmouth anglers. If you are fishing in shallow water and catching nothing but undersized smallmouth, you may be able to catch bigger ones by fishing several feet deeper.

During the cold months, smallmouth activity drops off. In laboratory studies, smallmouth fed very little at temperatures below 50°F (10°C) and they lay motionless on the bottom at temperatures below 40°F (4°C). In their natural surroundings, smallmouth respond to temperature in much the same way.

OXYGEN. Smallmouth can tolerate an oxygen level of 2.5 parts per million, while largemouth can survive at 2.0. This slight difference may explain why largemouth are better able to tolerate stagnant water. But neither species fares well at oxygen levels this low. Feeding and growth are severely reduced if the level remains below 5 parts per million for an extended period.

In most smallmouth waters, the oxygen level is adequate throughout the depths that smallmouth prefer. So measuring oxygen levels will not help you locate the fish. But in highly fertile waters, smallmouth may be confined to shallow water in summer because the depths lack sufficient oxygen.

PH LEVEL. Smallmouth are found in waters with a pH from 5 to 9. Although the best smallmouth populations are usually found where the pH is from 7.9 to 8.1, there is no research to indicate that smallmouth prefer any specific pH level. Canadian researchers found that smallmouth were unable to successfully reproduce at pH levels from 5.5 to 6.0.

TEMPERATURE PREFERENCES AND OXYGEN REQUIREMENTS OF VARIOUS FRESHWATER FISH

Species	Preferred Summer Temp.	Oxygen Requirement*
Smallmouth Bass	67–71°F (19–22°C)	2.5 ppm
Largemouth Bass	68–78°F (20–25.5°C)	2.0 ppm
Bluegill	74–80°F (23–27°C)	3.5 ppm
Walleye	65–75°F (18–24°C)	4.0 ppm
Northern Pike		1.4 ppm
Under 7 pounds (3.2 kg)	65–70°F (18–21°C)	
Over 7 pounds	50–55°F (10–12.5°C)	
Brook Trout	52–56°F (11–13.3°C)	5.0 ppm
Rainbow Trout	55–60°F (12.7–15.5°C)	1.5 ppm
Black Bullhead	78–84°F (25.5–29°C)	Less than 1 ppm

*Minimum requirement (in parts per million) for long-term survival at summertime temperatures. Oxygen requirements decrease at lower water temperatures.

CURRENT. Smallmouth prefer moderate current, usually in the range of 4½ to 15½ (1.4 to 4.7 m) feet per second. This range is slower than that preferred by trout, but faster than that favored by largemouth bass. With a little experience, you will be able to recognize the right current speed.

In most streams, smallmouth are more numerous in pools with noticeable current than in pools where the water is completely slack.

In lakes, smallmouth often concentrate around river mouths or in areas with wind-induced current, such as a trough between two islands or a narrow channel between two major lobes of a lake.

DEPTH. Smallmouth are generally considered fish of the epilimnion, the upper layer of water in a lake that is stratified into temperature layers.

They are most likely to be found in shallow areas adjacent to deep water. The depths offer smallmouth refuge from intense light and boat traffic.

In waters that have both smallmouth and largemouth, the smallmouth are usually slightly deeper. Generally, smallmouth stay deep enough that they are not visible from the surface.

In spring, summer, and early fall, smallmouth are seldom found at depths exceeding 30 feet (9 m). But in late fall and winter, they often congregate in tight schools at depths down to 60 feet (18 m).

CLARITY. Although smallmouth will tolerate murky water for short periods, they rarely live in water that remains murky year-round. As a rule, waters where the usual visibility is less than 1 foot (30 cm) do not hold substantial smallmouth populations.

If the water is murky in one portion of a lake but clear in another, chances are that smallmouth will be most numerous in the clearer area. Similarly, smallmouth are usually more plentiful in clear reach of a stream than in a muddy reach. And in extremely fertile lakes, smallmouth bite best in spring, before intense algal blooms cloud the water, and in fall, after the algae have died back.

BOTTOM TYPE. In most waters, smallmouth are found over a bottom consisting of clean rocks or gravel. This type of bottom is usually rich in smallmouth foods including crayfish and larval insects like dragonfly nymphs and hellgrammites. But in lakes where most of the basin consists of rock, smallmouth often prefer sandy shoal areas, especially those with a sparse growth of weeds. The sandy, weedy areas will hold fewer crayfish and insect larvae, but more baitfish.

SPAWNING HABITAT. To spawn successfully, smallmouth need a rock, gravel, or hard sand bottom. Nests on silty bottoms are seldom successful. Stream smallmouth nest in light current, but avoid swift current. The best spawning areas have boulders or other large objects to protect one side of the nest. Waters that tend to remain muddy for long periods of time following a heavy rain are not well suited to successful smallmouth spawning. The suspended silt makes it difficult for the male to defend his nest and silt deposited on the eggs prevents them from absorbing enough oxygen.

COMPETITOR SPECIES. Populations of other species that compete with smallmouth for food, living space, or spawning habitat can greatly affect the size of the smallmouth population and the way the smallmouth behave. Compared to most other freshwater gamefish, smallmouth are poor competitors. If a body of water contains a large number of shallow-water predators like largemouth bass or northern pike, chances are it will not support a dense smallmouth population.

Competition with other fish species can be a major factor in determining smallmouth location. Most reservoirs in the mid-South, for instance, have good populations of largemouth and spotted bass. If largemouth are numerous, smallmouth and spotted bass are normally found in the main-lake portion of the reservoir where the water is relatively deep and clear. Largemouth tend to dominate the upper portion where the water is shallower and the clarity lower. Largemouth also concentrate in shallow creek arms and wherever there is weedy or brushy cover. In reservoirs with fewer largemouth, the smallmouth and spotted bass may occupy the upper as well as the lower portion.

FEEDING & GROWTH

In waters where they are numerous, crayfish can make up to 80 percent of the smallmouth's diet.

If you have ever caught a smallmouth and examined its stomach contents, chances are you found bits and pieces of crayfish. In waters where crayfish are plentiful, they make up at least two-thirds of the smallmouth's diet.

Because crayfish inhabit the same rocky areas that smallmouth do, they make a convenient target for feeding bass. Other important items in the smallmouth's diet include fish, adult and immature insects, and tadpoles.

The diet of smallmouth bass may vary from season to season, depending on the availability of food. In a five-year food-habits study conducted in Nebish Lake, Wisconsin, crayfish made up 83 percent of the smallmouth's diet in September, but only 14 percent in May. Insects make up 34 percent of the diet in May, but only 4 percent in July.

Smallmouth feed very little during cold-water periods. Normally, they begin feeding in spring when the water temperature reaches about 45°F (8°C). Food consumption peaks at water temperatures around 78°F (25.5°C). When the water temperature drops below 40°F (4°C) in fall, practically no feeding takes place. However, in some high-competition waters, smallmouth continue to feed through the ice-cover season.

Smallmouth bass differ from most freshwater gamefish in that males and females grow at about the same rate. Smallmouth in lakes and reservoirs usually grow faster and reach a larger size than those in streams. And smallmouth in southern waters generally grow faster than those in the North. The table below shows how growth rates vary. In Norris Lake, Tennessee, for instance, a 6-year-old smallmouth measures 18 inches (46 cm) and about 4 pounds; in Lake Opeongo, Ontario, a smallmouth of the same age measures only 12 inches (30 cm) and about 1 pound (0.45 kg).

Although smallmouth grow much faster in the South, their maximum size varies less from North to South than would be expected. Smallmouth live as long as 18 years in the North, but seldom longer than seven years in the South. Higher metabolic rates cause faster burnout in southern waters.

GROWTH RATES OF SMALLMOUTH BASS AT DIFFERENT LATITUDES

Length at Various Ages (inches/centimeters)										
					Age					
Lake Name and Latitude	1	2	3	4	5	6	7	8	9	10
Lake Opeongo, Ont. (46°N)	2.1	5.2	7.7	9.1	11.1	12.2	13.5	14.5	15.5	-
	5.3	13.2	14.6	23.1	28.2	31.0	34.3	36.8	39.4	-
Northern Lake Michigan (45°N)	3.9	6.3	8.1	9.7	11.5	13.2	14.6	15.8	16.8	17.4
	9.9	16.0	20.6	24.7	29.2	33.5	37.1	40.1	42.7	44.2
Lake Simcoe, Ont. (44°N)	4.2	6.3	8.6	10.9	13.0	14.6	15.8	16.9	17.0	-
	10.6	16.0	21.8	27.7	33.0	37.1	40.1	42.9	43.2	-
Quabbin Lake, Mass. (42 ½°N)	3.5	6.7	10.2	12.9	14.7	16.1	16.7	17.1	17.3	17.5
	8.9	17.0	25.9	32.8	37.3	40.9	42.4	43.4	43.9	44.5
Pine Flat Lake, Cal. (37°N)	5.5	8.9	12.5	14.7	16.6	17.9	18.3	-	-	-
	14.0	22.6	31.8	37.3	42.2	45.5	46.5	-	-	-
Norris Lake, Tenn. (36°N)	3.1	8.9	13.3	15.8	17.4	18.0	18.6	20.9	-	-
	7.9	22.6	33.8	40.1	44.2	45.7	47.2	53.1	-	-
Pickwick Lake, Ala. (35°N)	5.9	10.7	13.5	16.6	18.5	20.4	21.0	21.6	-	-
	15.0	27.2	34.3	42.2	47.0	51.8	53.3	54.9	-	-

COMPETITION

Experienced smallmouth anglers know that smallmouth behave differently in different bodies of water, so you should alter your fishing strategy to suit the situation. The level of competition in a particular body of water can make a big difference not only in your fishing strategy, but also in your choice of fishing waters.

Competition can affect your choice of lures and baits and your method of presentation. A fast-moving crankbait, for example, is more likely to trigger strikes in high-competition waters. Smallmouth in these waters are conditioned to chase their food. The fish that gets to the minnow first may be the only one that eats.

In low-competition waters, crankbaits and other fast-moving lures have less appeal. Smallmouth examine their food more closely, so a slow presentation will usually draw more strikes.

If you must fish after a cold front or under other adverse weather conditions, choose a body of water where the competition level is high. When food is scarce, smallmouth must continue to feed despite changing weather.

The level of smallmouth competition can also determine the time of day when fishing is best. In low-competition waters, smallmouth normally feed most heavily in early morning and late afternoon, when light levels are relatively low. But in high-competition waters, they usually feed all day.

Good habitat, such as a cool, clear lake with a rocky shoreline (shown), usually means smallmouth are abundant and the competition level high.

Heavy fishing pressure is likely to reduce the smallmouth population enough to keep the level of competition low.

Predators that occupy shallow water, like northerns and largemouth, compete with smallmouth. If they are numerous, competition is high.

HOW WEATHER AFFECTS SMALLMOUTH

Weather plays a major role in smallmouth fishing. If you had a choice as to when to fish, your odds would undoubtedly be best during a period of stable weather. Changes in the weather disrupt the smallmouth's feeding schedule. They may continue to feed, but peak feeding times are not as predictable. Exactly how changes in weather affect small- mouth depends on time of year, type of water, and even type of cover. Following are the weather conditions that have the most influence on smallmouth fishing:

CLOUD COVER. Smallmouth normally bite better when the skies are overcast rather than clear. Although smallmouth are not as light-sensi- tive as walleyes, low light causes them to move into shallow water and feed more heavily.

But clear weather is nearly always better in early spring, because the sun warms the water and urges smallmouth to begin feeding.

The degree to which cloud cover affects smallmouth fishing depends on the clarity of the water. In lakes that are extremely clear, daytime fishing is usually poor when skies are sunny. In these waters, small-mouth do much of their feeding at night. But in lakes of moderate clarity, they feed sporadically throughout the day even though the skies are clear.

WIND. Windy weather generally spells good smallmouth fishing. The waves scatter the light rays so less light penetrates the surface and smallmouth feeding increases.

In a shallow body of water, a strong wind stirs up the bottom, making the water so murky that smallmouth cannot see well enough to feed. Fishing remains slow until the water starts to clear.

Windy weather may also cause poor fishing when smallmouth are in the weeds. The movement of the vegetation caused by the wave action seems to make them extra-cautious.

RAIN. Rainy weather usually improves smallmouth fishing, especially when the surface is calm. Overcast skies combined with rain droplets dimpling the surface decrease the amount of light that penetrates. And the sound seems to reduce the chance of spooking the fish.

Rain has practically no effect on fishing on a windy day. Because light penetration is already low and the level of background sound is high, smallmouth are not as spooky as in calm weather.

A warm rain in early spring can make a big difference in fishing success. The water temperature may rise several degrees in one day, resulting in an insect hatch which causes semi-dormant smallmouth to start feeding.

A heavy rain usually means poor fishing in streams. Runoff clouds the water so smallmouth cannot see your bait as well. And rising water spreads the fish over a larger area, so finding them is more difficult.

Storms accompanied by lightening and loud thunderclaps cause small-mouth to stop biting. Fishing stays slow for several days if the storm is severe.

COLD FRONTS. Smallmouth often go on a feeding spree before a storm, but if the temperature drops dramatically and the skies clear fol-lowing the storm, catching them becomes tough.

The negative effects of a cold front are most noticeable in spring and summer, especially if the front follows a period of warm, stable weather.

Smallmouth feed heavily during the warm weather, so they can afford to stop for a few days after the cold front passes.

Cold fronts usually do not slow feeding in fall. In fact, it seems as if smallmouth sense the approach of winter and begin feeding more heavily. Anglers willing to brave the elements can enjoy some of the year's best fishing.

The effects of a cold front on smallmouth, as on many other freshwater gamefish, are more severe in clear lakes than in murkier lakes or in rivers.

HOW WIND AFFECTS SMALLMOUTH FISHING

Wind-induced currents draw smallmouth into narrows (top) and into troughs between islands or between an island and the lakeshore. The current attracts baitfish and the narrows or trough concentrates them.

Onshore winds wash plankton in to shore and churn up the water, causing a mudline (shown). Baitfish move in to feed on the plankton and the light level is low enough for smallmouth to feed in the shallows.

Rough water scatters the light rays that strike the surface, causing much less light to penetrate than if the surface were calm. The lower light level causes smallmouth to move shallower and feed.

Crosswinds blowing over the underwater extension of a point or over a reef wash plankton and insect larvae loose from the bottom and carry them to the downwind side. The drifting food attracts baitfish and smallmouth.

How Moon Phases Affect Smallmouth Fishing

Many smallmouth-fishing authorities prefer to fish on the days around the full moon, particularly the days just before it. They maintain that night fishing is better around the full moon. However, daytime fishing may be slower, especially in clear lakes.

Summertime anglers on southern reservoirs do most of their smallmouth fishing at night, during the full moon. Some maintain that smallmouth bite better in the full moon, but others say that the biggest reason for fishing at that time is to see where they are going.

Most fisheries biologists and angling experts discount the importance of moon phase. They consider time of day and the weather much more important.

To evaluate the effects of moon phase on smallmouth fishing, researchers contacted conservation agencies throughout the country. They compiled records of the biggest smallmouth and the dates when they were caught, then correlated those dates with the moon phase. No information is available on what time of day the fish were caught, but most were probably taken in daylight hours.

PERCENTAGE OF BIG SMALLMOUTH CAUGHT IN EACH MOON PHASE BY REGION

Total Percentage Caught in United States					
Moon Phase	Eastern States	South-Central States	North-Central States	Western States	Total
New	25%	21%	27%	23%	24%
First Quarter	26%	34%	36%	32%	30%
Full	25%	34%	24%	18%	26%
Last Quarter	24%	11%	13%	27%	20%

Fishing success, as indicated by a sample of more than 200 big smallmouth caught around the country, is generally best during the first-quarter and full moon and poorest around the last-quarter moon. In the south-central states, for instance, anglers caught about three times as many fish during the first-quarter and full moon as in the last quarter. Figures for each phase include data from 3 days on either side, for a total of 7 days.

SPAWNING BEHAVIOR

Smallmouth bass can spawn successfully in lakes or streams and the areas they choose for spawning in stream differ very little form the area they choose in lakes.

A typical spawning site is near an object like a rock or log, which shelters it from strong current or wave action. Such an object also makes it easier for a male to guard the nest because predators cannot sneak in from behind. Nests are usually in water 2 to 4 feet (0.6 to 1.2 m) deep, although they have been found in water as deep as 20 feet (6 m). Smallmouth almost always nest on sand, gravel, or rubble and avoid mud bottoms.

Males begin building nests in spring, when the water temperature stabilizes above 55°F (13°C). The male uses his tail to fan out a circular nest with a diameter about twice as great as his own length. On a rubble bottom, he simply sweeps debris off the rocks. But on a sand or gravel bottom, he fans out a depression from 2 to 4 inches (5 to 10 cm) deep. A male nests in the same general area each year and will sometimes use the same nest.

Females move into the vicinity of the nest a few days later. When a male spots a female, he rushes toward her and attempts to drive her to the nest. At first, she swims away, but she returns again later. Eventually, the male coaxes her to the nest. Spawning usually occurs at a water

Smallmouth typically spawn on gravel or small rock areas in water from 1 to 8 feet deep.

temperature of 60 to 65°F (16 to 18°C), about 3 degrees cooler than the typical spawning temperature of largemouth bass.

As the spawning act begins, the fish lie side by side, both facing the same direction. Then the female tips on her side to deposit her eggs and the male simultaneously releases his milt. Females deposit an average of 7,000 eggs per pound of body weight.

The female leaves after spawning, but the male remains and vigorously guards the nest again any intruders. He will attack fish much larger than himself and may even bump a wading fisherman who gets too close. The amount of time required for hatching depends on water temperature. At 54°F (12°C), the eggs hatch in ten days; at 77°F (25°C), two days. On the average, 35 percent of the eggs hatch.

The male guards the fry on the nest for 5 to 7 days and usually continues to guard them for another week or two after the school leaves the nest. Of the fry that leave the nest, only about 10 percent survive to fingerling size.

Anglers can destroy smallmouth nests by stepping on them or by catching the guarding male. If panfish are numerous, they quickly consume the eggs or fry once the male is gone.

GROWTH STAGES

Fry are transparent when first hatched. They have a large yellowish egg sac that nurtures them through the first 6 to 12 days of life. Black coloration begins to appear within a few days after the fry hatch. This explains the origin of the term black bass.

Fingerlings are 3 to 5 inches (7.6 to 12.7 cm) long by the end of the first summer. The tail fin has a brownish-orange base and a distinct whitish margin.

HOMING

The homing tendency of smallmouth bass is among the strongest of all freshwater gamefish. In a lake or reservoir, a smallmouth may spend most of its time along a stretch of shoreline only 100 yards (91 m) long. In a stream, a smallmouth may stay in one pool that fulfills all its needs for food and cover.

Smallmouth may leave these home areas to find good spawning habitat or a deep wintering area, but during the rest of the year they stray very little.

Each spring, smallmouth return to the same area to spawn. Even high water does not discourage them from returning to their traditional spawning sites. So once you find a spawning concentration, you can bet the smallmouth will be there again the next year.

Even the wintering areas remain the same from year to year. In late fall, when the water temperature drops below 50°F (10°C), anglers familiar with the water know exactly which sharp-dropping points and steep breaks will hold the smallmouth.

Immature smallmouth tend to wander more than the adults. One possible explanation is that the large, more assertive smallmouth take over the best feeding and resting areas. The smaller fish are forced to move about to find suitable habitat.

Finding a lake or stream with a good smallmouth population can be difficult. Because smallmouth prosper in only the cleanest and clearest waters in a given region and because they are fairly easy to catch, a healthy population can be fished down quickly once the word gets out.

Natural resources agencies may not be able to give you much help because smallmouth are difficult to sample. A lake or stream may have lots of smallmouth, but few are found in fish-population surveys because they are very net-shy. They avoid gill nets, trap nets, and most other sampling gear, but can be sampled by shocking. Results of shocking surveys are available from some natural resources agencies.

You can sometimes get good information from tackle shops, marinas, and knowledgeable anglers who have firsthand experience on waters in the area where you will be fishing. You can also find good smallmouth waters by paying attention to fishing-contest results, newspaper reports, regional magazine articles, and local outdoor programs on radio and television. If a lake or river is consistently producing smallmouth, chances are you will find out about it through these sources.

The surest way to find a good lake or stream is to hire a competent guide who specializes in smallmouth. He will take you to his prime waters and best spots. And once you get to know him, he may be willing to share his knowledge of other good smallmouth waters.

HOW TO RECOGNIZE SMALLMOUTH STRUCTURE

Smallmouth are like most other warmwater gamefish in that structure, which is the topography of the lake or stream bed, dictates where they are found.

A piece of structure that provides food, cover, and easy access to the depths may hold smallmouth through the entire year. They simply move deeper or shallower as the seasons change. But if the structure lacks one of these vital elements, smallmouth will move to different pieces of structure to find what they need.

If you find smallmouth spawning in 3 feet (0.9 m) of water on a sand-gravel point, you may find them on the same point in summer, but in 12 to 18 feet (3.6 to 5.5 m) of water, especially if there are boulders or weeds for cover. In late fall, they will probably stay on the same point but drop into 30 to 50 feet (10 to 15 m) of water.

But if the point lacks summertime cover, smallmouth cannot escape the sunlight, so they will move to structure that offers shade. If the point flattens out at 25 feet (7.6 m), smallmouth may stay there through summer, but will move to a deeper point or offshore reef in late fall.

A good locator/GPS unit is a must in checking potential smallmouth structure. Smallmouth are almost always found over a hard bottom. By carefully watching for a strong signal, you can quickly locate hard-bottomed areas at the likely depth range.

After examining your map, you may conclude there is a good chance of finding smallmouth along an irregular sandy breakline that runs the length of the north shore. Run the breakline at high speed and watch your locator for a particularly strong signal, which indicates an area of rock or gravel and mark these spots in your GPS. In only a few minutes, you can pinpoint numerous likely smallmouth spots.

Resort owners or marinas and dock operators may be able to identify specific points, humps, or other spots that have been consistently producing smallmouth. If you have a lake map, ask them to mark the spots for you. If you are lucky enough to find a local fishing expert who is willing to share some of his secrets, be careful about the questions you ask. Few serious anglers are willing to reveal their prime spots, but they will usually tell you what type of structure to look for and the best depths to fish.

Above-water indicators reveal a great deal about smallmouth structure, if you know what to look for. The examples on the following pages show how to interpret these clues.

The exact type of structure that smallmouth occupy in different seasons varies greatly, depending on the type of water. For suggestions on where to look for smallmouth in the waters you fish, check the examples.

If you do find smallmouth on a particular location, try to find other areas on the lake that offer similar structure. Depth is also something to watch closely. For example, if you are catching fish at 15 feet, you will most likely find fish at that depth in other parts of the lake.

Surface activity of baitfish can help you recognize structure that holds smallmouth. If the structure holds a lot of baitfish, you can often see them feeding on the surface in early morning or at dusk. In some cases, largemouth or white bass can be seen taking baitfish on the surface while smallmouth feed below.

Changes in soil composition along the shoreline (shown) usually reveal similar changes below water. If you see a line where the soil changes abruptly from sand to rock, visually extend the line into the water. Smallmouth often congregate along the rock margin.

Jagged bluffs (shown) with many lips and crevices above the water line indicate good smallmouth habitat below water. These irregularities provide shade and attract food items. A smoothfaced bluff lacks these nooks and crannies and holds fewer smallmouth.

Aquatic vegetation along the shoreline can also provide clues to bottom type. If cattails grow along shore, the bottom probably consists of mud. But bulrushes usually mean a bottom of hard sand or rock, materials better suited to smallmouth.

Degree of slope on the underwater portion of a point can usually be determined by the slope of the above-water portion. A gradually sloping point is normally the best choice in spring, a point with a steeper slope in summer and fall.

How to Recognize Good Smallmouth Cover

Finding productive smallmouth water and determining the type of structure most likely to hold smallmouth are vital to consistent fishing success. But there is still one more piece to the puzzle: you must be able to recognize the specific types of cover that smallmouth prefer.

The primary component of good smallmouth cover is shade, but small-mouth will not use the cover unless a good food supply and deep water are within easy reach. The best cover offers overhead protection as well as shade.

Let's assume that you have located a reef that looks perfect for small-mouth. It is surrounded by deep water and consists mostly of marble- to golf-ball-sized rock, with a section of scattered boulders along one edge. The entire reef has a good supply of smallmouth foods like crayfish, insect larvae, and baitfish, but only the section with the boulders of-fers adequate shade. This section will hold many more smallmouth than other parts of the reef.

The type of cover that smallmouth use may also be influenced by the number of shallow-water predators that are present. If a body of water has a high population of largemouth bass or northern pike, they will oc-

cupy the weedbeds and woody cover, forcing smallmouth to seek other cover options. But if there are few largemouth or northerns, the weedbeds and woody cover will probably draw smallmouth.

Rocks tall enough to cast a significant shadow make better smallmouth cover than flat rocks. A reef with large rocks continuing well into deep water holds more and bigger smallmouth than a reef that has rock on the top but sand or silt sloping into deep water.

TYPES OF COVER

Weeds that grow on a firm sand-gravel bottom, such as wild celery and bulrushes, are more attractive to smallmouth than weeds that grow on a soft bottom, like lily pads and cattails. Hard-bottom plants located along a breakline attract smallmouth, along with those on a shallow flat with deep water nearby.

Stumps with openings between washed-out roots offer overhead cover in addition to shade. This type of stump is much more likely to hold smallmouth than one with embedded roots.

Fallen trees that have thick trunks and limbs and slope sharply into the water are best for smallmouth. The thick trunk and limbs offer shade and overhead cover and the steep slope means that there is deep-water access. Spindly trees seldom hold smallmouth, but may be attractive to largemouth.

WHERE TO FIND SMALLMOUTH THROUGH THE SEASONS

Although smallmouth are less migratory than most other freshwater gamefish, you must be familiar with their seasonal movement patterns for consistent fishing success. In many waters, smallmouth stay in the same vicinity all year. The secret to finding them in different seasons may simply be to fish shallower or deeper.

Regardless of the type of water, smallmouth seasonal movements are controlled by the same factors and are surprisingly predictable.

SPRING. Smallmouth remain in a state of near-dormancy until the water temperature approaches 50°F (10°C). Then they begin moving toward their spawning areas. In streams, the spawning migration may begin at lower temperatures. The exact sites chosen for spawning depend on the type of water. Because smallmouth have a strong homing instinct, they normally spawn in the same area each year.

After recuperating from spawning, the females scatter to deeper water. Males move deeper once they abandon the fry. Both sexes remain in the vicinity of their spawning sires, if there is deep water nearby. Although they are feeding more heavily now than during the spawning period, fishing may be tough because they are not as concentrated.

SUMMER. Smallmouth are even more predictable in summer than during other seasons. Once they take up residence on a particular piece of structure or in a certain pool, they may not move for several months. This stay-at-home tendency can be partially explained by the smallmouth's strong liking for crayfish. Unlike most other types of smallmouth food, crayfish are linked to a specific location. They require rocks for protection and cannot move far from cover. But in waters where schooling baitfish are the primary food, smallmouth must move around to find them.

Deep water is particularly important in summer. With the surface temperature high and the sun directly overhead, smallmouth must retreat to deep water to find a comfortable temperature and light level. How deep they go varies with the type of water. In a clear lake, they may go as deep as 25 feet (7.6 m). In a murky lake that lacks oxygen in the depths, they may be restricted to water shallower than 12 feet (3.6 m). In a small stream, they may spend the summer in pools only 4 feet (1.2 m) deep because there is no deeper water.

EARLY TO MID-FALL. Early fall finds smallmouth in much the same locations as they were in summer, although they spend more of their time in shallow water. The shallows offer more food and because of the cooler surface temperatures and lower sun angle, smallmouth have no need to go deep.

In most lakes, the surface continues to cool and eventually reaches the same temperature as the water below the thermocline. When this happens, the lake turns over, meaning that all of the water circulates and the temperature becomes the same from top to bottom. You may catch one smallmouth at a depth of 5 feet (1.5 m) and another at 30 feet (9 m). The lack of a consistent pattern results in tough fishing.

In rivers, smallmouth remain in their early fall locations through mid-fall. They feed more as the water cools, so mid-fall fishing can be the best of the year, particularly for good-sized smallmouth.

LATE FALL AND WINTER. Following the turnover, the likelihood of finding smallmouth in the shallows diminishes. However, a few days of warm weather may draw baitfish into shallow water and attract smallmouth.

Once smallmouth retreat to deep water, they feed very little. Many anglers believe that smallmouth simply cannot be caught under these conditions, but if you take the time to do some thorough scouting, you can sometimes locate small but densely packed schools. Although smallmouth are not actively feeding, a slow presentation will tempt a few bits. And the fish you catch are likely to be big.

Stream smallmouth may move to deep pools if their mid-fall locations are too shallow for wintering. They continue to feed and fishing is good until the water temperature drops into the low 40s (4 to 7°C).

To get a better idea of the seasonal movements of smallmouth bass in the specific types of water you fish, refer to the following pages.

Fall offers some of the best trophy smallmouth fishing of the year.

MESOTROPHIC LAKES

These moderately fertile lakes rank among the top producers of small-mouth bass. The mesotrophic lakes best suited to smallmouth have clean, well-structured bottoms; enough sand-gravel or rock areas to provide spawning habitat and produce crayfish; and low populations of competitor species, especially largemouth bass and northern pike.

Several weeks before spawning, when the water temperature reaches the mid-40s (6 to 8°C), smallmouth in meso lakes begin moving from their deep wintering areas toward the areas where they will spawn. On calm, sunny days, they swim into the shallows to feed on minnows and insects. Dark-bottomed bays and shallow flats with lots of exposed boulders warm most quickly and are the first to attract smallmouth, especially if these areas are near the spawning grounds.

Periodic cold fronts during the pre-spawn period will drive most small-mouth to deeper water, usually back to the breakline. But the females stop making these in-and-out movements once their eggs near ripeness. They stay in deep water until the time comes to spawn.

Males build the nests in 2 to 8 feet (0.6 to 2.4 m) of water, usually in bays or along shorelines protected from the wind. The nests are generally next to boulders, logs, boat-mooring blocks, or any other solid object in the water. Smallmouth will also spawn in emergent vegetation, especially bulrushes, if largemouth are not using it.

Other spawning areas include rocky main-lake points and submerged humps. But water in the main lakes takes longer to warm, so spawning takes place a week or two later than spawning in bays or along sheltered shorelines.

After spawning, females return to deep water where they spend at least two weeks regaining their strength. They refuse to bite during this time. Males stay with the fry for up to three weeks.

When the recuperation and fry-guarding period is over, smallmouth begin feeding heavily. They may be found just about anywhere. Some roam the shoreline in search of small baitfish, others work muddy flats to find emerging insects, and still others move to rocky offshore structure where they can feed on crayfish. Because they seldom stay in one place for long, finding them may be difficult.

Smallmouth gradually move to deeper water and by the time the water temperature reaches 65 to 70°F (18 to 21°C), they have reached the locations where they will spend the summer. Although summertime structure is quite varied, it usually falls in a depth range of 10 to 20 feet (3 to 6 m).

The main ingredients of summertime smallmouth habitat are a good food supply, adequate cover, and easy access to deep water. The right type of bottom is also important. In most meso lakes, smallmouth prefer rock, gravel, or a combination of the two. But if the basin consists mostly of rock or gravel, the smallmouth are often found on sandy, weedy bottoms. Sandy areas are also a good choice in lakes where most of the bottom is muddy.

Smallmouth remain in their summertime haunts through early fall. But as the surface cools, they move into the shallows where they feed heavily until the turnover. They scatter while the turnover is in progress. When the surface water cools to the upper 40s (8 to 10°C), they move much deeper, usually to depths of 25 to 40 feet (7.6 to 12 m) and sometimes to depths of 50 feet (15 m) or more. Prime late-fall areas are in deep water just off summertime structure that borders large, open areas of the lake. Smallmouth tend to hold at the base of the drop-offs.

Although smallmouth become much less active in late fall, a period of warm, calm weather may draw them into shallower water and trigger some feeding. But when the water temperature drops below 40°F (4°C), they form extremely tight schools and become semi-dormant. A storm in late fall may spur some deep-water feeding. Only in high-competition lakes will smallmouth feed regularly in late fall and winter.

Sand-gravel bays protected from the wind are prime spawning areas. Some deep bays may hold smallmouth until fall.

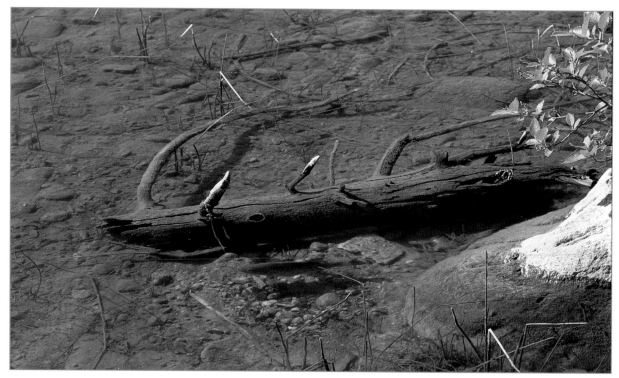

Woody debris over a firm sand or gravel bottom provides smallmouth with excellent nesting cover.

Bulrush beds adjacent to deep water are good spawning areas. They also serve as feeding areas through summer.

Docks, fallen trees, and other shallow-water cover near spawning areas concentrate pre-spawn smallmouth.

Dark-bottomed bays warm fastest, so they offer the earliest source of food for pre-spawn smallmouth.

Gradually sloping points are good spawning areas. Before and after spawning, smallmouth fold along the drop-off.

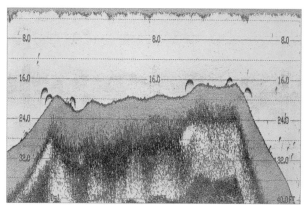

Deep humps near summertime smallmouth habitat attract smallmouth in late fall and into the winter.

Irregular breaklines that plunge sharply into deep water are good late-fall smallmouth spots.

Steep-sloping points concentrate smallmouth in late fall and continue to hold them into the winter.

Sandgrass growing along a moderate drop-off is likely to hold smallmouth from early summer to early fall.

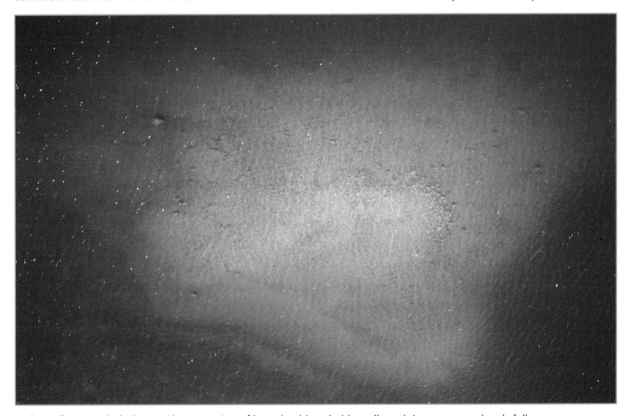

Rocky reefs, particularly those with a scattering of large boulders, hold smallmouth in summer and early fall.

Cabbage beds adjoining deep water make ideal spots for smallmouth to ambush food, particularly in summer.

Sand-gravel humps, especially those with sparse weed growth, rank among the top summertime smallmouth spots.

Flats near deep water are major feeding areas from early spring into early fall. Good flats have cover like rocks or logs.

Moderately sloping points draw smallmouth after spawning and continue to hold them into early fall.

OLIGOTROPHIC LAKES

The cold, infertile waters of most oligotrophic lakes are best suited to lake trout, northern pike, and walleyes. But many of these lakes have warm, shallow sections that more closely resemble mesotrophic lakes. These sections often hold tremendous numbers of smallmouth bass.

The key to finding smallmouth in oligotrophic lakes is learning to identify these prime areas. Because most oligotrophic lakes have an abundance of rocky habitat that looks good for smallmouth, the best areas may not be easy to recognize.

Depth is the major consideration. If half of a lake averages 100 feet (30 m) deep and the other half 30 feet (9 m) deep, you can bet that the vast majority of smallmouth will be found in the 30-foot portion, where the water is warmer and food more abundant. If you do not have a contour map of the lake, the easiest way to identify smallmouth water is to look for clusters of islands, preferably islands surrounded by large shoal areas.

Smallmouth may winter in the deeper portions of oligotrophic lakes, especially if the shallow portions lack deep holding areas. But when the water temperature rises to the mid-40s (6 to 8°C) in spring, smallmouth begin moving toward the shallower areas.

Areas that seem suitable for spawning are almost everywhere, but the sites actually chosen are in the areas that warm earliest. Protected bays or shoals around island clusters are excellent spawning areas.

Prior to spawning, smallmouth hold along the first major drop-off out from the spawning area, provided that the drop-off leads into water at least 15 feet (4.5 m) deep. A period of calm, sunny weather warms the water enough to draw smallmouth into the shallows, but they move out again when the water cools. When the water temperature reaches the mid-50s (12 to 14°C), males stay in the shallows and begin to fan out nests.

The nests are usually in 2 to 6 feet (0.6 to 1.8 m) of water next to a boulder, especially one that is partially exposed rather than completely submerged. Exposed boulders will absorb more heat from the sun, so they warm more quickly and in turn warm the water around them.

Because the water generally warms more slowly in oligotrophic lakes than in other types of waters, smallmouth may spawn at temperatures cooler than normal. It is not unusual for spawning to start at 55°F (13°C). The spawning period lasts from 6 to 10 days, although not all

Using natural looking baits such as flies presented with a fly rod is a good choice in oligotrophic lakes.

Smallmouth often spawn near exposed boulders because they warm from the sun more quickly and in turn warm the water around them.

smallmouth spawn at once. A sudden cold snap, a common occurrence on oligotrophic lakes, may cause smallmouth to abort their spawning activity and leave the nests. If spawning activity is aborted several times, females may re-absorb their eggs.

The slower warming of these lakes also means that the females need extra time to recuperate from spawning. And the fry develop more slowly, so the males spend more time guarding them. The recuperating and guarding periods last about a week longer than in a typical meso lake. Both males and females then scatter in search of food. Some can be found in shallow, mucky bays while others feed in deep water. Finding a consistent pattern is difficult at this time. To further complicate matters, some males may still be guarding their fry and some females still recuperating.

Smallmouth may not have to move far from their spawning areas to find summertime habitat. Most oligotrophic lakes that hold smallmouth are in the northern states or southern Canada where surface temperatures seldom rise above the low 70s (21 to 23°C). Many of these lakes have a light to moderate bog stain, so sunlight does not penetrate as deep as in clear mesotrophic lakes. As a result, smallmouth seldom need to move to deep water.

The best summertime smallmouth habitat generally has a bottom of base-ball- to basketball-sized rock. This type of bottom has plenty of hiding places for crayfish, insect larvae, and other invertebrates. It also offers good cover. Smallmouth are rarely found over a bottom of large slab rock. Typical summertime depths range from 8 to 15 feet (2.4 to 4.5 m). Easy access to deep water is less important in oligotrophic lakes than in mesotrophic lakes.

As in meso lakes, smallmouth may prefer sandy, weedy bottoms, especially if the rest of the basin consists primarily of rock. The weedy habitat attracts more baitfish. It is not unusual to find summertime smallmouth in sandy bars or over sandy offshore humps. Smallmouth will stay near their summertime habitat until the fall turnover. They may remain there after the turnover, if the structure drops rapidly into 30 to 50 feet (9 to 15 m) of water. If not, they move to deep reefs of rocky points that slope sharply into the depths.

Although smallmouth continue to feed through late fall, finding them can be difficult. They form very tight schools, usually next to rock piles or deep weed beds. Or a school may tuck into a sharp inside turn along the breakline. Once the water temperature drops below 40°F (4°C), smallmouth become nearly dormant. But in high-competition lakes, they may continue to feed through the winter.

Drop-offs adjacent to spawning sites are the primary staging areas for pre-spawn smallmouth bass.

Shallow, sandy bays warm earlier than the main lakes and make excellent spawning areas for smallmouth.

Points at the mouths of spawning bays hold post-spawn smallmouth until they are ready to move into the main lake.

Small creeks draining bog areas warm early. Smallmouth congregate around the mouth prior to spawning.

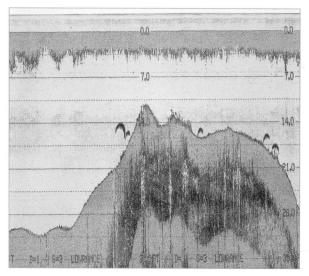

Deep reefs in shallower portions of the main lake hold small-mouth from late fall into the winter.

Breaklines where shoreline flats plunge into deep water are likely to draw smallmouth in late fall or winter.

Island clusters with a lot of shoal area provide good spawning habitat and usually hold smallmouth through summer.

Shallow, rocky reefs close to shore draw smallmouth after spawning and continue to hold them through summer.

Points that extend into the main lake then slope gradually into deep water are good summertime smallmouth spots.

Mouths of major inlets offer current, food, and warmer water. They attract smallmouth from late spring through summer.

Sandy bays with moderately deep water and some weeds hold good numbers of smallmouth in summer and early fall.

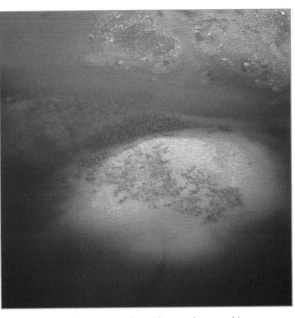

Sandy humps with scattered weeds are also good in summer and early fall, especially if the basin is primarily rock.

Points that extend into the main lake then drop sharply into deep water are the best late-fall and winter spots.

EUTROPHIC LAKES

These fertile lakes are shallow, warm, and weedy. They have silty bottoms and often lack well-defined structure. Eutrophic lakes are best suited to largemouth, but some hold a few smallmouth, often fish of trophy size.

Because of the silty bottom, spawning sites are scarce. Smallmouth will spawn on rocky points or along sand-gravel or rock shorelines in protected bays, usually at depths of 4 feet (1.2 m) or less. If there is no rock or gravel, smallmouth may be able to fan away the silt to reach a firm bottom.

Before spawning, smallmouth cruise the breakline in the vicinity of the nesting area. You can generally find them at depths of 5 to 10 feet (1.5 to 3 m). After spawning has been completed, they begin scattering to their summer locations.

In lakes with some structure, smallmouth spend the summer on points that drop into the deepest water, along inside turns on the breakline, and around offshore humps. In bowl-shaped lakes, they relate to the outside edge of the weedline.

As summer progresses, rising water temperatures drive the smallmouth to deeper water. However, most eutrophic lakes do not have adequate

Eutrophic lakes may offer some excellent trophy fishing opportunities. Highly eutrophic (fertile) lakes may not support smallmouth due to high water temperatures.

oxygen below the thermocline during the summer months, so small-mouth must stay at depths of 15 feet (4.5 m) or less.

Smallmouth remain in their summertime locations until the submerged weeds begin to die off in fall. By late fall, you can find them at the base of points and humps, usually at depths of 20 to 30 feet (6 to 9 m). In structureless lakes, hard-bottomed areas that rise only 1 foot (30 cm) above the rest of the bottom may draw smallmouth. They remain in these locations through winter, but do not feed regularly.

MID-DEPTH RESERVOIRS

Mid-depth reservoirs produce more big smallmouth than any other type of water. They have an abundance of shallow rock and gravel spawning areas, plenty of hard-bottomed structure adjacent to deep water, and a good supply of smallmouth foods like crayfish and shad. The large reservoirs in mid-South states like Kentucky and Tennessee are the best producers of big smallmouth. They have a much longer growing season than reservoirs in the North.

Smallmouth generally spend the winter in deep water off shoreline points or steep-sloping banks or in deep areas of the old river channel. As the water starts to warm in spring, they begin moving toward their spawning areas.

Shallow creek arms warm earlier than other areas of the reservoir and are the first to attract pre-spawn smallmouth. Shallow points in the main reservoir and eddies in the tailrace also attract them. Because the upper end of a reservoir warms earlier than the lower end, pre-spawn movements take place sooner on the upper end.

Most mid-depth reservoirs are fairly clear, so smallmouth build their nests in deep water, usually 3 to 10 feet (0.9 to 3 m), but sometimes as deep as 15 feet (4.5 m). Nests are usually on gradually sloping bottoms of rock or gravel mixed with clay. As in other types of waters, small-mouth nest near boulders, logs, or stumps.

At the upper end of a large reservoir, smallmouth may complete spawn-ing a month earlier than at the lower end. As a result, smallmouth at the upper end may be moving toward their summer locations while those at the lower end are just starting to spawn.

After the nest-guarding and recuperation periods, most smallmouth move to shoreline points and sloping banks where the bottom is composed of rock, gravel, clay, or a combination of these materials. Hard-bottomed offshore humps are also prime summertime locations. Typically, the best summertime spots are adjacent to water at least 40 feet (12 m) deep.

In many cases, smallmouth simply drop deeper on the points and banks where they spawned. If a creek arm is deep enough, smallmouth may stay here all summer rather than moving to the main lake.

The surface temperature of mid-depth reservoirs in the South often ex-ceeds 80°F (27°C) in summer, so smallmouth are forced to go deep. It is not unusual to catch them at depths of 25 to 35 feet (7.6 to 10.6 m). In the North, typical summertime depths for smallmouth range from 10 to 20 feet (3 to 6 m).

Flooded timber is not as important to smallmouth as it is to large-mouth, but trees and stumps near deep water may hold smallmouth in summer. Timbered flats adjacent to the old river channel often attract fair numbers of smallmouth.

In fall, when the surface temperature drops into the 60s, smallmouth move into shallower water on the same banks, points, and humps where they spent the summer. You can find them at depths of 10 to 20 feet (3 to 6 m) until the surface temperature drops below 50°F (10°C). Then they begin to move deeper. By late fall, most smallmouth are found deeper than 30 feet (9 m). A warm spell in late fall or winter will draw smallmouth much shallower and cause them to start feeding.

Many mid-depth reservoirs undergo a drawdown in the fall as a means to increase the storage capacity for spring run-off. When the reservoir is drawn down, the water level may drop as much as 30 feet (9 m). In the shallower upper reaches of the lake, smallmouth may have no choice but to retreat to the old river channel or move farther down the lake to find deep water.

Some smallmouth spend the winter in the tailrace of an upstream res-ervoir, if the reservoir drains from the surface. Smallmouth avoid swift current by nesting behind boulders or staying in eddies.

Creek arms with active inlet streams warm quickly in spring, attracting pre-spawn smallmouth from the main lake.

Rock or gravel shorelines, especially those in protected creek arms, make ideal spawning areas.

Timbered flats along the old river channel are prime nighttime feeding areas for smallmouth in summer.

Steep portions of a breakline hold more smallmouth in fall than portions that slope more gradually.

Points extending into the old river channel make good summer habitat because smallmouth can easily reach deep water.

Main-lake points that are composed of gravel, rock, and clay hold smallmouth in summer, fall, and winter.

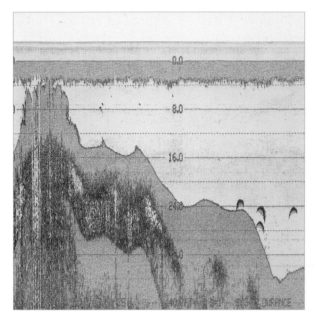

Secondary drop-offs on points in creek arms draw smallmouth in summer, primary drop-offs in spring.

Submerged roadbeds, particularly those built along steep banks, make good feeding areas for smallmouth in summer.

Main-lake humps that are within easy reach of deep water are likely to draw smallmouth in summer.

Fallen trees along steep-sloping banks are good summertime smallmouth spots, much better than trees on gradual slopes.

SHALLOW RESERVOIRS

Shallow northern reservoirs, often called flowages, may offer good smallmouth fishing, especially if they have fairly clear water and a rocky basin. Shallow southern reservoirs seldom hold smallmouth; the warm, weedy conditions favor largemouth.

Many shallow reservoirs have extensive areas of flooded timber. The old river channel is often only a few feet deep and there are no significant creek arms. As a result, river and creek channels have less effect on smallmouth movement patterns than in mid-depth reservoirs.

Smallmouth in shallow reservoirs spawn along rocky shorelines and points sheltered from the wind or on offshore reefs. They may spawn in silt-bottom bays, if there are enough stumps or logs for cover. Spawning sites range from 2 to 8 feet (0.6 to 2.4 m) deep and are almost always near a drop-off.

Prime summertime habitat includes rocky reefs or sand-gravel humps that top off near the surface and slope gradually into deep water. If there are distinct points adjacent to deep water, these also are good summer spots. The best summertime habitat often has some submerged weed growth.

As the surface starts to cool in early fall, smallmouth return to the vicinity of their spawning areas. But when the surface temperature falls into the low 50s (10 to 12°C), they move to deeper water, where they spend the late fall and winter in the old river channel or in other deep areas of the reservoir.

CANYON RESERVOIRS

Canyon reservoirs sometimes have limited smallmouth populations, but most of these deep, cool impoundments lack the shallow-water cover that smallmouth need. In those that do have smallmouth, the only suitable structure may be submerged ledges along the steep rock walls. In many instances, smallmouth use these ledges through the entire year.

Spawning usually takes place on ledges that are covered with sand or gravel and have boulders for cover. Such ledges are often found at the mouths of inflowing streams. Some smallmouth spawn on gravel shoals in the stream itself. Canyon reservoirs generally have very clear water, so smallmouth may spawn as deep as 20 feet (6 m).

After the spawning period, smallmouth drop into slightly deeper water, sometimes suspending just off the spawning ledges. As the water warms, they move progressively deeper. On sunny summer days, you may find them as deep as 80 feet (24.4 m). Smallmouth are drawn to anything along the sheer banks that provides shade. Docks, clumps of brush, and rockslides are examples of commonly used cover.

Smallmouth begin to move shallower as the water cools in fall. Often, they return to the same areas where they spawned. Canyon reservoirs in the Southwest remain warm enough that smallmouth continue to feed through the winter.

SMALL- TO MEDIUM-SIZED RIVERS

In many parts of the country, particularly in areas with numerous natural or man-made lakes, small- to medium-sized rivers offer a virtually untouched smallmouth fishing opportunity.

The best rivers have cool, clean water, moderate current, a winding stream course, and deep pools combined with rock or gravel riffles.

A few weeks before spawning, smallmouth move out of the deep pools where they winter. These pools may be many miles, usually downstream, from the areas where they will spawn and spend the summer. As smallmouth work their way toward their spawning areas, they feed in riffles and along current margins. When not feeding, they drop into the slack water of pools and eddies so they do not have to fight the current.

Shortly after they arrive at their spawning areas, males begin to build nests, usually along the edge of the stream where there is a slight current and a bottom of sand, gravel, or rock. Most nests are in 1 to 3 feet (0.3 to 0.9 m) of water. If good spawning sites are scarce in the stream itself, smallmouth may swim up small tributaries to find the right conditions.

After the spawning period, the key to finding smallmouth is to look for current margins where they can rest in slack water and dart into the current to grab drifting food. During this early part of the summer, they remain in fairly shallow water, usually less than 5 feet (1.5 m) deep.

By midsummer, most good-sized smallmouth have retreated to deeper pools. The best pools are generally below shallow riffles and have gravel or rock bottoms with boulders, deadfalls, logs, rock-ledges, or undercut banks for cover. Smallmouth remain in these deeper pools through early fall.

When the water temperature drops into the 60s (16 to 20°C), smallmouth begin feeding more heavily, usually along current margins similar to those used in early summer. This period of heavy feeding continues until the water temperature drops to the low 50s (10 to 12°C).

As the water temperature continues to fall, smallmouth move out of the shallows and into the deepest holes. If there are no deep holes in the vicinity of the summer habitat, smallmouth will swim long distances to find the necessary depth, sometimes 10 miles (17 km) or more. They hold in crevices between rocks or behind any object that shelters them from the current. They stay in these deep holes through winter and feed very little.

Gravel deposits on inside bends provide good spawning sites. Smallmouth feed on these same bars through fall.

Undercut banks, especially those with a lot of exposed roots, are excellent smallmouth spots in summer and fall.

Pools below riffles hold smallmouth in summer and fall. They feed along the upper lip and rest in the deeper downstream end.

Fallen trees and logjams attract minnows and insects and create slack-water pockets. They are best in summer and fall.

Springs attract smallmouth in summer because of their cooler water; in late fall and winter because of their warmer water.

Seasonal flooded pools warm quickly, drawing pre-spawn smallmouth to feed on minnows and insects.

Large boulders make it easy to pinpoint eddies where smallmouth feed and rest in summer and fall.

Rocky points extending into the current also create eddies used by smallmouth in summer and fall.

Steep ledges formed where the current cuts into the limestone bank make good smallmouth habitat in summer and fall.

Eddies alongside the swift water below a dam draw smallmouth after spawning and hold well into the fall.

Deep holes with no current draw smallmouth from miles away in late fall. They spend the winter in a near-dormant state.

BIG RIVERS

Big rivers that carry only a light silt load may have excellent populations of smallmouth. Such rivers have a diversity of natural and man-made habitat that provides good conditions for spawning, an abundant supply of food, and deep water for wintering. But muddy rivers with silt-covered bottoms seldom support many smallmouth.

Most smallmouth winter in deep areas of the main river channel. As the water temperature begins to rise in spring, they leave the deep holes and begin feeding on flats or in eddies along the channel margin, near the locations where they will spawn. Many of them move into areas where the water is warmer, like sloughs off the main channel or into the mouths of tributaries. Spawning in sloughs and tributaries takes place 1 to 2 weeks earlier than spawning in the main channel.

Prime spawning sites include gravel shorelines, riprap banks, and stump fields with a hard bottom. Seldom will smallmouth spawn in midstream, unless there is a boulder or log to afford protection.

Following the spawning period, smallmouth gradually filter out of their spawning areas. They school up in eddies and pools where they can wait for food to be washed to them rather than waste energy chasing it. They remain in these post-spawn locations through summer.

Examples of good summertime habitat include eddies around islands, wingdams, and bridge pilings; rocky pools with some current; eddies below points and inside bends, especially where the water is deep and has lots of rocks or logs for cover; and eddies below dams, riprapped channel markers, and riprapped lighthouse foundations.

Smallmouth remain in their summer locations until the water temperature drops to about 55°F (13°C). Then, they gradually begin to work their way toward the deep holes where they will spend the winter. These holes, 15 to 30 feet (4.5 to 9 m) deep, are usually located in bends where the water is slack. Big-river smallmouth feed very little from late fall through winter.

Big rivers that have dams to control water levels offer prime smallmouth habitat. Because rocks are often used to divert river currents, man-made features are often abundant.

Shallow gravel bars are commonly used as spawning sites, if the current is not too swift.

Backwater areas with gravel or riprap shorelines and little current make ideal smallmouth spawning areas.

Islands with rock or riprap banks are good in summer and fall. Try eddies on the edges and downstream end.

Deep cuts connecting the main channel with backwaters concentrate smallmouth in summer and fall.

Channel markers are often placed on man-made rock piles. The downstream eddies hold smallmouth in summer and fall.

Marinas warm early and offer lots of cover. Smallmouth move in before spawning and may stay through summer.

Tributaries that bring in warm water attract smallmouth from spring through early summer.

Riprap highway or railroad embankments offer food and cover. They often hold smallmouth from spring through fall.

Pilings of bridges, piers, and docks create small eddies that smallmouth use for summertime feeding and resting areas.

Wingdams are prime smallmouth feeding areas in summer and fall. Active smallmouth usually lie along the upstream lip.

Deep holes in the main river channel provide protection from the current and draw smallmouth in late fall and winter.

PRIME SMALLMOUTH WATERS

To determine the best smallmouth-fishing waters in North America, researchers conducted a pool of state and provincial natural resources agencies and expert fishermen. The most productive waters in each of the major smallmouth fishing regions are shown below.

NORTHERN NATURAL LAKES REGION. This region produces more smallmouth bass than anywhere else in the world. Laced among thousands of cool, clear glacial lakes that hold smallmouth are thousands of miles of smallmouth rivers and streams. Although the Great Lakes are in this region, they will be discussed separately.

Most of the lakes in the northern portion of this region are cold and infertile, falling into either the oligotrophic or mesotrophic categories. In the southern portion of the region, most of the lakes are mesotrophic or eutrophic. Many waters in the northern portion are located in wilderness areas, like the Boundary Waters Canoe Area Wilderness in northern Minnesota and the Quetico Provincial Park in southwestern Ontario. Access to these waters is limited; many can be reached only by portaging a canoe. Even though they are not as productive as waters farther south, they receive very little fishing pressure, so catches of 50 to 100 smallmouth a day are not unusual.

The region has a tremendous diversity of smallmouth waters ranging from 100-acre (40 ha) unnamed lakes to Lake of the Woods, which covers nearly 1 million acres (400,000 ha). In the western part of the region, most anglers pursue walleyes and northern pike, so smallmouth are often overlooked. In many lakes in the eastern part, smallmouth take a back seat to trout and landlocked salmon.

Because the waters are so diverse, the best fishing times vary widely. But in most cases, fishing is good from late May through mid-July and from

September through early October. Smallmouth in this region generally run from 1½ to 2½ pounds (0.6 to 1.1 kg) and top off at about 7 pounds (3 kg). Excluding fish caught in the Great Lakes, the largest smallmouth ever taken in the region was a 9-pound, 4-ounce (4.2 kg) fish caught in Long Lake, Michigan in 1950.

GREAT LAKES. The shallow, warmwater portions of the Great Lakes offer excellent smallmouth fishing, as do many of the connecting rivers, canals, and smaller lakes. The deep, open waters of the Great Lakes are too cold for smallmouth.

There are several reasons for the top-rate smallmouth bass fishing in the Great Lakes and their connecting waters. Because of the vast expanses of water, the Great Lakes have the capacity to produce huge numbers of smallmouth. Compared to the trout, salmon, walleye, and yellow perch fishing, the smallmouth fishing has drawn little attention. Unlike walleyes and lake trout, smallmouth have not been harvested by commercial fishermen.

Throughout most of the Great Lakes, the best smallmouth fishing is found in shallow warmwater bays and around islands and shallow underwater reefs. The deep waters are better suited to trout, salmon, and other coldwater species.

Some islands and reefs in the Great Lakes are so isolated that they are seldom fished. But anglers who are willing to travel 30 miles (48 km) or more by boat can enjoy some of the finest trophy-smallmouth fishing to be found anywhere. The best-known smallmouth fishing area in the Great Lakes is the Bass Islands area in Lake Erie. Although this area has been fished heavily for many years, it continues to produce impressive numbers of good-sized smallmouth.

Fishing in shallow warmwater bays and connecting rivers and canals is generally best from late April through June. Around main-lake reefs and islands, smallmouth bite best from mid-June until early August. For those willing to brave the weather, main-lake fishing can also be good from September to early November.

A typical Great Lakes smallmouth weighs from 1½ to 3 pounds (0.7 to 1.4 kg), but 5- to 6-pounders (2.25 to 2.7 kg) are taken with surprising regularity by anglers familiar with the waters. In 1964, one of the largest smallmouth ever recorded was caught in Lake Ontario. It weighed 11 pounds, 8 ounces (5.2 kg).

MID-SOUTH RESERVOIR REGION. These waters produce the world's biggest smallmouth. In addition to the world-record smallmouth weighing 11 pounds, 15 ounces (5.37 kg), several other smallmouth over 10 pounds (4.5 kg) have been caught in this region.

The best mid-south reservoirs are in mountainous areas and have plenty of deep, cool water. Shallower reservoirs in the region have few smallmouth because the water is too warm in summer.

Most mid-south reservoirs have super-abundant crops of shad. The excellent food supply combined with the long growing season account for the large size of the smallmouth. In addition, most southern anglers concentrate on largemouth, so smallmouth receive less fishing pressure.

Smallmouth fishing in this region peaks in March and April, slows during the warm summer months, then picks up again in September and stays good through November. In summer, you can catch some smallmouth by fishing at night. Stringers of 3- to 4-pound (1.4 to 1.8 kg) smallmouth are fairly common in this region and 5- to 7-pounders (2.25 to 3 kg) are not unusual.

Although the reservoirs get the most attention, many rivers in the Ozark and Ouachita Mountains also have good smallmouth populations. The best fishing is in remote areas where access is limited.

EASTERN RIVERS REGION. Historically famous for its smallmouth fishing, this region continues to provide quality angling despite heavy fishing pressure. Smallmouth fishing is actually improving in some rivers because of stricter water quality standards.

Originally, smallmouth were found only in the Ohio River drainage system. But widespread stocking has established smallmouth in virtually every major river system in the region. The best smallmouth rivers in this region are in hilly or mountainous country where difficult access keeps fishing pressure to a minimum.

Smallmouth in the northern part of the region begin to bite in March; those in the southern part, in April. Fishing remains good through October.

In the northern part, smallmouth generally run 1 to 2 pounds (0.45 to 0.9 kg), with an occasional 4- to 5-pounder (1.8 to 2.25 kg). They grow larger in the southern part, averaging 2 to 3 pounds (0.9 to 1.4 kg) with a few in the 6- to 7-pound (2.7 to 3 kg) class.

While the vast majority of smallmouth in the eastern rivers region are caught in rivers and streams, some of the deeper, colder reservoirs also have good numbers of smallmouth. The Hiwassee Reservoir in North Carolina produced a 10-pound, 2-ounce (4.56 kg) smallmouth in 1953.

MIDWESTERN RIVERS REGION. Because of the heavy agricultural use of this region, most of the lakes have silted in and become too fertile for smallmouth. But many rivers and streams have fair to good smallmouth fishing. The upper reaches of the rivers usually offer the best smallmouth fishing because the water is clear and cool and the bottom free of silt. Farther downstream, the rivers carry more silt and may be too warm.

In some spring-fed streams, the cold upper reaches hold trout, the cool middle reaches have smallmouth, and the warm lower reaches support only rough fish like carp and bullheads.

Smallmouth in Midwestern rivers and streams begin to bite in mid- to late April. The best fishing is usually in May and June, although some smallmouth are caught through October. Smallmouth in these waters average 1 to 2 pounds (0.45 to 0.9 kg) with an occasional fish topping 5 pounds (2.25 kg).

Many of the lakes in this region have heavy algal blooms and are too silty to support smallmouth. But a few have a limited smallmouth fishery. Because of the minimal quantity of smallmouth and the abundance of food in these fertile lakes, fishing is usually difficult. But when you catch a smallmouth, it is likely to be a big one.

NORTHERN CALIFORNIA RESERVOIRS. The rivers feeding these reservoirs were stocked with smallmouth in the early 1900s. When the rivers were dammed, smallmouth began to proliferate in the reservoirs and are now providing some outstanding fishing. Some of these deep, clear reservoirs have trout and salmon in the depths and smallmouth in the warmer, shallower water. Fishing is best from mid-March through April and from mid-August through mid-October. Most of the smallmouth range from 1½ to 3 pounds (0.45 to 1.3 kg). The Claire Engle Reservoir produced a 9-pound, 1-ounce (4.1 kg) smallmouth in 1976.

SOUTHWESTERN RESERVOIRS. Like northern California reservoirs, these steep-sided canyon reservoirs often have trout in the depths and smallmouth in the shallower portions. Some shallower reservoirs and a few rivers in the Southwest have also been stocked with smallmouth and are producing good fishing. Fishing is generally best from December through March. Night fishing can be good from May through July, but the fish generally do not run as large. Smallmouth in this region typically weigh from 1 to 3 pounds (0.45 to 1.3 kg) with an occasional 6-pounder (2.7 kg).

PACIFIC NORTHWEST. Trout and salmon are the primary targets of anglers in this region, so smallmouth receive very little attention. But good smallmouth populations are present in major rivers such as the Columbia and Snake and in some of their largest tributaries. The smallmouth start to bite in spring, as soon as the rivers recede and clear up. Fishing remains good though July. September and October are also good times. Most of the smallmouth run from 1½ to 2 pounds (0.7 to 0.9 kg), but several 10- to 11-pounders (4.5 to 5 kg) have been taken by survey crews while shocking in the Columbia River in Washington.

Chapter 8
EQUIPMENT

In many cases, the equipment used for finding and catching smallmouth bass is identical to that used for catching largemouth. That information has been previously covered in the largemouth section of this book. When applying this information to your fishing situation, be sure to review that section when making equipment choices.

In general, you will want to downsize this equipment used for largemouth. Smallmouth are typically found in clearer water than largemouth, so lighter line is often used to cast the smaller baits needed to fool them.

Spinning gear is used much more often and having a smooth drag on your reel is very important to battle tough-fighting smallies. And unlike largemouth, there is a smaller "core" group of lures you can use to catch smallmouth. Because of this, you do not need to have nearly as much equipment to go smallmouth fishing.

The following section will help you to get a good selection of rods and equipment together to catch smallmouth wherever they are found.

RODS, REELS & LINE

Smallmouth anglers often only need a few rod and reel combos to catch fish.

For maximum sport, smallmouth anglers should use the lightest rod and reel that suits the conditions. A light outfit not only makes the most of the smallmouth's magnificent fighting qualities, but is easier to cast for long periods of time and is ideal for tossing the small lures and baits that smallmouth usually prefer. The only reason for using heavy tackle is to fish in timber, brush, or other heavy cover, or to cast large lures.

RODS. Experienced smallmouth fishermen carry several rods, each intended for a different fishing situation. This way, they are prepared to use a variety of lures and baits and do not waste time re-rigging every time they try a new presentation.

If you do not wish to carry several outfits, your best choice is a general-purpose outfit. A 5½- to 6½-foot (1.6 to 1.9 m) graphite spinning outfit, spooled with 6- to 8-pound (2.7 to 3.6 kg) line will fit most smallmouth fishing situations; this will handle lures weighing from $\frac{1}{16}$ to $\frac{5}{8}$ ounce (1.8 to 17.7 g).

Smallmouth do not necessarily take a lure or bait as vigorously as they fight, so any rod you select should be sensitive enough to detect subtle strikes. Most experts prefer graphite rods as their stiffness makes them very sensitive and enables you to set the hook fast and hard. In some instances, high-quality fiberglass rods will do the job better, such as when you are crankbait fishing.

Before buying a rod, check its graphite modulus, the quality of the guides, and check to see how the rod balances in your hand with the reel you are going to use attached. In general, a rod with a higher-modulus graphite will perform better than those with lower grade. In most cases, employees at the store where you purchased the rod should be able to step you through different levels of rod quality.

SPINNING REELS. The most important consideration in selecting a spinning reel for smallmouth fishing is a smooth, reliable drag. Many anglers make the mistake of buying a cheap spinning reel to save a few dollars. Then, the first time they hook a good-sized smallmouth, the drag malfunctions and the smallmouth snaps the line.

The only sure way to test a drag is to spool line on the reel, then pull on it to be sure it comes off smoothly. If you cannot test the drag this way, check to see how much adjustment is required to go from a light drag setting to a heavy one. Generally, the best drags are those with the largest amount of adjustment between settings.

Another consideration is the gear ratio. A spinning reel with a gear ratio of at least 5:1 enables you to retrieve lures rapidly and take up slack line when a smallmouth suddenly changes direction. But a high gear ratio is not the best choice for retrieving lures with a lot of water resistance, such as big crankbaits.

Many spinning reels have small-diameter spools, which make the reel light and compact, but a small spool causes the line to come off in tight coils. Limp monofilament line is the best choice for spinning reels rather than stiffer co-polymers and fluorocarbons, which have more memory and have a greater tendency to remain coiled.

BAITCASTING REELS. These should also have a smooth drag. A narrow-spooled model with a magnetic brake system minimizes the problem of backlashing, especially when casting light lures into the wind. A button to disengage the anti-reverse is also a good feature in a baitcasting reel.

Most baitcasting reels have a built-in anti-reverse. The handle will not turn backward, so you must rely on the drag when a smallmouth makes a run. But on a big run you can disengage the anti-reverse and thumb the spool instead of relying on the drag. This way, your line will not break if the drag malfunctions.

FLY-FISHING OUTFIT. A 7-weight, 8½-foot (2.6 m) fly rod with a sturdy single-action fly reel is a good all-around choice for smallmouth. The reel you select should have enough capacity for your fly line and at least 50 yards (45.5 m) of 12- to 20-pound (5.4 to 9 kg) Dacron backing. A 7-weight floating line allows you to cast anything from a delicate dry fly to a bulky bass bug. For special-purpose fly tackle, refer to the recommendations from an employee at a local fly shop.

LINE. Smallmouth anglers commonly rely on monofilament line. Be sure to select premium-grade monofilament because cheap mono may have weak spots caused by an inconsistent diameter. Limp monofilament is usually the best choice. It is easier to cast than stiffer line and because it flexes more, your lures will have better action.

However, most brands of limp mono have a high stretch factor. Some stretch as much as 30 percent. A high stretch factor makes it more difficult to detect strikes and set the hook. If your fishing technique requires a long cast or is in deep water, then low-stretch co-polymers or fluorocarbon would be a better choice. The other situation for using co-polymers or fluorocarbon is if you are fishing in heavy cover or in an area with a snaggy bottom.

Although the low-visibility is an advantage in clear water, you may have difficulty detecting subtle strikes because you cannot see the line twitch. If the water clarity is low, you can use heavier line as it is not visible to the fish and is much easier for you to see.

Light line is still the best choice in most situations. It lets you cast farther, allows your lure to run deeper without restricting its action, and makes it easier to feel bites.

When fly fishing, floating and sink-tip fly lines from 6- to 8-weight are recommended for smallmouth fishing. Lines with weight-forward tapers cast the large wind-resistant flies used for smallmouth more easily than double-tapers or level lines.

FISHING QUALITIES OF VARIOUS TYPES OF LINE

Type	Stretch	Abrasion Resistance	Memory	Diameter	Visibility	Knot Stretch
Monofilament	High	Low	Low	High	Medium	High
Co-Polymer	Medium	Medium	Medium	Medium	Medium	Medium
Fluorocarbon	Low	High	High	Medium	Low	Medium

BOATS, MOTORS & ACCESSORIES

Depending on the type of water you fish, the best craft for smallmouth may be a high-powered bass boat, such as those featured in the large-mouth section. But in many cases when fishing for smallmouth, an aluminum or fiberglass semi-V, a jon boat, or a pair of waders are the best option. Smallmouth anglers who fish a variety of waters often have two or three boats. We will feature boats that are more specific to small-mouth anglers in this section.

SEMI-V BOATS. The term semi-V indicates that the boat has a V-shaped bow, but a relatively flat bottom at the stern. The V-shaped bow serves to part the waves and the flat bottom makes the boat stable. There are two basic types of semi-Vs: aluminum and fiberglass.

Aluminum semi-Vs are light, so the bow rides up on the waves instead of cutting through them, resulting in a rough ride. Fiberglass semi-Vs are heavier, so they ride more smoothly and are less affected by wind. They are also quieter than aluminum, but tend to be less durable around rocks and more expensive.

Fiberglass Semi-Vs are popular on big lakes because the hull is flared at the bow to deflect waves to the side. Without the flared bow, spray flies up and the wind blows it back into the boat. Fiberglass semi-Vs used for smallmouth fishing range from 16 to 19 feet (4.9 to 5.8 m) and are normally rigged with 35- to 90-horsepower motors.

Most smallmouth anglers prefer a semi-V with tiller steering. A tiller gives you much better boat control than a steering wheel, especially for backtrolling. Other desirable equipment includes a locator and a transom or bow-mounted electric trolling motor. Some of the more expensive semi-Vs come equipped with bass-boat features like live-wells, carpeted floors, air-pedestal seats, and elevated casting decks.

JON BOATS. The stability and light weight of a jon boat make it ideal for river fishing for smallmouth. Many rivers lack developed boat landings, but a pair of anglers can easily carry a 14-foot (4.3 m) jon boat to the water. A small-horsepower outboard provides all the power you will normally need. With jon boats bigger than 16 feet (4.9 m), anglers may choose a 10- to 15-horsepower outboard.

Some anglers customize their jon boats with a bow-mounted trolling motor, locator, rod holders, and a bait well. But others would rather go light. They rely solely on their outboard, check the depth visually or with a push pole, and keep their bait in a cooler.

CANOES. Anglers who regularly fish difficult to reach waters prefer canoes. They are inexpensive, durable, and light enough for one person to carry on his shoulders when portaging around dangerous rapids or from one lake to another. Because of their light weight, they are easy to paddle long distances. Most canoe anglers travel light; the only extra equipment is a portable locator, paddles, and an anchor rope. For an anchor, they tie onto a rock.

Where motors are permitted, use a square-stern canoe or one with a bracket for mounting a motor alongside the stern. A side-mount bracket will usually take a 2- to 4-horsepower outboard. If you prefer, you can attach an electric motor to the stern or simply attach the electric motor to the gunwale. Even a small electric motor will push a canoe at a surprising speed.

ELECTRONICS

Electronics for smallmouth are identical for those you would use for largemouth featured earlier in the book. Anglers fishing large water should have a quality mapping, locator/GPS unit. A portable flasher is an indispensable tool for most types of smallmouth fishing because of the rivers and smaller streams they inhabit. It enables you to find depths quickly and if you know how to interpret the signal, you can even check the bottom type and determine if fish are present.

WADING GEAR

One major difference in largemouth and smallmouth equipment is that a great deal of smallmouth fishing can be done by wading in small streams and rivers. For this type of fishing, you will need a good pair of waders or hip boots.

The major considerations in buying waders or hip boots are the type of leg material and the type of sole. Most wading gear used in smallmouth fishing is made of lightweight breathable materials or neoprene.

It pays to buy high-quality waders rather than cheap rubber wading gear. High-quality waders are very durable, whereas cheap ones will probably tear or develop leaks after you wear them a few times.

For wading on slippery rocks, choose waders or hip boots with felt soles, or glue pieces of felt or carpet to your soles. Lugged soles are best for sandy or muddy bottoms.

Another consideration in buying waders is whether to select a boot-foot model or a stocking-foot model with separate wading boots. Stocking-foot waders are less bulky, so you can wade more easily in current and are best if you have to walk long distances.

Cut pieces of felt to fit your soles and heels, then attach them with shoe-repair cement. You will have good traction, even on slippery rocks.

Sprinkle the inside of rubber waders or hip boots with baby powder to make them slide on easily. Powder removes the sticky texture.

Dry damp waders or hip boots using a hair dryer. Set the dryer on low heat, then let it blow into each leg for 10 to 15 minutes.

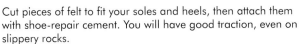

Chapter 9

SMALLMOUTH FISHING FUNDAMENTALS

To catch smallmouth bass consistently, you must understand a few basic fishing principles that always apply, regardless of the technique you see.

- Smallmouth are object-oriented, meaning that they like to get next to something. Their favorite type of object is rock. They are sometimes found around weeds, but are not as weed-oriented as largemouth.

- In a given body of water, smallmouth can usually be found deeper than largemouth, but shallower than walleye.

- Smallmouth tend to school by size, so if you are catching nothing but small ones, try a different area.

- Smallmouth have different personalities in different types of water. In lakes, rivers, or reservoirs with high competition between smallmouth, they tend to be aggressive, so aggressive presentations will work. But in low-competition waters, they can be very finicky. Here, a slow, tantalizing presentation draws the most strikes.

- Small-sized smallmouth are more aggressive than large ones and generally inhabit shallower water.

- If smallmouth are feeding on schooling baitfish, you can catch them suspended in the water column. Otherwise, smallmouth are typically caught near the bottom.

- Smallmouth tend to be more vulnerable to surface presentations than largemouth.

- In most waters, smallmouth bite best in early morning. In clear lakes, they may bite best at night, especially in summer.

- Object fishing is effective when smallmouth are in the shallows. Look for boulders, logs, stumps, brush piles, or any other visible object that provides shade.

- Small lures and baits are best when fishing for smallmouth bass. A smallmouth would prefer a 4-inch plastic worm, for instance, while a largemouth would prefer an 8-inch worm.

BOAT CONTROL

One of the biggest problems for the average fisherman is learning to control his boat. The wind and current constantly seem to work against him. So he spends too much time fishing in unproductive water or presenting his bait at the wrong speed.

The smallmouth's skittishness makes boat control even more important, especially in clear water. If you are casting to a shallow reef, for instance, and allow your boat to drift too close, you may as well look for a new fishing spot because the fish will spook.

Once you locate the fish, the objective of most boat control techniques is to keep the boat at the precise depth. To accomplish this, a depth finder is essential. Expert anglers keep their eyes glued to their depth finders.

You can control your boat much easier with a tiller than with a steering wheel. A tiller allows you to steer and operate the throttle with one hand, leaving the other hand free for fishing. And you can turn more quickly with a tiller, so you can make a faster adjustment when the depth changes.

Ideally, you should have an electric motor in addition to your outboard. With an electric motor matched to your boat, you can maneuver in all but the windiest weather. A bow-mount works better for some techniques, like motoring along a shoreline while casting into the shallows. The transom-mount is a better choice for backtrolling.

Trolling Techniques

To most anglers, trolling means motoring forward slowly while pulling their line behind the boat. By trolling forward, you can go fast enough to troll with crankbaits and other fast-moving lures. When forward trolling, fishermen in the front of the boat must be careful to keep their line from tangling in the propeller.

However, it is difficult to present live bait and some types of lures slow enough by trolling forward, so you should also know how to backtroll.

Backtrolling enables you to move more slowly because outboard motors are geared lower in reverse. Also, the transom becomes the leading end and its flat surface has more water resistance than the bow.

Another big advantage to backtrolling is the ease of following an exact depth contour. And wind has less effect on the transom than on the bow, so you are less likely to be blown off course. When trolling forward, you cannot make depth corrections as quickly.

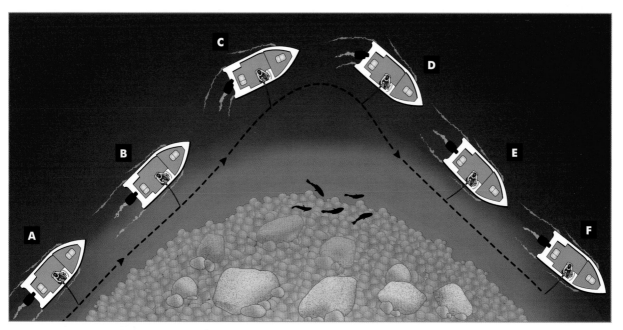

Forward Trolling. A to B. Depth holds at 15 feet (4.5 m). No course adjustment necessary. B to C. Depth reads 17 feet (5.2 m) at C. You turn sharply, but the bow is well past the drop-off. C to D. You continue to turn sharply, but your line passes well outside of the school of smallmouth. D to E. The boat is back on the 15-foot contour, but your line is still over much deeper water. E to F. The line is finally back to the 15-foot contour, but has not passed by the fish.

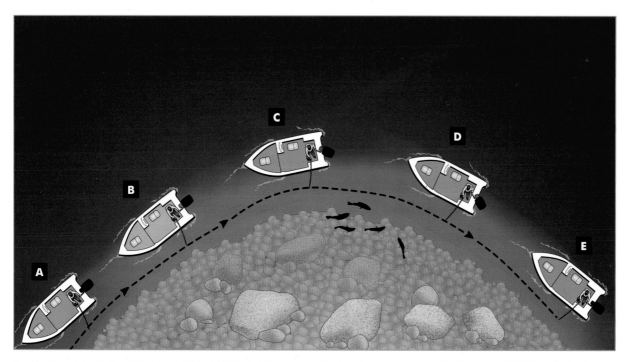

Backtrolling A to B. Depth holds at 15 feet (4.5 m). No course adjustment necessary. B to C. Depth reads 17 feet (5.2 m) at C. Turn the motor sharply to get back to 15-feet contour. C to D. Continue turning sharply so your line will pass through the school of smallmouth on the end of the point. D to E. Straighten the motor and continue following the 15-foot break. Your line will pass by the fish holding on the point.

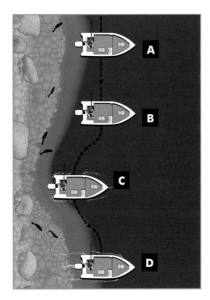

Drifting an irregular breakline.
A to B. Wind moves boat parallel to drop-off. No course adjustment needed. B to C. Boat begins to drift away from drop-off. Motor backward to pull boat back to drop-off. C to D. Boat begins to drift into shallow water. Motor forward to push boat back to drop-off.

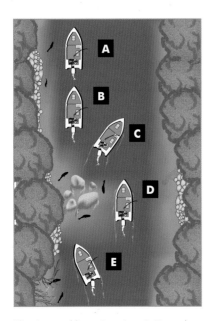

Slipping and hovering. A to B. Keep the motor straight so the boat slips parallel to the shoreline while you cast. B to C. Turn the bow to starboard so you can cast to the upstream side of a rock pile. C to D. To fish the end of the rock pile, continue turning to starboard. Straighten the handle, then accelerate slightly so the boat hovers. D to E. Turn the bow to port to return the boat to position for fishing shoreline cover.

Drifting

The major advantage to drifting is that you do not have to run your motor continuously and risk spooking the fish. If you need to make course adjustments as you drift, an electric trolling motor will do the job.

Drifting is generally not recommended in water less than 10 feet (3 m) deep because smallmouth often spook at the sight of a moving boat or from its shadow, even if the motor is not running.

Drifting works well in still or moving water. In still water, you can drift along a breakline or make a series of parallel drifts to cover a reef. In current, you can drift along while casting to likely cover or jigging vertically.

When the wind exceeds 15 mph (24 kmh), your drift speed will probably be too fast. To solve this problem, attach adrift sock—a parachute type device that is put in the water to control your drift speed. Or use your motor to slow your drift as described in the section on slipping.

Slipping & Hovering

Slipping means running your motor against the wind or current to slow your drift. The boat still moves in the direction of the wind or current, but you can present your bait more slowly and work likely spots more thoroughly than you could by drifting.

Because of the counteracting forces, slipping is a difficult technique to perfect. In a river, the safest method is to point the bow into the current and run the motor in forward; in a lake, some anglers prefer to point the transom into the wind and run the motor in reverse.

By running your motor at the speed that exactly counteracts the wind or current, you can hold the boat nearly motionless while working a likely spot. This technique is called hovering.

The biggest problem in perfecting the slipping technique is learning to steer. The basic concept is to steer as if the boat was moving ahead, even though it is slipping backward.

Anchoring

When you find a school of smallmouth or when you suspect smallmouth are concentrated in a relatively small area, anchor your boat. Anchoring allows you to work the school more thoroughly and to use techniques that would otherwise be difficult, like slip-bobber fishing. And anchoring is often the only practical way to control your boat in strong winds.

When smallmouth are skittish, anchoring is the best boat-control technique. If you repeatedly troll or drift over a school in shallow water, you may catch a fish or two, but you could probably catch a dozen or more by anchoring.

But anchoring is effective only when done properly. For instance, if you pull up on a shallow reef, throw out your anchor with a big splash, and let it clank down on the rocks, you will send smallmouth scurrying to the depths. Instead, quietly lower your anchor in deep water and let the wind position the boat so you can cast to the reef. Carry an anchor heavy enough to insure that it does not slip.

HOW WORK A REEF FROM ONE ANCHOR POSITION

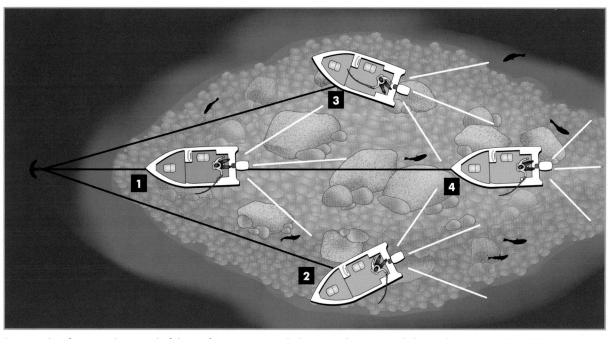

Drop anchor far enough upwind of the reef so you can work the upwind portion with the anchor rope tied to (1) the bow eye. To work one side of the reef, let out some more rope and tie it to a cleat near (2) the starboard bow. The side of the boat acts as a sail, so instead of riding directly downwind of the anchor, the boat swings to port. To work the other side of the reef, tie the rope to a cleat near (3) the port bow; the boat will swing to starboard. To work the downwind side, let out more rope and attach it to (4) the bow eye.

HOW TO PLAY A SMALLMOUTH

The aerial acrobatics of a good-sized smallmouth can humble even the most experienced fisherman. When a smallmouth grabs your bait, then rockets out of the water shaking its head, the hook often comes flying back at you.

Everyone is going to lose some smallmouth. There is no way to avoid it. But there are some things you can do to increase the percentage of smallmouth that you land:

• Avoid using a stiff, fast-action rod, unless you are experienced at playing hard-fighting fish. A rod with slower action bends over more of its length, so it is more forgiving of mistakes in playing the fish. The drawback to a slower action is that you will have more trouble setting the hook.

- Be sure to test your drag before you start fishing. When a smallmouth strikes and starts making a run, there will not be enough time to tinker with your drag.

- Set the hook hard. Some anglers set the hook two or three times to be sure the barb is sunk.

- Keep your line tight. One of the smallmouth's favorite tricks is to take your bait in deep water, then bolt for the surface, leaving you with a pile of slack line. If you see your line coming up, reel rapidly to take up the slack. Otherwise, the fish will probably throw the hook when it jumps.

- Play the smallmouth out before bringing it close to the boat. If you horse the fish in while it is still green, it is more likely to throw the hook or break your line. Fishing the fish at a distance gives you more margin for error because of the increased line stretch.

- Drop your rod tip at the moment the smallmouth jumps, especially when it is close to the boat. By dropping the rod tip, you reduce the line tension enough to prevent a break-off.

TIPS ON LANDING AND RELEASING SMALLMOUTH

Lip-land a smallmouth by grabbing its lower jaw with your thumb inside its mouth. Do not attempt to lip-land a smallmouth that has been hooked on a crankbait or any other lure with more than one treble hook.

Release the smallmouth by gently setting it back in the water, rather than throwing it. If you plan on releasing a fish that has swallowed the bait, clip the line rather than attempting to dislodge the hook.

FISHING WITH ARTIFICIAL LURES

Smallmouth will strike almost any type of artificial lure, as long as it is similar in size to the food they normally eat. One of the most common mistakes in smallmouth fishing is using lures that are too big.

Most smallmouth are taken on lures from 2 to 4 inches (5 to 10 cm) long. Even trophy smallmouth prefer lures in that size range. Larger lures work better only in late fall, when the size of the natural food has increased, or at night.

A 6-inch (15.25 cm) minnow bait is a popular lure for largemouth bass, but is seldom a good choice for smallmouth. Although smallmouth occasionally will take a lure this long, a 4-inch (10 cm) model would be a more consistent producer.

Similarly, the ⅜- to ½-ounce (10.6 to 14 g) spinnerbaits that work so well for largemouth are usually a poor choice for smallmouth. A ⅛-ounce (3.2 g) spinnerbait would be much more effective.

As with most other gamefish, the clarity of the water is an important factor in choosing lure colors. Most smallmouth waters are relatively clear, so a wide selection may not be necessary and most anglers choose natural-colored baits. Bright lures may work well during the spawning period, however, because the bass are aggressive and not easily spooked. And although it seems contradictory, smallmouth are well-known for their penchant for the color chartreuse.

Experienced anglers know that smallmouth are particularly vulnerable to a stop-and-go retrieve. In many cases, smallmouth strike as soon as you stop reeling. This habit was confirmed in a laboratory study on predator–prey relationships. Researchers found that smallmouth usually attacked their prey immediately after it stopped swimming.

During periods of heavy runoff and low water clarity, noisy lures seem to work best. One of the best choices in this situation is a lipless crankbait with a rattle chamber. Another effective lure is an in-line spinner with a larger-than-normal blade for extra vibration.

Fishing with Jigs

If you were limited to only one lure for all of your smallmouth fishing, your best choice would undoubtedly be some type of jig. A jig will catch smallmouth in any type of water at any time of year. And you can work a jig through practically any type of cover and at any depth where smallmouth are likely to be found.

JIGGING BASICS. Jig fishing for smallmouth is much like jig fishing for largemouth or walleyes. Smallmouth generally strike as the jig is sinking, so you must keep a taut line at this critical stage. If you let the line go slack as the jig sinks, you will probably not feel the strike.

Even with a taut line, smallmouth strikes may be difficult to feel. In cold water or whenever a smallmouth is not in the mood to feed, it swims up to a jig and simply closes its mouth on it. You may feel a little extra weight or the line may go slack or move slightly to the side. If you do not set the hook quickly, the smallmouth will spit the jig.

Detecting these subtle strikes is much easier with a sensitive rod. A 5½- to 6½-foot (1.7 to 2 m) fast-action, medium-power graphite spinning rod designed for 6- to 8-pound (2.7 to 3.6 kg) line is a good all-around choice. For casting tiny jigs around shallow cover, many anglers prefer a 5- to 5½-foot (1.5 to 1.7 m) ultralight graphite spinning rod with 4- to 6-pound (1.8 to 2.7 kg) line.

The way you work your jig depends on the time of year and the mood of the smallmouth. During coldwater periods, a gentle twitch or slow lift is usually more effective than a sharp snap. But in warm water, a sharp snap may work better.

Because smallmouth prefer subtle colors, some expert fishermen use unpainted jig heads. The gray color has a natural minnow-like look, especially when the jig is tipped with a smoke-, pumpkinseed-, or green pumpkin-colored grub or tube bait. Other popular jig colors are black, brown, white, and green. Bright or fluorescent colors are used mainly in murky water and around spawning time, although chartreuse is always worth trying.

In most situations, tipping your jig with live bait is not necessary. In fact, tipping may result in fewer smallmouth because they tend to strike short. But tipping will probably improve your success at water temperatures below 55°F (13°C), in low-competition waters, and under cold-front conditions.

Instead of live bait, many experts use a 3-inch (7.6 cm) curly-tail grub for tipping their jigs. They have a true-to-life action and are nearly impossible to tear off the hook.

Versatile smallmouth anglers use several different jig-fishing techniques, including casting, jig-dragging, and vertical jigging. Each technique has its advantages and disadvantages.

CASTING. Casting with a jig is extremely effective in a wide variety of smallmouth fishing situations.

When smallmouth are holding in the shade of rocks, logs, or other objects, cast a jig and let it sink into their hiding spot. Often, a smallmouth will grab the jig before it hits the bottom.

To catch smallmouth in stream pools or eddies, cast a jig into the slack water. It will sink into the fish zone before the current sweeps it away.

When smallmouth are scattered along a breakline, drift or slowly motor along just out from it, cast a jig into the shallows, then retrieve down the drop-off.

To work a specific piece of structure, like a sharp point or small reef, anchor your boat and cast. If you suspect the smallmouth are in shallow water, anchor in deep water, cast into the shallows, and retrieve downhill. You will need a long rope to make the anchor hold. If the fish are deep, anchor in the shallows and retrieve uphill or anchor along the drop-off and retrieve parallel to the break.

For casting into shallow water, use a slow-sinking jig. A slower sink rate can be more attractive to smallmouth and results in fewer snags. Use a $\frac{1}{16}$- or $\frac{1}{8}$-ounce (1.8 or 3.2 g) jig in depths of 10 feet (3 m) or less. Some fishermen use a "shakey" head jig with a buoyant dressing. Others mold their own jig heads using tin instead of lead. Smallmouth like the shine of the tin head and the sink rate is much slower than that of a lead head.

JIG DRIFTING. This technique has not gained widespread popularity, but is one of the best ways to locate smallmouth. It enables you to cover a lot of territory while keeping your jig in the most productive depth range. It has become very popular for catching smallmouth in the Great Lakes or other bodies of water where there are large expanses of open water and the fish relate to subtle breaks.

The technique works best in water of moderate depth, usually from 15- to 35-feet (4.5 to 10.7 m). In shallower water, jig trolling may spook smallmouth; in deeper water, you may have trouble maintaining bottom contact.

Jig drifting requires moving the boat very slowly while precisely following a contour. The best way to control your speed and depth is with your electric motor.

To begin jig drifting, lower your jig to bottom. Let out only enough line so your jig can touch. Repeatedly lift the jig and lower it until you see the line go slack. Being able to see your line go slack after each jigging stroke is the key to successful jig dragging.

If you troll into deeper water, you will lose bottom contact, so the line will not go slack. Let out just enough line to reach the bottom, then continue trolling. If you troll into shallower water, too much line will drag on the bottom. You will not see your line go slack because the jig does not lift off the bottom even though you are lifting your rod. The best solution is to reel in your jig, then start over.

A round-head jig is a good choice for jig drifting because it sinks rapidly, enabling you to feel the bottom easily. Use a $\frac{1}{8}$- to $\frac{1}{4}$-ounce (3.2 to 7

g) jig in depths down to 20 feet (6 m). In deeper water or in windy weather, you may need a ⅜-ounce (9.5 g) jig. Avoid using bulky bucktail or large soft-plastic dressings that reduce the sink rate, making it difficult to maintain bottom contact.

VERTICAL JIGGING. One of the best deep-water techniques, vertical jigging, is especially effective in late fall and winter, when smallmouth commonly retreat to depths of 30 to 50 feet (10 to 15 m) and form tight schools. In summer, vertical jigging works well in waters of low to moderate clarity.

Working a jig in deep water requires hovering over a specific spot while jigging straight up and down. On a calm day, keeping the boat stationary is no problem. But on a windy day, you must point the transom of your boat into the wind, put your motor into reverse, and adjust the throttle to compensate for the wind.

If you are accustomed to jig fishing and have a sensitive touch, you can get by with a jig as light as ¼ ounce (7 g). But most anglers use ⅜- to ½-ounce (10.6 to 5.7 g) jigs for vertical jigging.

Because of line stretch when using monofilament at these extreme depths, detecting strikes may be difficult. Low-stretch co-polymer or flourocarbon line makes it easier to feel a slight tap or nudge.

HOW SMALLMOUTH TAKE A JIG

Strikes often feel like a light tap, a sensation created when a smallmouth inhales the jig in vacuum-like fashion.

If it detects something unnatural, a smallmouth expels the jig within a fraction of a second. Experienced fishermen know they must set the hook instantly at any hint of a strike.

Fishing with Vertical Jigging Lures

When smallmouth are tightly schooled in deep water, a vertical jigging lure is an excellent choice. You can hold your boat directly over the school and vertically jig so the lure is continually in the fish zone. And the constant jigging motion may irritate an uninterested smallmouth into striking.

Any jigging lure will catch smallmouth, but each type has its advantages and disadvantages.

Tailspins work well in water with few obstructions. The spinner blade on the tail turns as the lure is pulled forward and helicopters as it sinks. Helicoptering slows the sink rate, giving the fish extra time to strike. But tailspins are prone to snagging, so they are not a good choice in heavy cover.

The heavy lead body of a tailspin is ideal for long-distance casting. In clear water, for instance, you can cast to distant objects, yet keep your

boat far enough away that you do not spook the fish. Retrieve the tail-spin using a helicopter technique.

Vibrating blades are a good choice in murky water, but they also work well in clear water. The rapid wiggling action produces intense vibrations that smallmouth can easily detect with their lateral line. Most vibrating blades have two or more holes on the back for attaching a round-nosed snap. Placing the snap in the front hole results in a tight wiggle; the rear hole, a looser wobble. Like tailspins, vibrating blades are prone to snagging in heavy cover.

Although vibrating blades are most commonly used for vertical jigging, you can also use them for casting or trolling, much the way you would use a crankbait.

Jigging spoons have an attractive fluttering action when they sink. To a smallmouth, the action probably resembles that of an injured minnow. Jigging spoons are effective in heavy cover, like flooded timber or brush. If you get snagged, twitch the rod tip to make the spoon dance up and down. The long, heavy body often swings downward with enough force to free the hook from the snag.

One disadvantage to spoons is that the heavy body of a spoon can be a problem when playing a smallmouth. If the fish jumps and shakes its head, it can easily throw the spoon. If you keep a tight line, however, the chances it will throw it are greatly reduced.

The principles of fishing with a jigging lure are much the same as with a lead-head jig. Because smallmouth generally strike as the lure is sinking, you must keep enough tension on your line so that the impulse of the strike telegraphs to your rod.

For ¼- to ⅝-ounce (7 to 17.7 g) jigging lures, use 8- to 10-pound (3.6 to 4.5 kg) line. For lures over ⅝ ounce (17.7 g), use 12- to 14-pound (5.4 to 6.3 kg) line. Most anglers prefer a stiff 6- to 7-foot (1.8 to 2.1 m) bait-casting rod. This type of rod works especially well for jigging vertically. You can snap the lure sharply and if you drift into shallower water and develop slack line, the length still gives you enough sweep to set the hook.

These types of lures work best in the mid-summer period when fish are on deep offshore structure or in mid-winter when fish are in their winter staging grounds, often in deeper water. In both situations strikes will often feel like dead-weight on the end of your line rather than a firm hit. Lift up and reel while keeping tension on the line if this happens.

Fishing with Crankbaits, Minnow Baits, & Surface Baits

Even though a smallmouth can throw this style of bait more easily than most other lures, they account for a surprising number of trophy-class smallmouth, including the current world record.

Experienced smallmouth anglers start with small crankbaits and minnow baits, generally 2 to 4 inches (5 to 10 cm) in length. However, some anglers use baits up to 6 inches (15 cm) long when fishing for big smallmouth, but a plug that long may reduce the total number of strikes.

The best type of crankbait to use for smallmouth depends on the season, time of day, water and weather conditions, and mood of the fish. Effective types include standard lipped crankbaits, lipless crankbaits, and particularly minnow baits, which are often referred to as "jerkbaits."

SURFACE BAITS. These plugs work best when smallmouth are in the shallows or suspended and feeding on schooling baitfish. They are most effective during the spawning period and in water temperatures above 60°F (16°C). They typically do not work well in rough water. The best times to catch smallmouth on surface plugs are early morning, around dusk, or after dark.

In general, the best surface plugs for smallmouth are those that create minimal surface disturbance. Smallmouth differ from largemouth in that they will not tolerate as much commotion.

Propbaits are probably the best all-around surface plugs for smallmouth. Use a twitch-and-pause retrieve, moving your plug just enough to make the blades spin. When smallmouth are spooky or not in the mood to feed, long pauses usually draw more strikes than short ones. Some anglers wait as long as a minute between twitches. A steady retrieve seldom works for smallmouth. Make sure your propbait is properly tuned by blowing on the blades. If they do not spin freely, bend them until they do.

Surface stickbaits are more difficult to work than propbaits, but they typically work better over deep water. If the water is clear, they may draw smallmouth from depths as great as 20 feet (6 m). When retrieved with short, sharp jerk in a side-to-side "walk the dog" pattern, the most popular bait by far in this catagory is the Heddon Zara Spook. They come in several sizes and are considered a must in all smallmouth anglers' arsenals.

Chuggers/poppers are used mainly for largemouth, but the smaller versions will catch smallmouth if worked properly. The most common mistake is to twitch the chugger too hard, causing a big splash and spooking the fish. Instead, work it with short, gentle twitches followed by pauses to mimic an injured minnow.

Surface baits should be tied directly to the line, preferably with a loop-knot to allow for maximum action. A snap-swivel or steel leader may weigh down the nose of the plug so it catches too much water when retrieved. A 5½- to 6-foot (1.7 to 1.8 m) medium-power spinning or baitcasting outfit with 6- to 10-pound (2.7 to 4.5 kg) line is adequate for most surface plugs.

CRANKBAITS AND MINNOW BAITS. These baits will catch smallmouth under a much wider variety of conditions than most other lures. They work well in rough water and at water temperatures as low as 45°F (7°C). Crankbaits and minnow baits can be fished with steady retrieves or jerk-and-pause-retrieves at any depth where smallmouth are likely to be found.

Minnow baits come in floating, sinking, and neutrally buoyant models. Floaters tend to work best for smallmouth feeding near the surface. Most floaters have short lips and run at depths less than 5 feet (1.5 m). Long-lipped floaters can run as deep as 12 feet (3.7 m), but they will quickly return toward the surface on any pause.

When smallmouth are in very shallow water, twitch a short-lipped floater so it darts just beneath the surface, then floats back up. Pause occasionally between twitches as you would with a surface plug. A hungry smallmouth finds this erratic retrieve difficult to resist.

In deeper water, try a neutrally buoyant model and retrieve it with periodic jerks to change the direction. This is where the term "jerkbait" gets its name. Vary the length of the pauses and the length of the jerks until you find a rhythm the fish prefer.

Minnow baits are light for their size, so they can be difficult to cast. To make casting easier, use 6- to 8-pound (2.7 to 3.6 kg) line and a spinning rod with a light tip. To avoid dampening the plug's action, attach it with a loop-knot or small, round-nosed snap.

Standard crankbaits come in shallow- and deep-running models. Shallow runners have small, sharply sloping lips and track at 6 feet (1.8 m) or less. Deep runners have lips that are much longer and do not slope as sharply and track as deep as 12 feet (3.7 m). Some extra-deep runners track as deep as 20 feet (6 m).

Crankbaits can be cast a long distance and retrieved rapidly, so they will cover a lot of water. The large lip tends to deflect off obstructions, keeping the hooks from snagging. Because of their snag resistance, crankbaits are ideal for working rocky shorelines and reefs.

In cold water or whenever smallmouth are not in the mood to feed, a slow, stop-and-go retrieve is more effective than a fast, steady retrieve. But in warm water, the reverse is sometimes true.

Whether you are casting over a 5-foot (1.5 m) flat with a shallow-running crankbait or working a 15-foot (4.5 m) reef with a deep runner, try to keep the crankbait's lip banging the bottom and bumping obstructions. The interruption in the action triggers more strikes.

Deep-running crankbaits have a lot of water resistance, so most veteran anglers prefer medium-power baitcasting gear with 8- to 14-pound (3.6 to 6.3 kg) line. For most shallow runners, light- to medium-power spinning gear with 6- to 10-pound (2.7 to 4.5 kg) line is adequate. If your crankbait comes with a split-ring or snap, tie your line directly to it. If not, attach the lure with a small, round-nosed snap or a loop knot.

Minnow baits and crankbaits must be properly tuned for peak performance. If the plug veers to the side, it is out of tune. To make it run straight, bend or turn the attachment eye in the direction opposite of the way the plug is veering.

Lipless crankbaits have a tight wiggle that appeals to smallmouth. They work best when retrieved at medium to high speed. The vibrating action makes them especially effective in murky water.

Most models have beads or shot inside a rattle chamber to create even more vibration and noise. But because lipless crankbaits do not have lips, they may snag more easily than crankbaits.

You can fish lipless crankbaits at practically any depth. To fish in the shallows, begin your retrieve as soon as the plug hits the water. To fish in deeper water, feed enough line to let the plug reach the bottom before beginning your retrieve. To keep your lure the near bottom, pause it occasionally to let it sink. Lipless crankbaits are easy to cast because of their weight. A medium-power baitcasting outfit with 8- to 12-pound (3.6 to 5.4 kg) line works well in most situations.

Fishing with Spinners

Smallmouth are quick to notice any unusual flash or vibration. Spinners produce a good deal of both, explaining why they are so effective. Spinners commonly used for smallmouth fishing include spinnerbaits, in-line spinners, and weight-forward spinners.

SPINNERBAITS. A spinnerbait is a good choice when smallmouth are in heavy cover or feeding on schooling baitfish. Its safety pin design

Spinners are a top choice for catching smallmouth bass because they imitate small baitfish so well.

makes it relatively snagless, it can be fished in shallow or deep water, and is one of the best lures for night fishing.

Smallmouth prefer spinnerbaits smaller than the ones normally used for largemouth. Most smallmouth anglers use ⅛- to ¼-ounce (3.2 to 7 g) models, but some use panfish models weighing as little as ¹⁄₃₂ ounce (0.9 g). Spinnerbaits are usually fished with a soft plastic trailer, such as a twister tail to reduce the sink rate.

To fish a spinnerbait in shallow water, cast well past an obstruction like a boulder or stump, then reel steadily. Keep your rod tip high so the spinner blades bulge the surface. Try to make the lure bump the obstruction. The change in action often triggers a strike.

In deeper water, let the spinnerbait helicopter to bottom, reel a short distance, then let it helicopter to bottom again. Using this technique, you can walk it down a drop-off or keep it at a constant depth.

For night fishing, use a fairly large spinnerbait, from ⅜- to ½-ounce. A Colorado blade sends out more vibrations than other blade styles, making it easier for smallmouth to find the lure. Smallmouth seem more aggressive at night, so the larger size does not discourage strikes. Large spinnerbaits also work well during the spawning period and in late fall, when smallmouth begin their pre-winter feeding spree.

A medium-power spinning outfit with 6- to 10-pound (2.7 to 4.5 kg) line works best for fishing small spinnerbaits. But in most cases a medium to medium-heavy power baitcasting outfit with 12- to 17-pound (5.4 to 7.6 kg) line is better suited to most spinnerbaits or when fishing in heavy cover.

IN-LINE SPINNERS. A favorite of many old-timers, the in-line spinner is not as widely used for smallmouth as it once was. Nevertheless, it is still an excellent smallmouth lure. Its decline in popularity is probably due to the increasing popularity of other smallmouth lures, like jerkbaits.

Standard spinners work best in shallow water, especially for casting to rocks, stumps, and other visible cover. Simply toss the spinner a little past your target, then retrieve steadily, just fast enough to make the blade turn. To make the spinner run a little deeper, attach split-shot to your line about 1 foot (30 cm) ahead of the lure.

A spinner with a blade no larger than size 3 works best. Some anglers attach a piece of nightcrawler or a small minnow to the back of their spinner.

For maximum fun, try an ultra-light spinning rod with 4- to 6-pound (1.8 to 2.7 kg) line. To avoid line twist, attach the spinner with a small ball-bearing swivel.

Fly Fishing for Smallmouth

Anyone who has battled a big smallmouth on a fly rod would be quick to agree that few other types of fishing are as exciting. When a smallmouth smashes a fly and catapults into the air, even an experienced angler has a tough time maintaining his composure.

Not only is fly fishing for smallmouth a lot of fun, it is extremely effective. Flies imitate natural smallmouth foods more closely than most other lures. The most popular smallmouth flies are subsurface types, including streamers, crayfish and leech imitations, nymphs, and surface types, including bugs and dry flies.

STREAMERS. The elongated shape of a streamer usually imitates that of a baitfish. Among the top streamers for smallmouth are jigging flies. They work better than other types of streamers in still water, because the weighted head makes them move with an appealing up-and-down

Whitlock Eelworm

Marabou Streamer

Male Dace

Zonker

action; in addition, they work well in current. Marabou streamers also are effective in still or moving water. They have a long, flowing wing that gives them an attractive breathing action. Hackle-wing and bucktail streamers are most effective in current; they lack sufficient action in still water.

Many streamer patterns are tied in both weighted and unweighted versions. A few have monofilament weedguards. Streamers in sizes 2 to 6 are most popular for smallmouth fishing.

When fishing a streamer in current, quarter your cast upstream, then let the streamer sink and drift naturally until it swings below you. If a curve or belly forms in your line during the drift, use your rod tip to mend the line. Flip the line into the air and straighten it without lifting the fly from the water.

When the fly has swung below you, retrieve it with short jerks to imitate a minnow struggling against the current. Strikes may come at any time during the drift or retrieve.

Cast well upstream of cover like a boulder or log, so the streamer will have time to sink before reaching it. An un-weighted streamer fished on a floating line is the best choice where the current and depth are moderate. Use a weighted streamer or a sink-tip line in deeper or faster water.

In long, still pools or in lakes, cast around likely cover, let the streamer sink, and then retrieve it with foot-long (0.3 m) pulls to imitate a darting baitfish. At times, a steady retrieve or a series of short twitches may work better.

For fishing in still water at depths less than 5 feet, a floating line is usually best. For depths from 5 to 10 feet (1.5 to 3 m), switch to a sink-tip line. For greater depths, you will need a sinking line.

Streamer fishing requires the same basic equipment used for most other types of fly fishing. In streams, most fishermen prefer 6- to 7-weight rods and lines; in lakes, 7- to 8-weight. All lines should be weight-forward tapers. With floating lines, use 7½- to 9-foot (2.3 to 2.7 m) leaders; with sink-tip or sinking lines, 3- to 4-foot (0.9 to 1.2 m) leaders. Leader tippets range from 6- to 12-pound-test (2.7 to 5.4 kg), depending on the size of the fly and the type of cover. For maximum action, attach your fly with a loop knot.

CRAYFISH AND LEECH FLIES. These flies mimic some of the smallmouth's favorite foods. Crayfish flies have realistic claws made of hair or feathers. Leech flies have a long tail made from marabou or a strip of chamois. Marabou leech patterns in dark brown or black also make excellent hellgrammite imitations. Many crayfish and leech flies are

Schley Crayfish

Dave's Softshell Crayfish

Wooly Leech

Lectric Leech

weighted and some have mono weedguards. Sizes 2 to 6 work best for smallmouth.

Drift a crayfish fly in current much as you would a streamer. When the drift is complete, crawl the fly back along the bottom or swim it just above bottom with a series of short pulls. Crayfish flies that sink rapidly can be fished in current with a floating line; those that sink slowly require a sink-tip line.

In lakes, crayfish flies take smallmouth on rocky points, reefs, ledges, and other places where crayfish are found. Make the longest cast you can, let the fly sink to bottom, then retrieve it slowly with short pulls. Choose your line according to depth, as you would in lake fishing with streamers.

Crayfish and leech flies require the same basic fly-fishing equipment used with streamers.

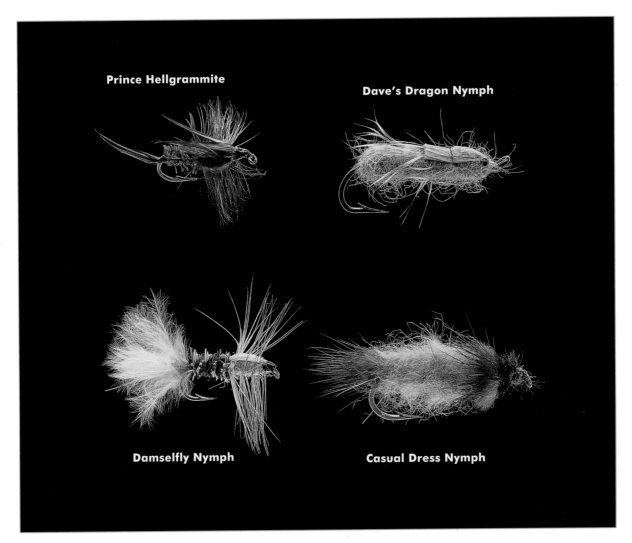

Prince Hellgrammite

Dave's Dragon Nymph

Damselfly Nymph

Casual Dress Nymph

NYMPHS. Big nymphs rank among the top lures for river smallmouth. They also work well in lakes. Nymphs resemble immature forms of aquatic insects, an important part of the smallmouth's diet. They are effective whether or not a hatch is in progress. Nymphs that imitate hellgrammites or the larvae of dragonflies and damselflies are most popular for smallmouth. Sizes 6 to 10 work best.

Different types of aquatic insects move through the water in different ways, so you can use a wide variety of presentations when fishing nymphs. You can let them drift with the current or retrieve them with long, slow pulls or gentle twitches followed by pauses. A weighted nymph sometimes works best if you let the current roll it along bottom, like an immature insect tumbling or crawling over the rocks.

Strikes may be hard to detect when fishing with nymphs. Sometimes a smallmouth swims up and simply closes its mouth on the nymph. Anytime you feel a tick or notice the tip of your line twitch or stop moving, set the hook.

Hard-bodied Popper

Hard-bodied Slider

Mouserat

Dahlberg Diver

BUGS. Sometimes called bass bugs, these floating flies generally work best in early morning and around dusk, when smallmouth are feeding in the shallows. They are most effective in calm water.

Bugs have bodies of hard cork or plastic or of clipped deer or elk hair. Hard-bodied bugs are more durable, but hair bugs feel more like real food. A smallmouth will hold a hair bug slightly longer, giving you an extra instant to set the hook.

Before you fish a hair bug, treat it with a floatant. If it starts to sink, dry it with a powdered dessicant and then reapply the floatant.

Smallmouth prefer bugs in sizes 1 to 6. For fishing in heavy cover, select a bug with a monofilament weedguard. Bugs have a lot of wind resistance, so they require a heavy rod and line, usually 7- to 8-weight. Your rod should be 8 to 9 feet long. Use a bug-taper line, which will lay a bug out faster and easier than an ordinary weight-forward line.

The following types of bugs work best for smallmouth fishing:

POPPERS. The cupped or flattened face produces a popping or gurgling sound. Most poppers imitate frogs, mice, or insects. Many have rubber legs, which give them a remarkably lifelike look.

Most poppers are designed for still water. The face will dig into a current, creating too much disturbance and making it difficult to lift the popper off the water for a new cast.

In most cases, the best retrieve consists of slight twitches that produce only moderate pops or no pops at all. Pause a few seconds between twitches. If you jerk the popper too hard, you will pull it away from the cover too soon, and the loud popping may spook the fish. If a twitch-and-pause retrieve does not produce, try twitching the popper more rapidly with no pauses.

Pencil poppers, which are long and very thin, should be fished with a darting retrieve to imitate an injured minnow. Because of their slender shape, they work as well in current as in still water.

SLIDERS. Designed to imitate a minnow struggling on the surface, these flies have a bullet-shaped body which makes them easier to cast than a popper.

Sliders do not create as much surface disturbance as poppers, so they sometimes work better when smallmouth are spooky. They do not dig like a popper, so you can fish them in current or still water.

You can retrieve sliders with a twitch-and-pause technique or a slow, steady pull. Occasionally, smallmouth prefer them skittering across the surface and kicking up spray.

DIVERS. The head design causes these flies to dive when pulled forward, much like a frog. Most have a long wing made of feathers or a fur strip. Divers work well in either still or moving water.

When retrieved with a short pull followed by a pause, a diver plunges beneath the surface, emitting a stream of air bubbles, then floats back up. If you strip in line rapidly without pausing, a diver will stay underwater. And when fished with gentle twitches and pauses, it reacts much like a slider.

Because of its surface and subsurface action, a diver will often take smallmouth when other types of bass bugs fail.

OTHER BUGS. A wide variety of bugs are shaped like frogs, moths, mice, dragonflies, or other smallmouth foods. Generally, they have less action than other types of bugs. As a result, they cannot attract fish from much distance. They work best when cast precisely to a rise or to shallow cover. These bugs are normally retrieved slowly, with slight twitches followed by long pauses.

DRY FLIES. A dry fly can be identified by its prominent hackle collar, which helps keep it afloat. Although dry flies are not as popular for smallmouth as bugs, they sometimes work very well in rivers, especially when a hatch of large mayflies or stoneflies is in progress. Under these conditions, dry flies in sizes 4 to 6 are the best choices.

The most productive way to work a dry fly for smallmouth is to angle your cast downstream, allow the fly to drift over a likely spot, then skate it there by holding your rod tip high. Smallmouth nearly always prefer the skating action to a dead drift.

Like hair bugs, dry flies should be treated with a floatant before fishing. Paste floatants last longer than liquid types and should be applied sparingly with the fingertips.

For skating a dry fly, use a 9- to 9½-foot (2.7 to 2.9 m) rod matched to a 6-weight floating line, and a 9- to 12-foot (2.7 to 3.7 m) leader with a 7- to 10-pound (3 to 4.5 kg) tippet.

Cast the fly just to the side of a log, brush pile, rock, or other cover likely to hold a smallmouth. Aim the cast parallel to the water or slightly below parallel. If you aim the cast too high, the line and leader will be slack when they settle in the water.

Lower your rod tip close to the water as the last few feet of line shoot to the target and unroll. The rod, line, and leader should point directly at the target, with no slack. This way, you can set the hook instantly should a bass strike when the fly hits the water.

Hold the line against the rod handle with the forefinger of your right hand. Strip in line with your left hand, letting it slip beneath your finger. Between pulls, pinch the line securely against the handle in case a fish should strike. Keep your rod tip low throughout the retrieve.

Set the hook by sharply lifting the rod with a stiff wrist. At the same time, pull the line down with your left hand. Keep the rod nearly parallel to the water; raising the tip high would not increase your hooking power and could tangle the line on the rod if you miss the fish.

Fishing with Soft Plastics

Modern soft-plastic baits appeal to smallmouth because of their natural look and lifelike texture. Soft-plastic worms, tubes, crayfish, and creatures in 3- to 5-inch (7.6 to 12.7 cm) sizes are more effective than the larger soft plastics typically used for largemouth.

You can rig soft plastics Texas-style for fishing in weeds, brush, or other dense cover. Or you can rig them with an exposed hook for fishing on a clean bottom. Your hooking percentage will be higher with the hook exposed.

Soft plastics are normally weighted with a bullet sinker, above a drop-shot weight, or behind a Carolina rig. They can also be fished on a jig head, either with the hook exposed or buried in the plastic. Some jig heads are designed specifically for soft plastics and come with a keeper molded into the head that allows you to rig them weedless.

Hollow-bodied tube baits or "tubes" are very popular for catching smallmouth. Most anglers choose 3- to 4-inch (7.6 to 10 cm) versions in natural colors such as pumpkinseed, green pumpkin, or some type of baitfish color. Internal jig heads that are specifically designed for fishing with tubes are available at any top sporting goods store.

Normally, soft plastics are retrieved with a lift-and-drop jigging action, much as you would retrieve a jig and minnow. Smallmouth often grab the lure as it sinks, so you must keep your line taut to detect a strike. But when smallmouth are not feeding, you may have better success by simply crawling the lure on the bottom or "dead-stick" it by just leaving it on the bottom for up to a minute.

When fishing soft plastics rigged Texas-style, use a medium- to heavy-power baitcasting outfit with 10- to 12-pound (4.5 to 5.4 kg) line. You need a fairly stiff rod to drive the hook through the soft plastic and into the fish's mouth. A medium-power spinning outfit with 6- to 8-pound (2.7 to 3.6 kg) line works better when using soft plastics with exposed hooks.

Big smallmouth love soft plastics!

FISHING WITH LIVE BAIT

Finding good live bait for smallmouth can be difficult. Bait shops may not carry shiners, soft-shelled crayfish, hellgrammites, or other effective baits, so you may have to catch your own. But the effort is well worth it because there are many situations in which these live baits will outfish artificial lures by a wide margin.

When the water temperature is below 50°F (10°C), live bait presented very slowly is often the best choice for smallmouth. With their metabolic rate slowed by the cold water, they are not as likely to chase a fast-moving lure.

Live bait is also the best choice when weather changes, like cold fronts or slow feeding activity. In low-competition waters, smallmouth inspect their food closely before striking, so there is no substitute for real food.

Smallmouth take most types of live bait by inhaling them along with a volume of water. This photograph shows a smallmouth sucking a minnow into its mouth and expelling its excess water through its gills. The slight tap that you often feel once a smallmouth picks up your bait results from this sharp suction.

But there are disadvantages to live-bait fishing. In most cases, strikes are more difficult to detect. A smallmouth does not always attack the bait with a slashing strike; more often, it simply inhales the bait and swims away slowly. Detecting this subtle pick-up requires a good sense of feel that must be developed through experience.

Another disadvantage of live bait is that you cannot cover as much area as you could with an artificial. With a crankbait, for instance, you can fan-cast a good-sized reef in just a few minutes and catch any active smallmouth. Covering the same area with live bait might take an hour or more.

Smallmouth will take a wide variety of live baits, including minnows and other baitfish, crayfish, nightcrawlers, leeches, spring lizards, grass-hoppers, and crickets.

MINNOWS AND OTHER BAITFISH. During most of the year, 2- to 4-inch (5 to 10 cm) minnows work best, but in late fall, some fisher-men use minnows as long as 6 inches (15 cm).

Shiners rank among the top smallmouth baits, but they may be difficult to keep alive, especially in summer. If you bought your shiners from a bait shop where they were held in cold water, you will have to keep them in cold water.

If you catch your own shiners or buy shiners held at lake temperature, you can keep them alive in a well-aerated cooler. About every hour, add some fresh lake water.

Minnows

Common shiners and golden shiners are not as difficult to keep alive as other types of shiners and generally do not require cold water.

Fatheads and sucker minnows are much hardier than shiners and are easy to keep alive in even the hottest weather. However, they are much less effective than shiners.

Redtail chubs and creek chubs are not as hardy as fatheads, but hardier than shiners. Their large size makes them a good choice in late fall.

Other baitfish used for smallmouth include shad, popular mainly in the southern part of the smallmouth's range; madtoms or willow cats are favorites in big rivers; eels, an extremely hardy and effective bait popular along the West Coast; and practically any other type of small fish commonly found in local water.

CRAYFISH. In many waters, crayfish make up the bulk of the smallmouth's diet, so it is not surprising that they are an excellent smallmouth bait, particularly in the summer.

Soft-shelled crayfish, if you can find them, work better than the hard-shelled type. But smallmouth eat plenty of hard-shells, so there is no reason to avoid using them for bait.

Crayfish

Do not use crayfish longer than 3 inches (7.6 cm) unless you are fishing for big smallmouth. An average-sized smallmouth will take a larger one, but you will have trouble getting a good hook-up.

While fishing, keep your crayfish in a flow-through style minnow bucket. For long-term storage, refrigerate them in a container with damp sphagnum moss or layers of wet newspaper.

NIGHTCRAWLERS. Although crawlers are mainly warm-weather bait, they will catch smallmouth well into the fall.

To insure that your crawlers stay lively, keep them in a large Styrofoam container or a cooler. On a hot day, they will die in an hour or less if left in the sun. You can keep crawlers for months if you store them in a refrigerator in a box of worm bedding or moss.

Nightcrawlers work best when allowed to trail from a single hook bait rig. They are less effective when gobbed onto the hook. When using a large crawler, you will increase your hooking percentage if you break it into two pieces.

Night Crawlers

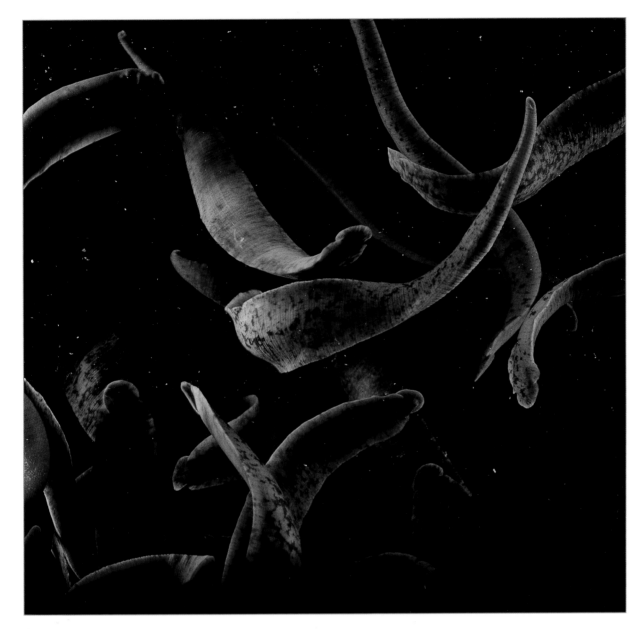

Leeches

LEECHES. In the northern part of the smallmouth's range, the undulating action of a leech makes it one of the most effective live baits. Like crawlers, leeches work best in warm weather. If the water temperature is below 50°F (10°C), they curl into a tight ball.

Only one species, the ribbon leech, is known to be good smallmouth bait. You can buy ribbon leeches in most bait shops throughout the north-central states. Their popularity is slowly spreading, but you may have difficulty finding them in other areas.

Smallmouth prefer leeches measuring 3 to 4 inches (7.6 to 10 cm) when stretched out, but some trophy specialists use jumbo leeches measuring 6 inches (15.25 cm) or more.

SPRING LIZARDS. These slender salamanders are popular smallmouth bait in the Southeast, but they are rarely used in other parts of the country.

Spring lizards are used in the adult form. You can find them under damp, rotting logs or under flat, half-submerged rocks along creek margins. They will stay alive in a container filled with moist leaves or moss. Keep them cool and make sure they can get air. For long-term storage, keep them in a refrigerator at about 45°F (7°C).

WATERDOGS. Many experts rate waterdogs as the tip bait for trophy smallmouth. Waterdogs range in length from 4 to 8 inches (10 to 20 cm), with the 4- to 6-inch (10 to 15 cm) sizes being most effective. Waterdogs are generally too large for average-sized smallmouth.

Lizards

Waterdogs

Waterdogs are the larval stage of the tiger salamander. Be sure you fish with the larval form; if your salamander does not have gills, it has transformed into the adult stage, which is not as effective.

Keep waterdogs in a cooler filled with water no warmer than 50°F (10°C). If you change the water once a week, they will live for months.

FROGS. Veteran river anglers know that frogs are excellent smallmouth bait in fall. When the fall frog migration begins, smallmouth sometimes hug the bank, waiting for an unsuspecting frog to hop in.

Frogs no more than 3 inches (7.6 cm) long work best. With bigger ones, you will have trouble hooking the fish.

One of the best ways to keep frogs is to put them in a wire-mesh box. Cut a 6-inch (15 cm) hole in the top and attach a piece of inner tube with a slit large enough for your hand. This way, you can grab one frog without the rest jumping out.

Keep frogs at a temperature of 70°F (21°C) or less and do not let them dehydrate.

Frogs

Hellgramites

HELLGRAMMITES. In the opinion of many accomplished smallmouth anglers, the hellgrammite, which is the larval stage of the dobsonfly, is the best bait for stream fishing. Dragonfly nymphs and other large aquatic insect larvae also make good smallmouth baits.

Like crayfish, hellgrammites are a natural smallmouth food. Most are no more than 3 inches (7.6 cm) long, so they are much easier for a smallmouth to swallow. They live under rocks in riffle areas. Bait shops rarely stock hellgrammites, but you can catch your own by turning over rocks and holding a fine-mesh net just downstream. Handle them carefully because they have strong pincers that can give you a painful nip.

You can keep a day's supply of hellgrammites in a plastic container filled with damp leaves or moss. To keep them for an extended period, put them in a large container filled with water and some type of aquatic vegetation. Keep the water cool and aerate it with an aquarium pump.

Hellgrammites are one of the toughest baits. They can be cast repeatedly without tearing off the hook and will stay alive indefinitely.

Grasshoppers

Crickets

GRASSHOPPERS AND CRICKETS. These insects are usually considered to be panfish bait, but they also work well for smallmouth. They are most effective for stream fishing, especially on warm summer days when smallmouth feed heavily on floating insects.

A handy container for keeping crickets and grasshoppers is a coffee can with a plastic lid. Punch small holes in the can and lid for air. Most bait shops that sell these baits will carry special containers for keeping them.

For extended storage, add a damp paper towel and some cornmeal and keep the container in a cool place. The insects will stay alive for weeks.

Live-Bait Techniques for Smallmouth

How you present your bait depends mainly on the depth of the water you are fishing. When smallmouth are at depths of 10 feet (3 m) or less, simply tie on a hook and pinch a split-shot or two about 18 inches (46 cm) up the line. In deeper water, a slip-sinker rig is a better choice. You will need more weight to reach bottom, so if your sinker is not rigged to slip, smallmouth may feel too much resistance and drop the bait.

Slip-bobber rigs work well for fishing schools of smallmouth, especially when they are not in the mood to feed. And you can set your depth so the bait rides just above rocks or other snags.

Another technique that is less popular, but very effective, is freelining. This is the most natural of all live-bait presentations because the bait swims freely, with no drag from a sinker. This is a very popular technique for minnows and other baitfish.

With any live-bait technique, the most important consideration is to present the bait to make it look natural. This means using as little weight as possible, small hook, and light, low-visibility line with no heavy leader. Many live-bait specialists use clear 4-pound-test line for practically all of their fishing.

A 6- to 7-foot (1.8 to 2.1 m) medium-power, medium-action spinning rod is a good choice for most types of live-bait fishing. A slower-action rod reduces the odds of snapping the bait off the hook when you cast and is more forgiving should you mistakenly tighten the line when a smallmouth is biting.

Split-Shot Fishing

This technique is ideal for smallmouth because they spend so much of their time in relatively shallow water. A split-shot rig takes only seconds to tie and is easy to use.

The most important consideration in using a split-shot rig is the amount of weight. Too much and the rig will sink quickly and wedge in rocks or other snags. Too little and a lively bait will keep it from sinking. By using just enough shot to barely sink your bait, you can swim the rig along bottom without snagging, yet the bait can move freely and keep its natural look.

Slip-Sinker Fishing

When a smallmouth swims away with the bait, it feels no resistance because the line slides freely through the sinker.

Normally you can use a ¼-ounce (7 g) slip sinker for depths of 20 feet (6 m) or less. But you can also use a heavier one because the sinker slips on the line. The extra weight allows you to keep your line more nearly vertical, so you will feel bites more easily and get fewer snags.

You can fish a slip-sinker rig in shallow water, much like a split-shot rig. But slip-sinker rigs are usually trolled along a breakline. You can cover a lot of water and easily fish as deep as 40 feet (12 m).

Most anglers backtroll when using a slip-sinker rig. Because of the slower speed and better boat control, you can keep your bait in the fish zone more easily than you could forward trolling.

Keep your bail open and hold the line with your finger when slip-sinker fishing. A smallmouth often makes a fast run after it grabs the bait. If your bail is closed, you cannot release your line in time.

When the fish stops running, reel up the slack until you feel some resistance before setting the hook. Smallmouth may swim a long distance and put a lot of slack in the line. If you do not reel up the slack, you will not have enough leverage to set the hook.

Smallmouth often rocket toward the surface after grabbing the bait. With a slip-sinker rig, the sinker stays near the bottom, resulting in a lot of slack. If the fish takes more than 10 feet (3 m) of line and continues to run, quickly reel up the slack and set the hook.

Slip-Bobber Fishing

A slip-bobber rig is a good choice when smallmouth are not in the mood to feed. Even a full-bellied smallmouth will take a nip at stationary bait if it wiggles in front of his nose long enough.

You can adjust your slip-bobber knot to keep your bait dangling just off the bottom, so the rig works well over rocks or other snags. And when smallmouth are tightly schooled, a slip-bobber rig enables you to keep you bait in the fish zone more of the time than you could with any other method.

Adjust your slip-bobber rig so the bait dangles 6 to 12 inches (15.25 to 30.5 cm) off the bottom. Slide the bobber stop up the line the same distance you want the bait to sit below the surface. About 18 inches (46 cm) above the hook, pinch on enough split-shot so the bobber barely floats.

A spinning outfit is best for this technique because it allows you to get the bait out easily with the soft cast needed to keep bait lively. Most anglers choose 6½- to 7½-foot graphite rods with a soft tip that allows them to "feel" the bait in the water. When you feel a fish, sweep the rod backward with a steady pull and begin reeling. The light hook will set itself.

When your bobber goes down, wait a few seconds, tighten your line until you feel weight, then set the hook. If you wait too long, the smallmouth will feel resistance and let go.

Freelining

Freelining allows you to present your bait more naturally than you could with any other technique. Simply tie on a hook and let the bait swim about with no sinker to restrict its movement. A very small split shot can be used if you are having trouble casting.

Lob-cast your bait so it lands over a shallow rock bar or alongside a boulder, log, or some other type of shallow-water cover. Let the bait swim freely, but keep your line just tight enough so you will feel a bite. After a minute or two, twitch the bait or move it a short distance, then let it swim again.

Use a fine-wire hook and 4- to 6-pound (1.8 to 2.7 kg) line for freelining. A thick-shanked hook will weigh down the bait and heavier line will prevent it from swimming naturally.

TIPS FOR FISHING WITH LIVE BAIT

Keep shiners alive in warm weather by adding ice to your minnow bucket to chill the water. Try to keep the water at about the same temperature it was at the bait shop.

Carry your leeches in a specially designed bucket that enables you to change water easily. When you lift the inner bucket, water drains through the holes, but the leeches stay in.

Hold your bait on the hook and keep it from covering the hook gap by threading on tabs made from a rubber band (top) or plastic lid (middle). Or tie rubber bands on the shank (bottom).

Chapter 10

SPECIAL SITUATIONS

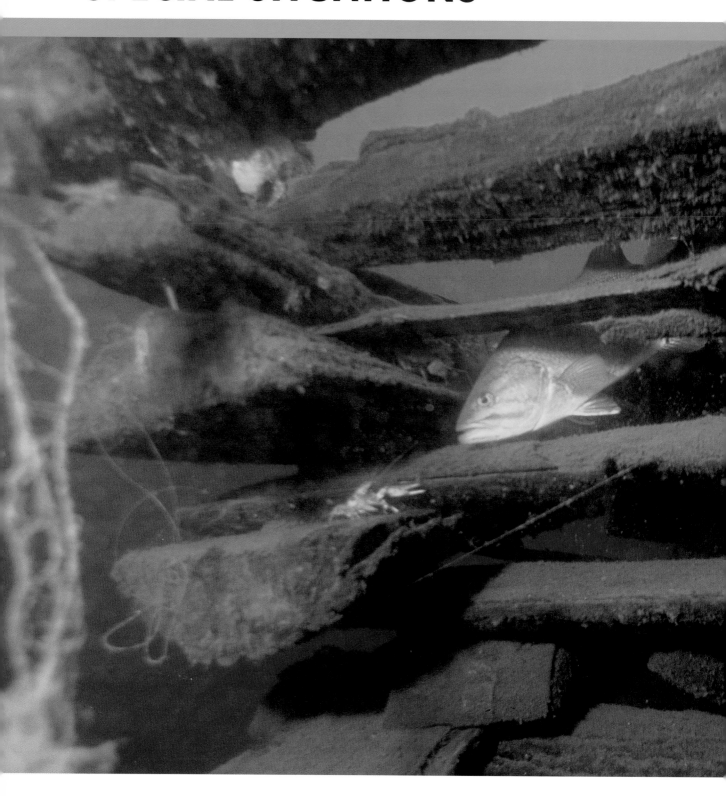

To be a good smallmouth angler you will need to have a good general knowledge of smallmouth bass. These have been covered in the previous chapters in *The Big Book of Bass*.

Unfortunately, knowing the basics is only the start. Throughout the year there will be numerous variables that you must factor in when you head out on a smallmouth fishing trip. They are related not only to the time of the year, but to the specific types of habitat you will encounter on the lake, stream, river, or reservoir you are fishing.

Whether it's spawning, rocks, dirty water, or night fishing, there are techniques you can use to catch more fish and make the best of what is often viewed as a tough situation by most anglers.

In the following pages we will try to take you through many common smallmouth fishing scenarios and help you dissect them, in the hope that you will become a better smallmouth angler.

The ability to adjust to situations while you are on the water and knowing when to do so is the major difference between average and very good anglers.

Many times you must piece together several situations at the same time and try figure out the most likely location of the fish. Trial and error is often a big part of deciphering smallmouth in special situations.

FISHING DURING THE SPAWNING PERIOD

Smallmouth fishing is never easier than during the spawning period. When males are defending their nests, they will attack anything that comes too close, including an angler's lure or bait. On occasion, a wading fisherman has been startled when a smallmouth swam up and bumped his boots.

Catching the females is not so easy. They stay in the vicinity of the nest before spawning, but in deeper water. If the nests are in 2 feet (0.6 m) of water, for instance, the females may be in 8 feet (2.4 m), usually on the first significant drop-off out from the nesting area. Females do not feed much during this period, so they pay little attention to a fisherman's offerings. But if you work this deeper water thoroughly, you may coax a few to bite.

Females are even more difficult to catch once they have finished spawning. You may catch a few starting about two weeks later, but in some water, they refuse to bite for three weeks or longer.

Nest-guarding males will take almost any kind of lure or bait, especially if it appears to pose a threat. As a result, precise casting is a must. A male will attack a lure or bait that passes directly over its nest or a few inches to the side, but will often ignore one a few feet to the side. Although subtle colors work best for smallmouth most of the year, bright or fluorescent colors often work better around spawning time.

Small jigs, from ⅟₁₆- to ⅛-ounce (1.8 or 3.2 g), are effective at depths down to 10 feet (3 m). The breathing action of a marabou jig gives it an especially threatening look. A jig also has a more menacing look if it sinks slowly. You can reduce the sink rate by adding a large soft-plastic tail or by using a tin-head jig instead of a lead head.

Single-blade spinnerbaits, usually ¼-ounce (7 g) models, are a good choice where the nest is surrounded by weeds, logs, or brush. Reel until the lure is over the nest, then stop and let it helicopter. The male will probably grab it before it reaches the bottom. Standard spinners work well over a clean bottom and their smaller size may be more appealing.

Surface lures like propbaits and poppers also work well. Let them rest motionless over the nest for 30 seconds or more before retrieving. You can often coax a strike by jiggling your rod tip so the lure ripples the surface without moving ahead. Floating minnow baits can be fished much the same way or they can be retrieved faster to reach smallmouth at depths down to 5 feet (1.5 m).

Fly fishing can be extremely effective because you can cast with pinpoint accuracy. And you can cover a large area quickly because you do not have to reel in after each cast. In shallow water, a nest-guarding male will usually hit a popper, diver, or other bug fished on a floating line. In deeper water, a jigging fly on a floating line or a streamer on a sink-tip line would work better.

Normally, live bait is not necessary to catch spawning males. But it may catch more females. Any type of live bait will work, but leeches, crawlers, and spring lizards on split-shot rigs are most effective. Smallmouth consider a soft plastic lizard bait a menace to their nests and will often strike it voraciously.

Look for circular spots on bottom that reveal the location of smallmouth nests. They may be dark or light, depending on bottom type. Once you find a nest, chances are others will be at about the same depth.

When planning a trip to catch spawning smallmouth, you should have an idea of when they spawn. If you arrive too early or too late, the males will not be on the nests. To get an idea of when smallmouth spawn in the waters you fish, check the spawning timetable. To find likely spawning areas in your waters, refer to the seasonal location section.

Because of the male smallmouth's almost suicidal behavior, many conservation agencies close their waters to fishing during the spawning period. But many others believe that no significant harm comes from catching spawning smallmouth, so they leave the season open.

In areas where the season remains open, savvy anglers release any smallmouth they catch. If you handle them carefully, males will return to their nests immediately when released. To eliminate the possibility of injuring the fish, file or bend back the barbs on your hooks. Some anglers have caught the same smallmouth two or three times and it's returned to the nest each time.

APPROXIMATE DATE OF SPAWNING PEAKS AT DIFFERENT LATITUDES

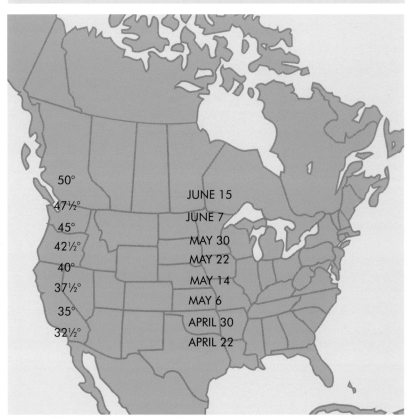

Spawning takes place much earlier in the South than in the North. At a given latitude, smallmouth may spawn several weeks earlier in a warm spring than in a cold one, and a month earlier in a shallow lake than in a deep one.

SMALLMOUTH IN THE WEEDS

Smallmouth often conceal themselves along the fringe of a weedbed as they lie in wait for unsuspecting baitfish.

Although smallmouth are not as weed-oriented as largemouth, weeds can be a key in locating them. Weeds make prime smallmouth habitat in oligotrophic lakes, especially if most of the lake basin is rocky. They are also important in rocky mesotrophic lakes. The rocky habitat holds some smallmouth, but you can generally catch more and bigger ones if you can find a sandy-bottomed hump, point, or bay with sparse weed growth. The weeds support a different type of food chain: fewer insects and crayfish, but more baitfish.

Weeds are not as important in most other types of waters. In lakes where weeds grow virtually everywhere in the shallows, smallmouth will seek the typical clean-bottomed habitat, such as rock piles and gravel patches.

Smallmouth may be found in both emergent and submerged vegetation, usually the types that grow on firm bottoms. Seldom will you find them in cattails or other weeds associated with soft bottoms. Low-growing or scattered weeds normally hold more smallmouth than tall or dense varieties. It may be that tall or dense weeds interfere with a smallmouth's ability to catch its prey.

The best smallmouth weeds are within easy reach of deep water. A band of weeds growing along a drop-off is much more likely to hold smallmouth than a large, weedy flat with no deep water nearby.

When a smallmouth takes your bait and winds itself around a stem, you will need fairly stout tackle and heavier than normal line to pull it free. Medium to medium-heavy power spinning or baitcasting gear with 8- to 14-pound (3.6 to 6.3 kg) abrasion-resistant line is suitable for most types of weeds.

Fishing in Bulrushes

These tough, round-stemmed plants grow on sand or gravel bottoms, usually in water from 2 to 5 feet (0.6 to 1.5 m) deep. They extend 3 to 6 feet (0.9 to 1.8 m) above the surface, so their total height may exceed 10 feet (3 m).

Smallmouth are found in and around bulrush beds mainly during the spawning season. But if the bulrushes border deep water, smallmouth may feed in them through the summer and into early fall.

Bulrushes by themselves do not provide much cover, so the best stands have plenty of rocks or logs. They also have numerous open pockets, indentations along the margins, or boat lanes or other types of channels leading through them. Smallmouth hang around the edges of these openings so they can easily ambush baitfish. The openings also make it possible to present a lure without snagging.

When casting into a bulrush bed, try to keep the wind in your face. That way, the bulrushes will be bending toward you, so your lure will tend to slide off the stems instead of snagging.

Lures for fishing in bulrushes include surface plugs like chuggers and propbaits, Texas-rigged plastics, spinnerbaits, small brushguard jigs, fly-fishing lures like jigging flies and divers, and live bait on split-shot rigs with weedless hooks.

Fishing in Cabbage

Given a choice, smallmouth prefer the broad-leaved varieties of cabbage to the narrow-leaved types. Smallmouth are often found in cabbage beds in 4 to 16 feet (1.2 to 4.9 m) of water.

Smallmouth are most likely to use cabbage beds from late spring though early fall. Later, when the cabbage turns brown, they retreat to deeper water.

The cabbage beds best suited to smallmouth are those where the individual plants are spaced several feet apart. Smallmouth are rarely found in dense beds where the plants grow close enough together to form a canopy.

Cabbage has crisp leaves that shatter easily. A fast-moving lure will usually rip through the leaves without fouling and a slow-moving lure can be freed with a sharp snap of the rod.

Surface techniques are usually not as effective as mid-water or bottom techniques for fishing in cabbage. But in low light periods such as morning and evening a topwater may "call" the fish out of the weeds. You can also catch smallmouth in cabbage on spinnerbaits, lipless crankbaits, Texas-rigged plastics, or a slip-sinker rig with a bullet-style sinker to come through the weeds.

Retrieve a deep-running crankbait over sparse sandgrass. Make sure the lip occasionally digs the bottom. The lure usually rips through cleanly and the bottom disturbance may trigger a strike.

Fishing in Sandgrass

Sandgrass or muskgrass, technically called Chara, is a brittle, narrow-leaved plant that grows in water as deep as 35 feet (10.6 m). It often forms a blanket several inches thick covering a large area.

You can find some smallmouth in sandgrass in summer, but the best time is late fall. Sandgrass grows in deeper water than practically any other aquatic plant and often is the only deep-water cover.

Large sandgrass flats may hold some smallmouth, but these areas are difficult to fish because the smallmouth are scattered. A deep hump or point carpeted with sandgrass would be a better choice.

Fishing in sandgrass is tricky. If you use a jig or live-bait rig, the hook catches on the tiny branchlets. When you pull, one branchlet snaps and the hook stops abruptly as it catches on another. This creates a tugging sensation hard to distinguish from a bite.

Fishing in Other Weeds

Although smallmouth prefer the previously shown weeds, they will use many other weeds when their favorite types are not available.

Savvy smallmouth anglers do not hesitate to try any weeds that offer food and cover. Even weeds not normally associated with smallmouth, such as lily pads, can be productive at times. Be aware of the following species.

TYPES OF WEEDS

Milfoil: The feather-veined leaves grow in whorls around the stem. These plants resemble coontail, but coontail leaves are forked.

Wild Celery: The long leaves have a light-colored center stripe. Small flowers grow at the tops of long, spiraling stems.

SMALLMOUTH IN WOODY COVER

Woody cover makes ideal smallmouth habitat because it harbors small-mouth foods like insects and minnows in addition to providing shade and protection from larger predators. In rivers, woody cover also creates pockets of slack water where smallmouth can get out of the current.

The best woody cover is in areas where smallmouth can fulfill all of their needs without moving too far. Consequently, a fallen tree on a rubble or boulder bottom would attract more smallmouth than a similar tree on a mucky bottom. Crayfish and aquatic insect larvae living on the rubble or boulder bottom make it more appealing.

If the fallen tree is adjacent to deep water, it would be even more ap-pealing. Then smallmouth could easily move to deeper water should the light become too bright or the water temperature too warm.

Smallmouth make use of many kinds of woody cover. Besides fallen trees, possible smallmouth hangouts include standing timber, sub-merged logs, standing or toppled stumps, flooded shoreline brush, beaver lodges, and piles of beaver cuttings.

TREES, LOGS, AND STUMPS. Experts know that certain trees, logs, and stumps hold more smallmouth than others that look practically the same. Part of the difference lies in the bottom composition and the depth of the surrounding water, but there are also differences in the cover itself.

Smallmouth prefer cover that offers overhead protection as well as shade, so a toppled tree with a thick trunk and limbs is more attractive than one with a thinner trunk and limbs, assuming that the habitat is similar.

Standing timber offers some shade, but little overhead cover. It often draws largemouth, but is not as attractive to smallmouth. The lack of overhead cover also explains why a log lying flat on the bottom attracts fewer smallmouth than one that is somehow propped up from the bottom.

FLOODED BRUSH. In spring, when river or reservoir levels rise high enough to cover shoreline vegetation, smallmouth move into flooded brush. They stay in the brush as long as the water continues to rise or remains stable. But as soon as it begins to fall, they move deeper.

Anglers sink brush piles into deep water, but the water where you find naturally flooded brush is usually shallow. Brush will survive seasonal flooding, but once it is flooded permanently it soon rots away. This explains why new reservoirs have an abundance of brushy cover, but old reservoirs have very little, if any.

Seasonally flooded brush is usually too dense for smallmouth to hide between the branches. Instead of attempting to work your bait or lure through the brush, concentrate on any pockets or fish the edges.

BEAVER LODGES. The idea of fishing around beaver lodges never occurs to most smallmouth fishermen. The areas where beavers build their lodges usually look too shallow and marshy for smallmouth. What many anglers do not realize is that beavers excavate deep entrance holes and runs leading into their lodges. The combination of deep water and overhead logs and brush makes excellent smallmouth habitat.

Another reason that smallmouth like beaver lodges: the mud used to cement the logs and brush attracts many types of bait and aquatic insects, so smallmouth enjoy a built-in food supply.

When fishing in woody cover, remember the old adage "no guts, no glory." To catch the biggest smallmouth, you must work the thickest, shadiest part of the cover. This usually means casting into small openings in the branches instead of casting around the edges. There is no way to avoid getting snagged and losing some lures; that's the price you must pay for success.

If you do get snagged, simply break your line and tie on another lure. If you jerk the branches back and forth or move your boat into the cover to retrieve your lure, you will surely spook the smallmouth.

The techniques for fishing in woody cover are similar to those used in weeds. Most anglers cast with snag-resistant artificials like spinnerbaits, brushguard jigs, and Texas-rigged soft plastics. When rigging Texas-style, peg your bullet sinker to keep it from sliding away from your worm or grub.

You can fish live bait in woody cover by freelining or by casting a split-shot or bullet-sinker rig. Use a brushguard hook or a fine-wire hook that will bend enough to pull free if you get snagged.

If there are pockets in the cover, you can flycast with bass bugs or jigging flies, jig vertically with a jigging spoon, twitch a surface plug or minnow plug through the openings, or dangle live bait from a bobber. Other techniques for fishing in woody cover are shown.

Fishing in woody cover demands heavy tackle, like a medium-heavy or heavy power baitcasting outfit with 12- to 20-pound (5.4 to 9 kg) abrasion-resistant line. With heavy tackle, you are better able to free a snagged lure. And you can horse a smallmouth out of the cover before it has a chance to wrap your line around a branch.

Check the location of timber and brush in your favorite smallmouth water at normal water stage or during a drawback.

SMALLMOUTH AROUND MAN-MADE FEATURES

When reservoirs are filled, the rising water covers numerous man-made objects that later become good cover for many types of fish, including smallmouth bass. Man-made objects also attract smallmouth in natural lakes and rivers.

Stone or concrete foundations, particularly those located on hills, are considered the top smallmouth fishing spots in many reservoirs. Small-mouth feed in and around the foundation, then retreat to the deeper water surrounding the hill.

Submerged railroad grades are made to order for smallmouth. The coarse gravel on top of the grade makes a good feeding area and the sharp-sloping sides offer shade. Railroad bridges over roads and water-ways are usually removed before a reservoir is filled and the gaps in the grade make good hiding spots for smallmouth. Riprapped shorelines that offer numerous hiding places for minnow and crayfish often hold smallmouth.

Fish attractors, especially those constructed with brush, draw large numbers of insects and baitfish. So it is no surprise that they also attract smallmouth. Attractors placed along a drop-off or the edge of a creek channel usually hold more smallmouth than those placed on a flat bottom.

In the Great Lakes and other large natural lakes, smallmouth can be found around shipwrecks, collapsed seawalls and jetties, docks, light-houses, and ship channels, especially those blasted from rock.

HOW TO FIND MAN-MADE FEATURES

Study a lake map to find man-made features. Learn to recognize submerged buildings, roads, cemeteries, and old ponds.

Locate fish attractors by looking for signs or specially marked buoys (shown).

In many reservoirs, a cluster or line of brush shelters is marked with a sign on shore. These shelters are shown during a drawdown period and will be submerged once the water rises. Some-times shelters near shore are identified by marks on trees.

SMALLMOUTH IN ROCKS & BOULDERS

Smallmouth spend more of their time around rocks and boulders than any other freshwater gamefish. Fishing in this snaggy cover can be extremely frustrating, but there are many techniques to help you keep the problem of snagging to a minimum.

The best way to avoid snags is to keep your bait or lure riding just above the bottom. Smallmouth hiding among the rocks are accustomed to darting upward to grab food, so there is no need to drag the bottom.

If you attempt to drag your bait or lure along a bottom strewn with rocks, you will always get some snags, even if you use sinkers and hooks that manufacturers claim to be snagless.

Keeping your bait or lure just above the bottom sounds easy, but requires a great deal of concentration. Many anglers are not comfortable unless they can feel the bottom, so they continually drop their rod tip back to test the depth. Before long, the sinker or lure will wedge into the rocks.

To avoid snags, you must resist the urge to continually feel the bottom. Instead, touch the bottom once, then reel up a foot or two and try to maintain that depth. When casting, try to find the retrieve speed that will keep the lure or bait just off the bottom. If you are trolling or drifting, watch your depth finder closely. When the depth changes, adjust your line accordingly. Should you lose your concentration and fail to reel in line when the water gets shallower, you will probably get snagged. Should you fail to let out more line when it gets deeper, your bait or lure will pass too high above the fish.

When casting, use the lightest sinker that will take your bait to the bottom. This way, you can retrieve slowly, yet keep the sinker gliding above the rocks. If you are using artificials, select one intended for the depth at which you are fishing. If you are casting into 5 feet (1.5 m) of water, for instance, you will get fewer snags with a 1/16-ounce (1.8 g) jig than with a 1/4-ounce (7 g) jig.

When trolling in deep water, use a relatively heavy sinker so you can keep your line nearly vertical. This allows you to hold the sinker just off the bottom and the steep line angle reduces the chances of the sinker wedging in the rocks. The same principle applies to artificials. And keeping your line as short as possible makes it easier to feel your lure tick the bottom.

Although nothing is completely snag-free, you can substantially reduce the number of snags by using the right tackle. If you rig your bait on a floating jig head and use a bottom-walking sinker, for instance, you will get only about half as many snags as you would with a standard hook and sinker. And a long-lipped crankbait will deflect off the rocks better than a short-lipped model.

If snagging continues to be a problem, you can always use some type of snag remover or plug knocker. One of the simplest gadgets for freeing a snag is a large clip-on sinker attached to a string, then clip the weight to your line and let it slide down your line to knock the lure free.

When you combine the right tackle with the right technique, snagging will become the exception rather than the rule. And your smallmouth fishing will become more enjoyable and more successful.

RIVER FISHING

Some anglers maintain that river smallmouth fight more than their counterparts in lakes; others say that it just seems that way because of the flowing water. Either way, you are in for some excitement when you hook a river smallmouth.

In many parts of the country, river smallmouth offer an almost untapped fishing opportunity. If an area has a lot of natural lakes or reservoirs, these waters draw the vast majority of fishing pressure.

Smallmouth inhabit a wide variety of flowing waters, ranging in size from small creeks only 10 feet (3 m) wide to the largest rivers. The best smallmouth populations are in medium-sized rivers with recognizable pool and riffle areas. Big, slow-moving rivers with silty channels rarely have good populations of smallmouth bass.

The best time to fish rivers is during periods of low water. Smallmouth will be concentrated in deep holes and easy to find. When the water is high, they could be almost anywhere. Smallmouth bite better when the water is rising or stable than when it is falling. But if a torrential rain causes the water to rise quickly and become muddy, fishing is poor.

Smallmouth in rivers tend to be in shallower water than those in lakes. Most smallmouth rivers have enough current so there is continuous mixing, so smallmouth cannot find cooler water by going deep. Except in late fall and winter, when they move into deep holes, river small-mouth are seldom found at depths exceeding 10 feet (3 m).

River smallmouth avoid strong current, but they will tolerate a moderate current. In rivers that have both smallmouth and walleyes, smallmouth are found in water that moves slightly faster. In many cases they inhabit the same pool, but smallmouth spend more time in the upper portion of the pool, while walleyes are in deeper, slacker water farther downstream. Small-mouth and spotted bass divide up the habitat in much the same way.

With the exception of heavy rains, weather seems to have less effect on smallmouth in rivers than in lakes. They continue to bite despite cold fronts, severe thunderstorms, or extremely hot weather.

The ideal rig for most river fishing is a 14- to 16-foot (4.3 to 4.9 m) jon boat with a 10- to 15-horsepower outboard. A jon boat draws only a few inches of water, so it will float over shallow riffles. Yet the flat-bottomed design gives it good stability.

If the river has deep holes, a flasher comes in handy. But in most river-fishing situations, you can visually identify the prime smallmouth spots.

Many rivers can be fished without a boat and a lot of expensive equip-ment. All you need is a rod and reel, a few lures, and a pair of hip boots or waders.

Fishing Techniques

The secret to catching river smallmouth is learning to read the water. Eddies caused by boulders, logjams, pilings, and other above-water ob-jects that break the current are easy to recognize. And with a little expe-rience, you can also recognize eddies caused by underwater obstructions.

Every river has a few key spots that always hold smallmouth. Once you discover such a spot, you can catch the fish that are there and more will move in to take their place. Some always hold big smallmouth, others only little ones.

High-gradient rivers are not suited to smallmouth because the current is too fast. Smallmouth are seldom found in a river whose gradient, or slope, exceeds 25 feet (7.6 m) per mile.

After fishing a stretch of river once or twice, a river-fishing expert can identify practically all of these prime spots. By concentrating his efforts on these spots and bypassing less productive ones, he can catch as many smallmouth in an hour as the average angler could in a day.

Once you learn to identify these prime locations, the rest is easy. Smallmouth in rivers are generally not as fussy as those in lakes. They are conditioned to grab food as it drifts by, so they do not take much time to make up their mind.

The lead-head jig is probably the most consistent producer of river smallmouth. One of the major advantages of a jig is that it sinks quickly, so it will reach bottom before the current sweeps it away from the spot you are trying to fish.

A ⅛-ounce (3.2 g) jig works well in pools or eddies as deep as 7 feet (2.1 m). In deeper or swifter water, you may need a ¼- to ⅜-ounce (7 to 9.5 g) jig. You can reach the bottom more easily if you angle your casts upstream and retrieve downstream. But if the current is slow enough, it pays to cast downstream and retrieve upstream. Your jig will have better action and you will get fewer snags. However you retrieve the jig, always keep it bouncing bottom.

Standard spinners also work well for river smallmouth. Because they are conditioned to respond so quickly at the sight of food, the flash of a spinner blade immediately draws their attention. But standard spinners are limited mainly to shallow water. Unless the water is very shallow, angle your casts upstream. If you attempt to cast downstream, the water resistance causes the blade to turn too fast and forces the lure to the surface.

Small spinnerbaits are better than standard spinners for casting into snaggy cover like logjams, fallen trees, or brush piles.

Crankbaits and minnow baits allow you to cover a lot of water quickly. You can cast to pools, eddies, and riffles while drifting or wading. Or you can troll a long stretch of uniform cover, like a riprap bank.

Select a crankbait or minnow bait suited to the type of water you are fishing. A short-lipped floating minnow plug is an excellent choice for cranking through the riffle at the upper end of a pool, but a deep-diving crankbait is more effective for fishing the pool itself.

Look for smallmouth around heated discharges from power plants or municipal treatment plants during the winter months. The discharge water may be 70° F or higher, so smallmouth will be active enough to strike fast moving lures such as crank baits and minnow plugs.

The best way to work a pool is to cast into the fast water at the upper end, then crank the plug downstream so it moves faster than the current. Smallmouth are accustomed to lying at the upper end and grabbing food as it drifts into the pool.

Fly fishing is an excellent technique for river smallmouth because you can cast to precise spots, like a small pocket below a boulder. Subsurface flies such as streamers, crayfish and leech flies, and nymphs are the top choices. In summer, when smallmouth feed heavily on floating insects, bass bugs and dry flies also work well.

River anglers also use a variety of live-bait rigs. A slip-sinker rig works best for large baits, like frogs and crayfish, because you can let the fish run and give it ample time to swallow the bait. A split-shot rig is better suited to smaller baits, like leeches and nightcrawlers. Use just enough weight to keep the bait drifting naturally along the bottom. When you feel a bite, simply drip you rod tip back, then set the hook. A slip-bobber rig is a good choice for fishing an eddy. Set the bobber to the right depth, then let the current sweep it around. A slip-bobber rig is ideal for hellgrammites and crayfish, because it keeps them from crawling under the rocks.

Float Trip

One of the most enjoyable and most effective methods of fishing a river is to make a float trip. By floating, you can get away from the crowd and fish parts of the river that receive little fishing pressure.

If the river is deep enough, a float trip can be a one-man operation. You float as far downstream as you wish, then simply motor back up. But if there are a lot of riffles, you may not be able to motor upstream without hitting bottom. In this case, the trip requires a partner with a second vehicle.

The usual strategy is to drive both vehicles to a take-out location a distance downstream of the spot where you will put in. Leave one vehicle, then tow the boat to your put-in spot. When you have floated down to the take-out spot, pull the boat up on shore, then drive back to pick up the other vehicle.

Another option is to leave a bicycle at the downstream end, then pedal it back to your car after you complete the float.

On the average, you can cover about 7 miles (11 km) on a day's float. If you attempt to cover much more, you will probably have to bypass some good spots. After floating a stretch of river once, you will have a much better idea of how far you can go the next time.

Although a jon boat is the best choice for a float trip, many fishermen use canoes or small semi-Vs. On a two-vehicle float, you can get by with

a pair of oars instead of an outboard. But a small outboard comes in handy for motoring upstream to make a second float through a productive area.

If you catch several smallmouth in a certain pool or eddy, you should anchor and work the spot more thoroughly. Or pull your boat up on shore and fish the spot by wading.

Step-by-step, here's how to make a float trip:

1. Launch your boat at the upper end of the stretch you want to fish. Before launching, check the water stage. High water is dangerous; low water makes it difficult to float.

2. Work the edges of the fast water below the dam (photo) with a ⅛- to ¼-ounce (3.2 to 7 g) round-head jig. Cast upstream and bounce the jig along bottom as it drifts with the current.

3. Slip downstream while maneuvering the boat toward cover on either side of the stream. Then cast a shallow-running crankbait into pockets above and below the boulders.

4. Anchor upstream of a deep pool (photo), then cast a bullet-head jig downstream. The jig cuts easily through current, so you can work it in the fast water at the head of the pool.

5. Cast a ⅛- to ¼-ounce (3.2 to 7 g) spinnerbait into pockets between the branches of a fallen tree or logjam. Let the lure sink enough that it bounces off the submerged limbs.

6. Catch frogs along a marshy bank (photo), then drift them on a slip-sinker rig. Smallmouth lie in wait along the bank to grab frogs when they hop into the water.

7. Drift along a deep stretch using a 3-way swivel. Keep your line as nearly vertical as possible. If the sinker snags, you can break it off without losing the entire rig.

8. Retrieve a standard spinner with a size 1 or 2 blade over a shallow, rocky shoal (photo). Angle your casts upstream; if you cast downstream, the blade may turn too fast.

9. Pull your boat up on shore and throw out the anchor. Drive upriver with your partner to get the other vehicle, then return with the trailer so you can load the boat.

LOW-CLARITY WATER

Although smallmouth are generally found in clear water, there are times when you have to fish for them in water where you cannot see your lure more than a few inches below the surface. In eutrophic lakes and big rivers, low clarity is often a permanent situation. In smaller rivers and streams, heavy rains often cloud the water for days or weeks at a time.

When fishing for smallmouth in low-clarity water, keep the following principles in mind:

- Smallmouth are rarely found in water deeper than 10 feet (3 m) and are often at depths of 5 feet (1.5 m) or less.

- Fishing is usually poor before dawn, after sunset, and at night.

- Weather has less effect on smallmouth than it does in clear water, but calm, sunny weather is generally better than cloudy, windy weather.

- Artificial lures usually catch more smallmouth than live bait. Larger-than-normal lures work best.

- Lures that produce sound or vibration are more consistent smallmouth producers than those that do not. Bright or fluorescent colors usually work better than dull colors.

- Smallmouth are not as skittish as they are in clear water; line diameter is not much of a factor.

When planning your fishing strategy, it is important to know whether the low clarity is a permanent or temporary situation. If it is permanent, smallmouth will hold tight to cover, much as they do in clear water. And their senses are tuned to the low clarity, so they can detect minute vibrations that signal the presence of food. As a result, they will strike jigs and other lures that do not produce much sound.

If the low clarity is temporary, smallmouth roam the shallows looking for food. They may not notice a jig, but will be attracted by a sound-producing lure, like a lipless crankbait.

ULTRA-CLEAR WATER

If you fish for smallmouth early in the year, before algae blooms cloud the water, you may be able to see bottom in depths of 15 feet (4.5 m) or more. In deep, cold lakes, the water may stay that clear all year. Streams often become very clear in fall, when runoff is minimal and cooler water reduces algal growth.

Smallmouth behave much differently in ultra-clear water than in moderate- to low-clarity water, so you must adjust your fishing strategy according to the following principles:

- Smallmouth are usually found much deeper than in low-clarity waters. In clear lakes, they normally inhabit depths of 15 to 30 feet (4.5 to 9 m). They feed in the shallows in dim-light periods, but stay in shallow water in midday only if they can find shady cover.

- Fishing is usually best in early morning, around dusk, and at night. In clear southern reservoirs, experts do the majority of their fishing at night, especially during the summer.

- Weather has a major influence on smallmouth behavior. Overcast or windy days are usually best. Smallmouth bite better in periods of stable weather than in periods with frequent storms.

- Smallmouth seldom stray far from cover, so pinpoint casting and precise boat control are a must.

- Artificial lures that resemble real food are best. Dark or natural-colored lures usually outfish bright or fluorescent ones. Sound and vibration are less important than in low-clarity water.

- Smaller-than-normal lures generally work best.

- When fishing is slow, you may have no choice but to switch to live bait.

- Smallmouth are extremely skittish. It pays to hold noise and movement to a minimum and keep your distance from your casting target.

- Use 4- to 6-pound (1.8 to 2.7 kg) clear monofilament. Avoid using heavy leaders or large swivels.

Additional smallmouth that are in the area you are fishing will often follow a hooked-fish up to the boat, looking for food that is lost by the fighting fish. Another angler in the boat can have great success by casting in the area near a fish being landed.

NIGHT FISHING FOR SMALLMOUTH

Night fishing is the best solution to a number of smallmouth fishing problems. In ultra-clear waters, night fishing is productive because smallmouth do much of their feeding after dark, especially in summer. On heavily used lakes, the boat traffic often spooks smallmouth into deep water during the day, so they are forced to feed at night. Many southern smallmouth anglers prefer to fish at night because fishing is better and they can avoid sweltering daytime temperatures.

Night fishing is effective because smallmouth become much more aggressive under cover of darkness. Instead of holding tight to cover, they roam shallow shoals in search of food. And they are much less selective about what they strike, so you can use larger lures. In fact, bigger lures usually draw more strikes because they create more commotion.

When fishing at night, look for shallow shoals adjacent to the deeper areas where you catch smallmouth during the day. If you normally catch smallmouth in 12 feet (3.7 m) of water off the tip of a point, for instance, try fishing on top of the point in about 5 feet (1.5 m) of water after dark. Use the same pattern when fishing on offshore humps, shoreline breaks, or any other likely smallmouth hangouts.

If you can find a lot of points, humps, and other likely structure in a small area, you can cover them quickly and reduce the distance you have to travel. This can be a big advantage, especially when night fishing in unfamiliar waters.

The depth where you find smallmouth will vary from night to night depending on the weather, but seldom will they be deeper than 10 feet (3 m). Often, they feed in only 2 or 3 feet (0.6 to 0.9 m) of water.

Noisy lures are a good choice for night fishing. Lures like crawlers, propbaits, and buzzbaits attract smallmouth by causing a lot of surface disturbance.

Cover your boat light with red cellophane. You can see well enough to change lures and unhook your fish, yet your night vision is not affected.

TROPHY SMALLMOUTH

Anyone who spends much time fishing for trophy smallmouth has heard stories about the big one that got away. All smallmouth have a knack for throwing your hook, pulling your knot loose, or breaking your line, but trophy smallmouth magnify the problem many times. So when you land a big one, there is a great feeling of accomplishment.

In most parts of the country, any smallmouth over 4 pounds (1.8 kg) is considered a trophy. But in mid-South reservoirs, a smallmouth must be 6 or 7 pounds (2.7 to 3.2 kg) to attain trophy status.

Waters that consistently produce big smallmouth have several things in common. Most have a significant area deeper than 50 feet (15 m). The deep structure has flat shelves for feeding and resting. If the structure plunges rapidly into deep water, it is of little value to smallmouth.

Good trophy waters seldom have heavy fishing pressure. Heavily fished waters produce few trophies because anglers catch the smallmouth before they have a chance to reach trophy size.

Most waters that produce a lot of trophy smallmouth do not have large smallmouth populations. Where smallmouth are numerous, there is a lot of competition for food and living space, so they do not grow as large. If you are interested in trophy fishing, be prepared to put in some long days with only a strike or two for your efforts.

Water where baitfish are the main food source is more likely to produce big smallmouth than those where the major food is crayfish or insects. And waters dominated by small baitfish are more likely to grow trophy smallmouth than those where most of the baitfish are large.

In mid-South reservoirs, for instance, threadfin shad make up a large part of the smallmouth's diet. Because threadfins seldom exceed 6 inches (15.25 cm) in length, smallmouth in these waters often grow to trophy size. Farther north, however, most reservoirs are dominated by gizzard shad which grow to 18 inches (46 cm) in length. The total food crop in any body of water is limited and with so much of it consisting of oversized shad, smallmouth have less food that is usable and rarely grow to trophy size.

Your chances of catching a trophy smallmouth are generally better in reservoirs or natural lakes than in rivers. Most small- to medium-sized rivers lack the abundant baitfish crops needed for fast growth. Some big rivers, however, produce a fair number of trophy-caliber smallmouth.

It pays to do some research in advance to maximize your chances of locating good trophy water and being there at the time when the big ones are biting. State and provincial conservation agencies can give you some helpful hints, as can local bait shops and tackle stores. Outdoor magazines and newspapers that serve the area you are interested in can also help. Another source of information is the results of past fishing contests held in the area.

Most trophy hunters agree that big smallmouth bite better in spring, from 2 weeks before spawning until spawning ends; on warm summer nights; and in fall, when the water temperature drops to about 60°F (16°C). Fall fishing remains good until the water cools to about 45°F (7°C). Another good time to catch big smallmouth is in streams in the late summer, when water levels are low and the fish are confined to deep pools.

As smallmouth get older, their personality and behavior patterns undergo dramatic changes. They lose their aggressive nature and become much more selective about what they eat. They hang tighter to cover and do more of their feeding at night. And they spend more of their time in deep water.

To catch big smallmouth with any degree of consistency, you must be aware of these changes and tailor your fishing techniques accordingly.

Although trophy-sized smallmouth are very skittish, the following steps will reduce the chances of spooking them:

- When they are in water less than 15 feet (4.5 m) deep, do not run your outboard over them. Instead, hold your boat within casting distance with an electric motor or drop anchor.

- Avoid dropping anything in the boat.

- Keep a low profile and do not allow your shadow to fall on the spot you are fishing.

- Do not use big hooks or swivels, a heavy leader, or any type of highly visible terminal tackle.

- Use light, clear monofilament. Many trophy anglers prefer 4-pound (1.8 kg) mono and few use mono heavier than 8 pound (3.6 kg), unless they are fishing in heavy cover.

Big smallmouth almost always stay deeper than smaller ones. If you are catching 1- to 2-pound (0.45 to 0.9 kg) smallmouth in 10 feet (3 m) of water, you will probably have to fish 15 to 20 feet (4.5 to 6 m) deep to catch a trophy. But big smallmouth may feed in shallow water on a cloudy, windy day or at night.

In a given body of water, only a small fraction of the smallmouth spots produce trophy smallmouth. Typically, these spots have ample cover, easy access to deep water, and a good food supply nearby. A spot that lacks any of these components will hold only small to average-sized smallmouth.

When you catch a big smallmouth, note the location carefully because the spot may hold more. Even if it does not, there is a good chance it will at a later date. Once a trophy smallmouth is removed, another usually moves in to take its place.

If you know of some of these spots, work one for a few minutes, then move on to the next. If nothing happens, check them again in a few hours. Continue to check them throughout the day; the big smallmouth have to feed sometime. Concentrate only on these spots and resist the urge to try others that hold smaller fish, which are easier to catch.

Although larger-than-normal baits and lures work well for trophy smallmouth at certain times, they are no more effective than smaller ones most of the year. And big baits and lures definitely reduce your chances of catching average-sized smallmouth. Bright or flashy lures catch big smallmouth at spawning time or in murky water, but dark or natural colors usually work better.

Your choice of rod and reel depends on your fishing technique and the type of cover. You may need a stiff baitcasting rod and 14-pound (6.3 kg) line for fishing in dense brush or vertically jigging with a vibrating blade. But a light- to medium-power spinning rod works better in most other situations. Big smallmouth can be extremely line-shy and with a lighter outfit, you can use lighter line.

Inexperienced anglers often make the mistake of using heavy gear regardless of the situation, thinking it is needed to land hefty small-mouth. But if you learn to play the fish properly, you can land any smallmouth on light gear.

Release any big smallmouth you do not intend to mount. Even prime trophy waters contain a surprisingly low number of large fish, so it you keep the big ones for food, you jeopardize your future fishing.

ADVANCED BASS FISHING

Chapter 11

BEYOND THE BASICS FOR BASS: TRIED & TRUE TECHNIQUES

With the interest in tournament fishing for bass exploding, the methods used to catch bass are changing so quickly that it is often hard to keep up.

However, having the knowledge of several time-proven bass fishing techniques that you can employ under different conditions will allow you to catch bass wherever you live. On the pages that follow, this section will take you through numerous advanced methods for catching largemouth and smallmouth bass. Top bass anglers have used these techniques for decades. The key is the fact that these methods are still as effective today as they were when first discovered. Learning these techniques will make you a better bass angler.

We will not only tell you how to fish these techniques, but what the optimum conditions are for the technique and which equipment is best to use. Beyond the Basics is an advanced course on bass fishing that will give you the tools to become a better all-around bass angler.

The key to everything in this book is bringing it to the water. You can read every book ever written on bass fishing and if you do not ever transfer that information and apply it to the lake it will not matter. The techniques featured in this section came from anglers that had thousands of hours on the water perfecting these methods through trial and error.

SIGHT-FISHING SECRETS

Most veteran bass anglers cringe at the thought of fishing a clear lake on a calm, sunny day. The bass are either holding so tight to cover or hugging so tight to the bottom that you can't see them on graph. And even if you do locate some fish, getting them to bite is a real challenge. But one way to make the most of this situation is to sight-fish. This is an overlooked pattern that few anglers tend to think about once the fish are finished spawning. To do this, you are simply going out with the intent of spotting fish and then doing your best to get them to strike.

When & Where to Sight-Fish

Sight-fishing obviously requires clear water. As a rule, don't try to sight-fish where you can't see the bottom.

For maximum visibility, the surface should be calm, the skies clear, and the sun directly overhead. You won't see much on a breezy day because of the ripples and cloud cover makes it harder to see detail. When the sun is at a low angle, much of the light reflects off the surface rather than penetrating the water to illuminate the bottom.

If possible, do your sight-fishing along a protected bank. Even a barely perceptible breeze creates enough surface disturbance to obscure the visibility of fish in water that is exposed to the wind.

You can sight-fish whenever bass are in the shallows, which could be from the pre-spawn period well into the fall. In late fall, however, when the water temperature in the shallows drops to low, most of the bass head for deeper water. In the South, the critical fall water temperature is 55 to 60°F (12.7 to 15.5°C); and in the North, 45 to 50°F (7 to 10°C).

The best time to find bass in the shallows is after a couple of warm, sunny days in early spring. Bass move out of the main lake or reservoir, which is still very cold, into shallow bays, coves, and creek arms, which are a few degrees warmer. And most of the fish are cruising, looking for food and spawning sites, so they're easy to see. Cold fronts drive fish out of the shallows or they bury themselves in thick cover.

In reservoirs with shad populations, bass commonly herd the baitfish into the back ends of coves and creek arms in fall. The clearest creek arms are generally those nearest the dam. Try sight-fishing in these areas if you see circling gulls or other bird activity or lots of shad flipping on the surface.

Sight-fishing is difficult in water deeper than 10 feet (3 m), even if the clarity is adequate. Unless the surface is perfectly calm, which is rarely the case, distortion prevents you from clearly seeing the fish.

Dense bottom cover also reduces sight-fishing possibilities. It's easy to spot fish around rocks or fallen trees or even in brush piles, but not in lush weedbed.

OPTIMAL CONDITIONS

TYPE OF WATER: any clear body of water
SEASON: spring through fall
WATER TEMP: doesn't matter, as long as bass are in the shallows
WEATHER: calm, sunny
WATER STAGE: doesn't matter
WATER DEPTH: depends on clarity
WATER CLARITY: 3 feet (0.9 m) or more
TIME OF DAY: mid-morning to late afternoon

Clear, calm water is best for sight-fishing.

Sight-Fishing Techniques

The major challenge in sight-fishing is to spot the fish before it spots you. Otherwise, your chances of catching it diminish greatly. It will often dart toward deeper water, but even if it doesn't, it will probably refuse your lure.

To minimize the number of fish you spook, stand in the bow and move along with your trolling motor. Wear drab clothing and be sure to avoid reds, yellows, and whites. While blind casting, look as far ahead of the boat as possible. Move fast enough so you can cover a good deal of water, but not so fast that your momentum carries you over the fish. The easier it is to see into the water, the faster you can go. Always wear polarized sunglasses and try to keep the sun at your back; otherwise glare will prevent you from seeing into the water.

When you see a fish, immediately reverse direction with your trolling motor to keep your distance, reel in quickly, and cast to the fish before it sees you. Use a high-speed reel so you don't waste too much time retrieving the lure. Keep a low profile and don't make any sudden movements or unnecessary noises.

Bass in clear water tend to be super-alert and not as aggressive as those in murky water. This explains why many top anglers prefer a tube-bait. It looks natural and you can swim it like a minnow or slow-crawl it like crayfish. A $\frac{1}{16}$-ounce (1.8 g) weight is a good choice most of the time, but when the wind is blowing or you want the bait to stay on the bottom and mimic a crayfish, switch to a $\frac{1}{8}$-ounce (3.2 g) or a small brushguard jig.

If the fish is motionless, cast past it at an angle that will allow you to retrieve the bait 3 to 5 feet (0.9 to 1.5 m) in front of it. If the fish is swimming, lead it accordingly. Veteran anglers use a skip-cast, intended to mimic a skittering baitfish and draw the fish's attention. Skip-casting these light lures is easiest with a spinning outfit, preferably with a long-spool reel and light line, no more than 8-pound-test (3.6 kg).

Sometimes the fish will strike as soon as the bait hits the water or it may grab the bait as it's spiraling down. But the vast majority of strikes come in response to an excruciatingly slow retrieve, accomplished by moving the rod tip no more than an inch (2.5 cm) at a time to crawl the bait along the bottom. If the fish still refuses to hit, give the bait a sharp twitch to mimic a scooting crayfish; this last-ditch maneuver may draw a reflex strike. Should the fish fail to strike a bait retrieved a few feet (m) ahead of it, try reducing the distance to a few inches (cm).

After watching a few fish react to your bait, you'll soon learn to judge whether or not they're catchable. If a fish shows no response to the bait or bolts away, keep moving and try to find new fish. A fish that turns on the bait and tips down to inspect it, however, can probably be caught, so it pays to keep casting as long as it shows interest.

There's no way to avoid spooking some fish as you motor through the shallows. But the fish that move away usually don't go far. Remember exactly where you saw them and come back a little later. Knowing where they are, you may be able to get within casting range without alarming them.

When you see a fish take the bait or feel a strike, reel down until your rod is pointed at the fish, then pull back with a smooth sweep. The light-wire hook penetrates easily, so there is no need for a full-power hook set, which could snap the light line.

Once the fish is hooked, do your best to keep it away from any obstacles. But with such light line, you don't have much control. If it's obvious you won't be able to keep the fish from swimming into a brush pile or around a dock pole, for instance, don't keep fighting it; otherwise it will wrap your line around the cover. Instead, back off on the tension and let it swim. After it stops running, try to ease it back out of the cover. The method is not foolproof, but it gives you the best chance of landing the fish.

Angling for Spawning Bass: A Continuing Controversy

Sight-fishing can be deadly in spring, when bass congregate in the shallows to spawn. Often, the fish are protecting a nest and refuse to leave, even with a boat hovering overhead. If they do leave, they usually return a few minutes later.

Although nest-guarding bass can be extremely finicky, you can generally irritate them into striking by dabbling a tube bait or worm or some type of live bait in the spawning bed. In Florida, more than half of all trophy bass are taken during the spawning period, mainly by bobber-fishing with big golden shiners. Waterdogs, leeches, and crayfish also work well for nest-guarding bass.

Anglers and fisheries managers have long debated the subject of fishing during the spawning period. At present, only five northern states totally prohibit fishing around spawning time. Thirty-five states, mainly in the South, have year-round seasons. The remainder of the states allows year-round fishing but may have special size limits, bag limits, or catch-and-release regulations to control harvest.

Closed seasons appear to be justified in the North, where rapidly warming temperatures in the spring tend to compress the spawning season. Nest-building, spawning, and guarding of fry may all take place in a month or less, meaning all individuals that are going to spawn are doing so at about the same time. Because the fish are tightly concentrated in the shallows, they're extremely vulnerable to angling.

Several northern states have recently changed their regulations to allow catch-and-release fishing at spawning time. Some biologists, however, question whether a bass caught off the nest will return in time to protect it from predators. Studies are presently being conducted to answer this question. Other biologists maintain that it really makes no difference if the fish return to their nests in time, because it only takes a few successful nests to provide an adequate number of fry.

Fishing for bass during the spawning period is an age-old tradition in the South and there seems to be little reason to change. Because the water temperature stays considerably warmer in winter, the spring warm-up is much more gradual and the spawning period is greatly extended. A few fish spawn early and then leave, while others continue to trickle in, some as much as four months later. Consequently, spawning concentrations are lighter than in the North, lessening the need for protection.

DRAGGIN': REFINEMENT OF A TIME-PROVEN METHOD

In East Texas, it's called "draggin'"—most everywhere else, it's Carolina rigging. The technique originated in South Carolina decades ago, but never gained widespread popularity until the early 1990s when several major national tournaments were won using this technique. And with the new soft plastics now available, draggin' is more effective than ever. It may be one of the simplest and surest ways to catch numbers of bass.

TYPE OF WATER: weedy reservoirs that are drawn down in fall and rise in spring
SEASON: spring
WATER TEMPERATURE: low 50s to 70°F (teens to 21°C)
COVER TYPE: clean to sparsely vegetated bottom
WATER STAGE: high
WATER DEPTH: 5 to 15 feet (1.5 to 4.5 m)
WATER CLARITY: at least 1 foot (30 cm)
TIME OF DAY: anytime

A Carolina rig differs from a Texas rig in that the sinker is positioned well up the line, rather than riding on the nose of the bait. This way, the bait sinks much more slowly and has a more enticing action. With a Texas rig, the hook is always buried in the bait; with a Carolina rig, it may or may not be, depending on density of the cover. Texas fishermen have dubbed this technique draggin' because all you do is cast out and drag the bait in with a series of short pulls.

Originally, a Carolina rig consisted of an egg sinker, a barrel swivel, and an ordinary worm hook. Some anglers modify the rig somewhat by substituting a bullet sinker for the egg sinker and a wide-bend hook for the standard worm hook. Most people choose to add a glass bead behind the sinker to prevent it from damaging the knot on the swivel.

The standard rig uses a heavy bullet sinker, about 1 ounce (28 g). This much weight enables long casts, helps you "read" the bottom, and lets you fish practically any water depth. It also gets the bait to the bottom quickly and keeps it there, even on a fairly rapid retrieve or from a moving boat. As a result, you can cover more water in a given time than you could with a lighter Texas rig. The sinker may also attract bass by kicking up silt on the bottom and clicking against the glass bead.

Best Conditions for Draggin'

One great thing about the Carolina rig is that some variation of this technique can be used throughout the year and in a wide variety of waters, but it is most popular in spring, from the pre-spawn through the post-spawn period. Bass can be real fussy around spawning time so they're more likely to grab a slow-sinking bait. Draggin' also has an edge over most other techniques in calm, sunny weather, for the same reason.

Carolina rigs works best on a clean to sparsely vegetated bottom. It is not recommended for use in heavy vegetation or woody cover; the unweighted bait will not penetrate the cover as well as a Texas-rigged plastic or a brushguard jig.

Top anglers contend that the very best situation for draggin' is in a reservoir that is routinely drawn down in fall. The weeds, usually hydrilla, milfoil, or peppergrass, die off on structure exposed by the drawdown and, when the lake refills in spring, many shallow points and bars are weed-free. If you know how far the lake was drawn down, you know where the inside weedline will be. The depth of the weedline is the same all over the lake. You fish the clean-bottomed structure from the weedline on in or the fringe of the weed edge.

In early spring, before spawning begins, look for clean points in the back ends of creek arms. The weedline on these points hold fish throughout the day, but the action is fastest in late afternoon, because of the warming water.

Around spawning time, you'll still find some bass along the weedlines, but most of them have moved into shallower bushes, where they will nest. Work the weedlines in the morning, but move to the bushes on a sunny afternoon, because the warming water draws females into the shallows. When the bass are bedding, a tube jig, a floating minnow bait, or an unweighted lizard usually works better than a Carolina rig.

Once spawning is completed, a few stragglers remain in the spawning areas, but you'll find most bass on points, humps, and flats closer to or in the main lake. Start fishing inside weedlines on these spots in the morning. Later in the day, you'll also find bass in deeper bushes, especially when the water is high.

Because this technique relies mainly on visual attraction, it's most effective where the water is fairly clear. The visibility should be at least 1 foot (0.3 m) and preferably 2 (0.6 m) or more. In murkier water, a noisier bait, such as a spinnerbait, may be a better choice than a Carolina rig.

The Draggin' Technique

There's not a whole lot to fishing a Carolina rig. You don't have to be an accurate caster and there's nothing special about the retrieve. In fact, there are times when you'll catch more fish by setting the rod down in the boat.

You can use practically any kind of soft-plastic bait. A lizard is a good all-around choice during the pre-spawn period. Bass are active then, so a bigger bait with good action draws the most strikes. During and after spawning, a smaller, less conspicuous bait, such as a "Senko" or finesse worm, is a better choice. Normally, the bait is Texas-rigged so it doesn't foul with weeds and debris, but it can be fished with an open hook if the bottom is clean.

Green pumpkin and other natural hues will work for most Carolina rigging situations. In clear water, translucent baits are often the best choice but if the visibility is less than two feet, you can switch to solid-colored baits, usually with a touch of chartreuse on the tail.

The taller the vegetation, the longer the leader you'll need. Bass in the weeds are less active than those along the weedline and they often suspend near the weedtops. Some anglers use a leader up to 7 feet (2.1 m) in length to keep the bait high enough that the bass can see it.

In very clear water, you'll have better success with lighter line and a lighter sinker. Instead of 20-pound (9 kg) line and a 12-pound (5.4 kg) leader, use 12-pound line, an 8-pound (3.6 kg) leader, and a lighter rod

HOW THE INSIDE WEEDLINE FORMS IN A RESERVOIR

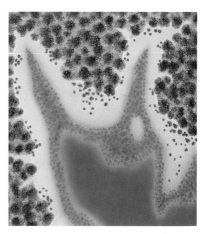

Fall drawdowns expose shallow, weedy structure, causing the vegetation to die. Weeds remain in areas still covered by water. When the water level rises in spring, bare spots remain on the shallow structure and the adjacent deeper areas are heavily vegetated. Weeds develop on the shallow areas as the season progresses. Look for bass where the fall draw-down creates shallow bare spots with deeper weeds nearby. Prime locations include shallow humps, points, and clean Vs in the back ends of coves and creek arms.

EQUIPMENT

ROD: 7-foot (2.1 m) medium-heavy power, fast-action graphite baitcaster
REEL: high-speed baitcaster
LINE: low-stretch 20- to 30-pound (9 to 13.5 kg) line with 12-pound (5.4 kg) mono or fluorocarbon leader
LURES: soft plastics, such as 6-inch (15.25 cm) lizard, 6- to 10-inch (to 25 cm) Ribbontail worm, or 4-inch (10 cm) creature

and reel. Instead of a 1-ounce (28 g) sinker, try a ¼-ounce (7 g). With this lighter gear, the technique is more like split-shotting.

Although draggin' works on any structure with a fairly clean bottom, you'll maximize your odds by pinpointing the inside weedline, positioning your boat just outside of it, and casting perpendicular to it. If you position the boat too far outside the weedline, you'll encounter dense weeds.

Using a 7-foot (2.1 m) long-handled rod, make a two-hand power cast. The long rod gives you extra distance and makes it easier to wield a long leader. Wait until the rig hits bottom, drag it about 4 to 6 inches

Shake your sinker while moving the rig forward as little as possible. The commotion and silt stirred up by the sinker trigger strikes when fishing is tough.

(10 to 15 cm) with your rod tip, pause, then drag it again. How long you pause depends on the mood of the bass. As a rule, the closer to spawning time, the longer the pause.

Sometimes strikes are aggressive, but more often, you'll just notice a bit more or less weight on the rod tip. Super lines will help telegraph these subtle takes. When you feel something different, reel up slack until you feel the rod "load" and set the hook with a sweep-set. A high-speed reel makes it easier to take up the slack and the long rod and low-stretch line give you a stronger hook set. There is no need to horse the fish in open cover. Take your time and let the fish play itself out before you attempt to land it.

DRAGGIN' TIPS

Work the shady side of isolated bushes (shown) between the inside weedline and shore to catch bass that are moving toward their spawning areas.

Custom-color soft-plastic baits by dipping them in a specially formulated dye, such as Dip-n-Glo.

Shake your sinker while moving the rig forward as little as possible. The commotion and silt stirred up by the sinker trigger strikes when fishing is tough.

Check your sinker for evidence of bottom composition. If you find mud in the sinker's hole, for instance, the bottom is probably too soft. Bass prefer a sandy bottom.

DROP-SHOTTING FINICKY LARGEMOUTH

OPTIMAL CONDITIONS

TYPE OF WATER: deep, clear lakes with sparse cover
SEASON: spring, summer, fall
WATER TEMPERATURE: above 55°F (12.8°C)
WEATHER: best under less than ideal conditions, such as sunny skies and cold fronts
WATER STAGE: normal, stable
WATER DEPTH: less than 20 feet (6 m)
WATER CLARITY: moderately clear to very clear
TIME OF DAY: anytime

Writers have dreamt up numerous ways to describe finicky bass. They're in a "negative feeding mode," they've got "lockjaw," they're on a "pressure bite," they've got the "post-spawn blues," etc., etc.

After trying every conceivable method to tempt these fussy biters Western anglers took a hint from their Japanese counterparts who had been quietly using a form of finesse fishing for years. The technique involves small, natural-looking baits, fished very slowly on a light wire hook and with light line. The "drop-shot" quickly caught on and is now widely accepted as a top technique for using finesse baits. And unlike a split-shot rig, the weight is actually below the hook so the bait stays suspended above the weight. Day in and day out, you'll get more bites on lighter line and smaller baits, this is why the drop-shot is so effective.

In areas that have been heavily fished by other anglers, drop-shotting is an excellent "cleanup" technique. Even wary fish that have been bombarded by big baits for days may grab a small soft-plastic bait presented very slowly riding just above the bottom.

When & Where to Try Drop-Shotting

When you're drop-shotting, you need to find specific areas on a piece of structure because drop-shotting is a slow, precise technique that does not cover much water. When you find likely holding area, you must work it thoroughly.

During the pre-spawn period, for instance, bass may congregate on long, slowly tapering points that top out at about 15 feet (4.5 m), with deep water around them. Using a graph, look for a rock pile, large boulder, clump of brush, a finger projecting off to the side, or anything different that might draw bass. The best points often dip a little at the end, then come back up again before dropping into deep water.

A graph can also help you find what some anglers refer to as "the activity zone," the layer of water where most fish and baitfish are spotted. Try to fish structure that is in this same zone.

Clear water is best for this technique; in low-clarity water, the fish may not notice such small baits. Drop-shotting is easiest in water up to 25 feet (7.6 m). With a rig this light, it can be difficult to fish in deeper water and to maintain good "feel." Because of the light line and the separation between the weight and lure, the rig is not well suited for use in brush or other heavy cover.

Drop-shotting is effective any time of day and in all but the coldest months of the year. At water temperatures below 50°F (10°C), the bass go deep and are more easily caught by vertically jigging a spoon. Another good cold-water technique is to fish a small plastic worm on a jig head, shaking it as it sinks and after it reaches bottom. The generic term for this technique is known as fishing a "shaky-head."

The mood of the bass also helps determine whether or not to use the drop-shotting technique. It's a good choice after a cold front, whenever fishing pressure or boating activity is heavy, under sunny skies, at spawning time, or anytime the bass are fussy. It may not be the best choice when the bass are actively feeding. Then they're more likely to strike larger, faster-moving baits, which also improves your odds for big bass.

The drop-shot technique is best in open-water situations. Lakes with an abundance of weeds or woody cover on the bottom cause too many problem with the light line used.

Drop-shotting works best on a rock pile or other "structure on the structure" type spots.

ROD: 6½- to 7-foot (2 to 2.1 m) medium power, high-sensitivity graphite spinning rod
REEL: spinning reel with smooth drag
LINE: 6- to 8-pound (2.7 to 3.6 kg) low-visibility line
BAIT: small plastic creatures, worms, and finesse baits

Drop-Shotting Techniques

What makes drop-shotting so effective under adverse conditions is the bait's lazy action. A Texas-rigged bait sinks rapidly because the weight stays with it. But a bait on a drop-shot rig sinks much more slowly, because the weight is separate. The slow sink rate is the key to tempting finicky bass.

Select the lightest size weight that will still allow you to maintain bottom contact. Special drop shot weights are readily available and a cylindrical weight is the best choice if you are around brushy cover.

Hook selection is also important. An ordinary worm hook is too heavy, so the bait will sink too fast and not sit properly in the water. A fine-wire hook slows the sink rate, giving the fish extra time to examine and grab the bait. And this type of hook penetrates more easily, an important consideration when using light line.

The distance between the hook and shot makes a difference too. Where the cover is sparse, a spread of about 15 inches (38 cm) is ideal. But in weeds or when the fish are suspended the spread must be greater, as much as 36 inches (0.9 m), so the bait stays above the cover, where bass can see it.

The technique is simple, but your presentation must be very precise in terms of location, speed, and depth. Once you find the structure on the structure, make a medium-length cast and feed line until the rig hits the bottom. A longer than normal rod and light line help in casting the lightweight rig. Light line also makes it easier to feel the bottom and detect subtle pickups.

Keeping your rod tip low, inch the bait in slowly along while gently shaking the rod tip, maintaining bottom contact at all times. When it reaches a prime spot, slow down even more to tempt any bass that are there.

Concentrate intently; if you detect any bump or hesitation or the bait just gets heavier, set the hook. With the sharp, fine-wire hook, there is no need for a powerful hook set that could snap the light line. Lift up with steady pressure while reeling.

Drop-shotting may not be the best way to catch big bass, but it's a great tournament technique because it's so consistent. You can catch a limit, then scale up (switch to larger baits) and go back to get some bigger bites.

The Crayfish Option

When fishing is really tough, even "finesse baits" may fail to draw a strike, but bass will seldom refuse a live 2½- to 4-inch (6.4 to 10 cm) crayfish. And crayfish account for more trophy largemouth than artificial lures.

Hook the crayfish through the horn, with a split shot for weight or no weight at all. This way, he can pull it ahead a short distance, let it scoot backwards, then pull it ahead again, making for a very natural presentation.

There are times when bass will eat any crayfish, hardshell or softshell, small or large. But when the fish are super fussy, it's important to select the smaller, softer-shelled crayfish.

You can also make a large crayfish appear smaller and less formidable by removing one or both claws. To remove a claw, squeeze it with your fingers and it will detach from the body neatly. If you rip the claw off, you may kill the crayfish.

Crayfish must be worked very slowly, so the best method is to anchor the boat near a likely spot and cast. Anchor from both the bow and stern so the boat can't move. Lob the crayfish out so it doesn't tear off the hook, then feed line until it reaches the bottom.

The retrieve is excruciatingly slow, sometimes taking as long as 5 minutes. When you feel a pickup, reel up the slack until you feel slight tension, then set the hook. A bass usually inhales the crayfish, so if you wait too long to set, you may hook the fish so deeply it won't survive.

Hook a crayfish through the bony horn with a small short-shank hook, size 4 or 6.

SOFT STICKBAITS: A HOT TECHNIQUE FOR STUBBORN BASS

At first glance, a soft stickbait is not much to get excited about; it has no legs, tentacles, or curly tail to give it action, so its appearance is certainly not lifelike.

But many would argue that this bait was one of the most significant bass-fishing innovations in many years when it began to show up in the early 1990s. Its near-neutral buoyancy and enticing dying-baitfish action works magic on big bass, even when they have the post-spawn blues.

One major drawback to these baits is the difficulty of fishing them in windy weather. They can be a problem to cast and when the wind catches your line, it pulls the bait through the water too fast. Because these baits must be fished so slow most of the time, they're not a good choice for covering lots of water.

The original soft stickbait, the Slug-Go, was introduced in 1990 and within a few years, its popularity swept the country. Then the Yamamoto Senko took over in popularity and became the standard choice. Today, fishermen can choose from dozens of different brands of soft-stickbaits.

When & Where to Try Soft-Stickin'

Soft-stickin' excels once bass move onto the spawning grounds. They're much less aggressive than they were in the pre-spawn period and they stay that way until late in the post-spawn. The bait's slow sink rate is a plus this time of year because the fish are in shallow water, usually less than 10 feet (3 m). Once they move deeper, soft-stickin' becomes less effective.

Concentrate on shallow creek arms and bays where bass are known to spawn. The best ones tend to be long and narrow, so the spawning beds are protected from the wind. They have only small creeks feeding them, so they stay fairly clear.

A soft stickbait produces practically no sound or vibration, so the water must be clear enough for bass to see it. As a rule, use soft stickbaits only when the visibility is a foot (30.5 cm) or more.

It works best under low-light conditions; early or late in the day or under cloudy skies. Under high sun, bass stick tight to the cover, where they're less aggressive and more difficult to reach with a soft stickbait, which won't penetrate the cover as well as a jig or Texas-rigged worm.

Work any visible spawning beds in shallow, sandy areas to catch nest-guarding males; work the areas between the beds for cruising bass. Your chances of catching the larger females are better around woody cover just outside the bedding area; females stage there before and after spawning.

The Soft-Stickin' Technique

The secret to catching bass on a soft stickbait is to keep your presentation slow. Just cast the bait, let it settle to the bottom, and retrieve it with short twitch followed by a pause, varying the pause length until you find the right cadence.

The bait is generally rigged with a long-shank offset hook, which keeps the center of gravity toward the middle of the bait and ensures that it sinks in a horizontal position. With a shorter-shank hook, the bait would nosedive and sink much faster. Heavier line, 15- to 20-pound (6.75 to 9 kg) line, helps slow the sink rate.

When rigged properly, the bait should have a slight upward bend at the head. This way, the bait will plane upward when you twitch it, then it glides back down.

Bass will usually grab the bait on the pause, as it settles. You may feel a tap, see the line jump, move off to the side, or just feel extra resistance. Then quickly reel up your slack and set the hook with a hard wrist snap. A beefy rod is a must to drive the big hook into the jaw and to horse a fish from the cover once it's hooked.

EQUIPMENT

ROD: 6½- to 7-foot (2 to 2.1 m) fast-action, medium-heavy to heavy power graphite baitcaster
REEL: narrow-spool high-speed baitcaster
LINE: 15- to 20-pound (6.75 to 9 kg) clear, low-stretch line
LURES: 6-inch (15.25 cm) soft stickbait (Senko)

The Budweiser Sharelunker Program

The chances of catching a 10-pound (4.5 kg) Texas largemouth have skyrocketed in recent years, thanks in part to the "Operation Share a Lone-Star Lunker Program," or "LSL," that started in 1996.

This co-op venture among the Texas Parks and Wildlife Department, various corporate sponsors, and anglers provides the TPWD with wild brood stock bass used to improve their propagation program. The program has changed names and is currently called the "Budweiser Share-lunker Program," or "BSP."

Anglers who turn in a bass weighing 13 pounds (5.8 kg) or more to TPWD are given a fiberglass replica of their fish, courtesy of the corporate sponsors. Taking eggs from large wild bass not only selects for large size, it increases genetic variability.

If only captive brood-stock are used, inbreeding can be a serious problem. Using wild brood stock also increases the chances that the offspring will spawn in the wild. And the fact that the parent was caught on hook and line increases the likelihood that the offspring will be catchable.

To date, more than 400 lunkers have been turned in by anglers, including a former state-record 17.65-pounder (7.9 kg) and the present state record, an 18.18-pounder (8 kg). Although a relatively small percentage of these fish have spawned in captivity, TPWD officials are confident that new facilities and techniques will improve spawning success. A new hatchery recently opened to care for these lunkers and to better duplicate natural conditions by precisely controlling water temperature and photoperiod.

Once TPWD is finished with the fish, they are returned alive to the anglers who caught them. Most are then released back into the waters from which they came. Several of the fish have been caught again and one fish was entered in the program a second time.

Not only has the BSP program created a positive relationship between anglers and fisheries managers, it has boosted public awareness of the importance of catch and release of largemouth bass. The program has also taught many fishermen how to properly handle big bass; tournament and recreational anglers are successfully releasing more bass than ever before.

PUNCHING THE MATS FOR BASS IN DENSE VEGETATION

Heavy weed growth or the very mention of it causes panic among boaters and lakeshore property owners. Aquatic plants can infest natural and man-made lakes, growing to depths of 20 feet (6 m) or more and sometimes forming a dense canopy at the surface or several feet below it. The matted plants interfere with boating and crowd out other aquatic plants.

For bass and bass fishermen, however, not all the news about heavy weed growth is bad. A thick canopy provides shade, security, and cooler temperatures for largemouth. In many lakes there's a big increase in the number and size of the bass since weeds have flourished. Many other natural and man-made lakes around the country also underwent a bass boom soon after weeds were established.

Two exotic species, milfoil and hydrilla, are the main species of plants that infest lakes in the U.S. and they can be fished with many of the same techniques. With so much of it in some lakes, most fishermen don't know where to find the bass. And even if they can find them, they often have trouble getting a lure to them.

When one of these species first invades a body of water, the bass may not be in the traditional spots they were prior to infestation and old techniques may no longer be as effective. But by understanding the locational patterns and using the angling techniques that follow, you'll catch more bass than ever.

These techniques will work on any weed-ridden natural lake or reservoir with moderate to clear water.

Understanding Dense Weed Growth

Most dense weed grows rapidly in spring, beginning when the water temperature reaches the upper 50s (14 to 15°C). There may be a second growth spurt in late summer. When the shoots reach the surface, they branch profusely and flower, forming heavy mats in the shallows. Even before the mats form, the dense growth prevents the lower leaves from getting enough sunlight, so they begin to drop off. By midsummer, the mats remain with surprisingly little vegetation below.

In deep lakes, the canopy may be several feet beneath the surface and dense surface mats form only near shore. The tendency of the plant to mat in shallow water means that the densest growth takes place in low-water years.

OPTIMAL CONDITIONS

TYPE OF WATER: any lake with heavy weed beds
SEASON: post-spawn through early fall
WATER TEMPERATURE: upper 60s (19°C) or higher
WEATHER: calm, sunny
WATER STAGE: normal, stable
WATER DEPTH: 15 feet (4.5 m) or less
WATER CLARITY: 2 feet (30 cm) or more
TIME OF DAY: late morning to early evening

Midsummer milfoil canopy provides ideal cover for largemouth bass.

Once these species gain a foothold in a lake, it soon overwhelms other native aquatic plants, sometimes crowding them out completely. They generally maintain their dominance for 5 to 10 years, then gradually decline in density.

Attempts to eradicate or control the spread of these species have been only minimally successful. Chemical treatments have never shown long-term results, although growth can be controlled with regular applications. Methods such as harvesting, dredging, and derooting may actually promote weed growth.

When & Where to Find Dense Vegetation Bass

Bass use dense weed throughout the year. They often spawn along the inside edges of shallow beds at depths of 1 to 4 feet (0.3 to 1.2 m), either in sheltered bays or along protected shorelines. After spawning, when the males have abandoned the fry, you'll find bass on flats adjacent to spawning areas. Look for dense clumps of weed that grow nearly to the surface, usually in water from 8 to 12 feet (2.4 to 3.7 m) deep.

If you're fishing a flat with a blanket of weed 4 feet (1.2 m) beneath the surface and you come across a small area with weeds 1 to 2 feet (30 to 60 cm) under the surface, that's a good place to find fish in the post-spawn period. Often these clumps are found on a slight rise, but they may also grow where the bottom is perfectly flat. On a calm, sunny day, the clumps are easy to spot. Those with schools of baitfish in or around them are the most likely to hold bass.

The depth at which you find post-spawn bass depends on their activity level. As a rule, the more active they are, the higher they'll be in the weed. Feeding bass cruise just beneath the canopy or even on top of it; bass in a neutral or negative mood stay near the bottom and move very little.

As summer progresses, largemouth move closer to the break at the outer edge of a weed bed, usually holding in 10 to 15 feet (3 to 4.5 m) of water. There, the sharp drop-off gives them easy access to deeper water. Bare spots on points or inside turns, or anywhere along the weedline, are the hub of summertime bass activity. These bare spots, most of which are less than 20 feet (6 m) in diameter, are simply hard-bottomed areas where plants can't take root.

When bass are most active, usually during low-light conditions, they move about and feed right on the bare spots. When they're less active, as is often the case on sunny days, they tuck into thick weed clumps near the bare spots and move about much less.

Bass using these bare spots in summer provide the year's best and most consistent fishing. A school of bass may hold on the same spot for weeks at a time. They remain in these locations until the plants begin to turn brown in late summer or early fall. Then the consistency of this pattern breaks down; the fish begin to move about more and spend more of their time feeding in shallower water.

By fall, most of the bass have abandoned the deep bare spots. You'll find them relating to shallower bare spots or areas of sparse weed growth, usually from 5 to 8 feet (1.5 to 2.5 m) deep but sometimes as shallow as 3 (0.9 m). Check bare spots within weed beds or along their sandy inside edges. Don't overlook such weed-free areas as boat channels or rock piles within a weed bed.

ROD: 6½- to 7½- foot (2 to 2.3 m) long-handled, medium-heavy power, fast-action, graphite baitcaster
REEL: baitcasting reel with gear ratio of at least 6:1
LINE: 20-pound-test (9 kg) or heavier co-polymer line or 40-pound-plus (18 kg) braid
LURE: ⅝- to 1-ounce (17.7 to 28 g) weedless bullet-head jig with a soft plastic trailer or Texas-rigged soft plastic

How to Punch the Dense Mats

Many novice anglers detest fishing in heavy weed because it's nearly impossible to pull a lure through it without fouling. And if you do hook a fish when casting, it will almost surely tangle in the weeds and escape.

Top anglers have developed a unique technique that solves the problem. Called punching the mats, it involves jigging vertically in the dense mats and using a stiff rod, heavy line, and high-speed reel to horse the fish to the surface before it can tangle.

The best jigs for punching have a bullet-shaped head with the attachment eye at the tip to minimize fouling and a large, strong hook that will improve your hooking percentage but won't bend when you hoist in the fish. Use the lightest jig practical for the conditions and a bulky trailer that will slow the sink rate. Dark colors or those that match common foods, such as crayfish, shad, or bluegills work best.

If jigs aren't working, try Texas-rigged soft plastics with a bullet-shaped tungsten weight and fish them the same way.

To locate bass in a weedbed, start at the downwind edge of the cover and move slowly into the wind. Then flip the jig into any opening in the milfoil (these can be from a few inches to a few feet [cm to m] in diameter). To keep your line as vertical as possible while you're moving forward, flip into openings slightly ahead of the boat. Always fish close to the boat, little more than a rod length away. This way, you can easily feed line and jiggle your rod tip to make the jig sink through the weedy tangle. It also allows you to horse a hooked fish straight up, so it won't wrap in the weeds.

When the bait hits the bottom, experiment with different jigging tempos until you find the pattern that works best. The more active the bass, the faster the tempo. When the bass are fussy, try "dead-sticking" them, letting the bait lie motionless for several seconds between each lift. Keep flippin' into different openings as you work into the wind.

With two anglers in the boat, both should stand on the front deck and work water ahead of the boat. If one stands in the back, he will be working water that the boat has already passed over.

Active bass usually inhale the jig on the drop, so you'll feel a tap or notice the bait stop sinking. But when the bass are finicky, they'll just pick the jig off the bottom and all you'll feel is a little extra weight.

Set the hook hard and crank the fish out of the cover as quickly as possible. If you give the fish a chance to swim around the weeds, it may escape by tangling your line or spook other fish in the school by tearing up the weeds. If you don't hook the fish, flip the jig into the same spot and try to coax another strike.

Sometimes you have to catch one bass to trigger others in a school to start feeding. It's not unusual to see a school follow a hooked bass to the surface during a wild frenzy.

If this happens, drop your jig back into the same hole, let it fall to bottom, then bring it up and work it just beneath the canopy where the active bass are most likely to be. You may want to switch to a lighter weight, about ½-ounce (14 g), that will sink through the upper zone more slowly.

Use your electric motor to slowly move along the weedbed and drop the jig into openings of the milfoil.

Once activated, some bass in the school may even begin feeding above the canopy. In this case, you may have better success by fan-casting the area with a spinnerbait, lipless crankbait, minnow bait, or topwater. Baits with internal rattles work best; bass can home in on them more easily, so you get more strikes and better hookups.

You'll catch more bass if you're careful not to spook the school. Put the fish you catch in your live well until you're done fishing a spot. A fish you release back to the same spot or one that breaks your line may alarm the school and they'll quit biting. Working into the wind also reduces spooking; when you hook a fish, the boat will blow away from the school, not over it.

When you find a school of bass, note the precise location, toss out a marker, and keep working it until the action stops. Then you may want to switch to a jig of a different size or color or to a Texas-rigged plastic. The change may trigger a few more fish to bite.

Be sure to mark any good spots in your GPS, then come back and try the spot again later; there may be a few rocks, taller weed, a deeper slot, or some other structural element that will draw bass back to the same spot over and over.

High winds make it difficult to jig openings in the submerged weeds. Not only will you have trouble seeing them, it's difficult to keep your boat in the right position. The wind also buffets your rod tip and deadens your feel, making it necessary to use a jig weighing at least 1 ounce (28 g).

In dead-calm conditions it may be necessary to try to keep quiet in the boat. Many anglers turn off their electronics to avoid spooking a school of bass. Also, when you catch a second fish in the same general area, you should throw out a marker bouy to give you a reference point as to where you are.

Other Dense Vegetation Techniques

After a few warm days in spring, when pre-spawn bass are holding in shallow water along the inner edges of milfoil beds, they'll hit practically anything you throw at them. It pays to use lures that cover a lot of water. Buzzbaits and spinnerbaits are ideal for working pockets in the weed and paralleling the edge. When the bass are not as aggressive, try a slower presentation, such as twitching a soft stickbait.

In summer and early fall, bass cruise the outer edges of weed beds when they're active and they tuck back into the weeds when they're not. When they're along the edges, you can catch them on a variety of baits, including medium- to deep-running crank-baits, ribbontail worms on shakey-head jigs, deep-running spinnerbaits, and the same bullet-head jigs discussed earlier. It's sometimes possible to use baits with open hooks, because the growth along the edges is sparse enough that fouling is not a big problem. Try to hold your boat right over the drop-off and cast parallel to the break.

Another good summertime pattern is fishing surface clumps of matted weed. Work edges and holes in the clumps with buzzbaits and spinner-baits, the clumps themselves with weedless spoons and hollow-bodied rats and frogs.

When bass move onto shallow weed flats in midfall, try slow-rolling a tandem-blade spinnerbait so it just bumps the weedtops, letting it helicopter into openings and slots. Or slowly retrieve a high-buoyancy, shallow- to medium-running crankbait over openings and along shallow edges of the flats. A buoyant lure is more likely to float off of the weeds should it foul. If you feel resistance, set the hook. A strike doesn't feel much different than hooking a weed stem. This technique produces fewer but bigger bass than you'd normally catch in summer.

Work matted milfoil with a surface lure, such as a weedless spoon, on a warm day.

FOOTBALL HEAD JIGS: MAGIC FOR BIG BASS

When pre-spawn largemouth congregate along steep ledges before and after moving into their spawning areas, they can be tough to catch. They're still in deep water and not very aggressive and the sharp-breaking structure makes fishing a real challenge.

This is a time to implement a little-known jig into action: the football head. Taking its name from the shape of the head, these heads began their popularity on rocky Western reservoirs where their unique shape allowed them to crawl through rocks better than any other jig style. Contrary to what you may think, the heavier versions often times hang up less than the lighter versions.

Unlike the methods commonly used by tournament anglers, this technique actually excels when the fish are holding on steep structure, particularly during the pre-spawn and mid-summer period. But the technique also works well when bass move to deep structure in late fall. The heavy jig with its unusual football-shaped head clinks against rocks and darts rapidly as it bounces down a steep bank and when used with a bulky, wriggling "spider-jig" body, it moves a lot of water.

The heavy football jig head enables you to stay in contact with the bottom, a near impossibility on steep structure if you use a lighter jig head or one with the attachment eye near the nose. The quick-sinking action is opposite to that recommended by most pros, but is similar to the darting movements of crayfish, which abound on the steep, rocky

OPTIMAL CONDITIONS

TYPE OF WATER: deep, clear, rocky bodies of water with deep offshore structure
SEASON: pre-spawn to late fall
WATER TEMPERATURE: 50 to 60°F (10 to 15.5°C)
WEATHER: windy, rainy is best
WATER STAGE: any stage; stable is best
WATER DEPTH: 10 to 35 feet (3 to 10.7 m)
WATER CLARITY: moderately clear to very clear
TIME OF DAY: early morning, late afternoon best

structure. The wild action often triggers "reflex" strikes from bass that are attempting to pick off crayfish before they zip under a rock.

The football head has some other advantages. Its shape keeps the jig head and hook riding upright and when the jig is worked slowly over a gravelly bottom, the head pivots each time it bumps into a pebble, making the body move up and down and creating an enticing action.

Although the technique evolved on western reservoirs, it will work wherever the bass are holding in deep, clear water and feeding on crayfish. Several big tournament wins in 2006 and 2007 vaulted this bait into the national limelight.

Where & When to Find Bass in Deep Reservoirs

The key to finding pre-spawn bass is knowing where to find their spawning areas and concentrating on adjacent deep water. In reservoirs of this type, largemouth spawn in the back ends of coves. Before they spawn, you'll find them along steep bluffs leading into the back ends. In shallower reservoirs look for reefs or ledges in front of the spawning areas.

Early in the pre-spawn period, when the water temperature reaches about 50°F (10°C), look for bass using these types of structure as they prepare to move into the coves. As the water warms and spawning time nears, they work their way farther into the cove, hugging the shore until they're adjacent to the spawning area. They'll stay there until the water temperature reaches the upper 50s, when they will move up shallow looking to spawn.

Bass tend to hold near any irregular features along the mouth of a cove. Look for rock-slides, points, indentations, and ledges with some kind of cover, such as a rubble pile or brush clump. Typical depths during the pre-spawn period are 10 to 35 feet (3 to 10.7 m), but the fish can be considerably deeper if the water is extremely clear. The best spots have water much deeper than that in which the bass are holding; this way, the fish can easily retreat to whatever depths they wish.

The same spots that draw bass during the pre-spawn period also attract them post-spawn and in fall. But the fall pattern is not as reliable, because baitfish movement scatters the fish about the lake. In summer look for offshore ledges or points with brush piles planted in deeper water. A good locator with a GPS is a must for finding and fishing these areas as you will often need to be very precise on how you fish them.

Water stage is not a major consideration, although the technique tends to be most effective under stable or falling conditions. In rising water, bass move onto shallow flats or into flooded brush where you would probably do better using other methods.

FEATURES THAT CONCENTRATE PRE-SPAWN BASS

Rubble piles on underwater ledges (shown) make ideal cover.

Irregular points plunging into deep water are best.

Shaded indentations hold bass on sunny days.

Rock slides indicate good underwater structure.

Football-Jigging Techniques

Fishing a football head jig is a simple proposition: cast it out, let it sink to the bottom, and retrieve it with a drag-and-pause technique starting with 3- to 6-inch (7.6 to 15 cm) pulls. Then adjust the length of the pulls and pause time until the fish tell you what they like. The biggest thing to remember is that you want the jig to be in contact with the bottom at all times.

Because of the fact that you are fishing rock, you are inevitably going to get hung up. Rather than continuing to pull and eventually breaking your line, simply use your trolling motor to maneuver back past the jig and pull it the opposite way you were fishing when it got stuck.

Occasionally you will have a situation where you are catching fish off a spot and they stop biting or you are fishing an area that you know has fish and can't get them to bite. In this scenario a good method is to occasionally "pop" the jig off the bottom several feet to trigger the fish into a reaction strike. The jig mimics a fleeing crayfish and can lead to vicious strikes.

EQUIPMENT

ROD: 6½- to 7-foot (2 to 2.3 m) heavy power, fast-action graphite baitcaster
REEL: high-speed baitcaster
LINE: 12- to 20-pound (5.4 to 9 kg) line
LURES: ½ to 1-ounce (14 to 28 g) football-head jig with a skirt and trailer or spider grub

JIG-DRIFTING: A NATURAL APPROACH FOR RIVER BASS

When it comes to locating bass in rivers, current can be your ally or your enemy. If you understand how bass respond to this variable, they become quite predictable and you can establish a consistent fish-catching pattern. If not, your success will be spotty.

You will often hear the same advice if you talk to top river anglers: "Learn where to find the fish at different water stages, present your bait naturally, and you will catch fish."

Many anglers rely heavily on jigs for fishing moving water, but you have to fish them much differently than you do in lakes. The jig should be light enough to drift with the current as it sinks. You'll get more bites if the bait approaches naturally from the direction the fish expects food to come from than if it plummets down from above.

By allowing the jig to drift naturally into openings in fallen trees, brush piles, and undercut banks, you can tempt strikes from fish that would otherwise be impossible to reach. The technique requires a slow, precise presentation, so it may not be the best way to catch bass when they're active enough to chase lures passing outside the cover such as a spinner-bait or crankbait.

The locational patterns discussed here apply to tidal rivers and in any good-sized river, assuming bass are relating to woody cover in current. The main difference in fishing tidal rivers is the constantly changing water level. It keeps bass on the move and causes them to turn on and off more quickly and more often than bass in waters without daily fluctuations.

Understanding Tides

Tidal fluctuations result mainly from the moon's gravitational pull on the earth's surface. This pull creates a bulge of water that stays under the moon as the earth revolves. Centrifugal forces create another bulge of about the same magnitude on the side of the earth opposite the moon. The earth makes one revolution relative to the moon about every 25 hours and during this time, a given point on the earth experiences a high tide as it passes under the moon, a low tide as it turns away from the moon, another high tide as it passes under the bulge opposite the moon, and another low tide as it turns toward the moon again.

Atlantic and Pacific coastal waters experience this typical pattern of two highs and lows every 25 hours; a low tide occurs about 6¼ hours after a high. But the shape of the ocean's basin and other geophysical factors sometimes interfere with the typical pattern. Consequently, some regions, such as the Gulf coast, experience only one high and one low every 25 hours; the low comes about 12½ hours after the high.

Tides vary considerably in different locations. Some places on earth have tides of 30 feet (9 m) or more; in others, the tide is only 1 foot (30.5 cm). And the amount of tidal fluctuation changes throughout the month. The greatest fluctuation (spring tide) takes place during the full moon and new moon; the smallest (neap tide) during the first and last quarter moon.

Weather conditions along the coast also affect water levels in the river. The levels are higher than normal with onshore winds, lower with off-shore winds. Water levels are higher than normal with a low barometer, lower with a high barometer.

As the tide rises in coastal areas, salt water flows up coastal rivers. The higher the tide, the farther its effects extend upstream. Tidal peaks occur at different times at different points on the river. How fast the

Fluctuating tides have a dramatic effect on bass location in tidal rivers. At high tide, look for bass scattered throughout marshes connected to the main river. As low tide approaches, you'll find the fish positioned along current breaks, where they can pick off food carried by water draining out of the marshes.

tide moves upstream depends on the configuration of the channel; the straighter and deeper it is, the faster the tide progresses.

The downstream reaches of tidal rivers are nearly as salty as seawater, the middle reaches are brackish, and the upper reaches are fresh. Bass are seldom found in brackish water for any amount of time. Knowing where the brackish water extends to will give you a pretty good idea of where you can start fishing. The extent of tidal influence varies in different rivers, depending on the amount of stream flow, gradient of the river channel, and location of dams or waterfalls.

In a high-gradient river, only the lower reaches are affected by tides. In a low-gradient river, however, the tidal influence may extend more than 100 miles (160.9 km) upstream. A dam or waterfall would prevent any tidal influence above that point, assuming the dam is higher than the tidal rise.

When & Where to Drift Jigs

The normal annual pattern for most river-dwelling bass is to spawn in still backwaters, then after spawning, move to a spot where current washes food to them. When the water temperature drops below 60°F (15.5°C) in fall, they retreat to deep, slack-water holes where they spend the winter. The jig-drifting technique is effective only when bass are relating to current.

Most bass rivers are fairly low in clarity, so the fish hold in shallow water, often less than 5 feet (1.5 m). If the clarity exceeds 2 feet (0.6 m), the fish tend to be warier and more of them hold in deeper water.

In tidal rivers, you must pay close attention to the daily tide cycle. As a rule, bass are easiest to catch during the last two hours of the outgoing tide. The falling water forces them to abandon flooded marshes and creeks and they move into deeper channels connecting to the main river or into the main river itself.

Bass forced out of a marsh or creek by falling water normally don't go far from the mouth. Look for them in small eddies that form behind a current break, such as a fallen tree, dock piling, weed bed, or any projection or pocket along the shoreline that creates an eddy.

Fishing is usually slow at dead-low tide, when there is practically no current, but picks up again during the first hour or so of the incoming tide. The fish are still relating to the same current breaks, but facing the opposite direction. As the water continues to rise, however, baitfish move back into flooded creeks and marshes to get out of the current and the bass follow. They're much more difficult to find when they're scattered in these large backwaters.

Any conditions that cause lower tides tend to improve fishing by further concentrating the bass around current breaks. Tides are lower during the full moon and new moon, for instance, than at other times of the month. You can identify prime low tides by referring to a weekly tide table.

Higher than normal tides, such as those caused by onshore winds, make fishing tough. High, muddy water caused by torrential rains also kills fishing.

One way anglers can improve their success is by moving upriver or downriver to avoid unfavorable tides or take advantage of favorable ones.

Before fishing a tidal river, check with local sources to learn what reach holds the most bass. As a rule, you won't find many bass downstream of the point where barnacles begin to appear, because the water is too salty. The lower part of the productive reach, however, usually produces the biggest bass.

ROD: 7½-foot (2.3 m) fast-action, medium-heavy to heavy power graphite flippin' stick
REEL: well-made baitcaster
LINE: 20- to 25-pound (9 to 11 kg) abrasion-resistant line or 45- to 80-pound (20 to 36 kg) braid
LURES: skirted brushguard jigs with a soft-plastic trailer

The Jig-Drifting Technique

The ideal way to drift a jig into a likely bass hangout is to position your boat in the current with the bow pointing upstream, while holding even with and just outside the cover. Then flip your jig far enough upstream of the cover so it reaches bottom just as it drifts into the fish's lie. Let the jig drift into the cover, then yo-yo it against the current by repeatedly pulling it back upstream and allowing it to drift into different pockets in the cover.

To achieve the proper drift, the weight of the jig and bulk of the trailer must be matched to the speed of the current. In very slow current, a jig that is too heavy won't drift at all. Fast current will blow away a jig that is too light and it won't stay in the strike zone very long. Use a brush-

Look for bass around old algae-covered pilings, which attract aquatic insects and baitfish. New pressure-treated pilings leach arsenic, which prevents algal growth.

guard jig with a stand-up style head, rather than cone style, because it will hook more fish. Most anglers choose dark colors, usually blacks, browns, blues, or combinations of them.

A long rod helps control the jigs drift and will reduce the amount of line needed to reach the cover. You'll normally use no more than 12 feet (3.7 m) of line, measuring from the rod tip. The more line in the water, the more the current drag and the less natural the presentation. Thin-diameter line will also reduce current drag.

When you feel a strike, set the hook immediately and try to pull the fish upstream, away from the cover. Your drag should be tight so you can keep enough tension on the fish to prevent it from swimming back into the brushy tangle.

If you suspect the cover is holding bass, but they're not interested in your jig, try "finessing" them with a smaller lure and lighter line such as 4-inch (10 cm) soft plastic rigged Texas-style on an offset jig hook. You could use a 4-inch worm, but a lizard or creature is bulkier and the legs give it extra lift, so it will drift better.

But this lighter jig may not be heavy enough to horse fish out of the cover. If the bass strikes outside the cover, set the hook right away and try to keep it from swimming back in. But if it strikes when the lure has drifted well into the cover, exert steady pressure and try to lead the fish heading out before setting the hook.

HOW TO DRIFT A JIG INTO DENSE COVER

Position your boat even with or just upstream of the cover you want to fish. This way, you can easily drift a jig into the cover and pull fish out.

Drift the jig beneath the cover, then twitch it while feeding line. Each twitch will allow the current to wash the jig a little farther into the tangle.

Set the hook at an upstream angle and lead the fish upstream. If you attempt to pull the fish cross-current, it will probably foul in the cover.

CRANKIN' THE WEEDS FOR LARGEMOUTH

If you've ever tried fishing a crankbait in a weedy lake, chances are you didn't do it for long—unless picking weeds off hooks is your idea of a good time.

When faced with dense weeds, most bass fishermen select other lures, such as spinnerbaits or weedless jigs. But top anglers don't see the weeds as a problem; they go right to their crankbait box. A crankbait will cover more water in less time than any other type of lure and they will often draw "reaction" strikes from neutral bass. Sometimes a crankbait will activate a whole school and divulge their location. When one fish strikes, it often activates the rest of them.

When you cover this much water, you not only find the active fish, you find the right vegetation and bottom type. If you suspect fish are in the area but they're not biting, you can work them with a slower, more thorough bait, such as a weedless jig or Texas-rigged worm.

Another advantage to crankbaits is that they're a good choice in windy weather, when it's hard to fish jigs, worms, or other baits that require a deft touch to achieve the right action and detect strikes. The best time to use crankbaits is whenever bass are holding along or just outside the weedline or over the weed-tops. They're usually not a good choice when the fish are tucked into deep weeds.

Techniques for Crankin' the Weeds

There's a lot more to crankin' than tossing out a bait and reeling it in. You must pay attention to your boat position and retrieve on every cast. If you allow your mind to drift, you'll catch more weeds than bass.

Crankbait selection is also critical. Not only must you choose a lure that runs at precisely the correct depth, its color and action must suit the water clarity and the mood of the bass. There is no sure way to predict which lure will work best, but the following guidelines will help.

The design of the lip affects running depth, as does line diameter. A deep-running crankbait will lose about a foot of depth for every .001-inch increase in line diameter. Shallower-running lures will lose proportionately less. Also, with thicker line, it takes longer for the lure to reach its maximum running depth.

The best colors vary from one body of water to another, but bright or fluorescent colors generally work best in dirty water, dull or natural ones in clear water. Most anglers believe a wide wobble is best in warm water, but the reverse is actually true. A lure with a wide wobble or lots of "roll" is most effective in cold water, because it still has adequate action at a slow retrieve speed. A lure with a tighter wiggle and less roll works better in warm water, because it's easier to retrieve faster.

Detecting strikes is seldom a problem when fishing crankbaits, but it can be in weedy lakes. Sometimes bass merely grab the lure and hold on, giving you the impression you've hooked a weed. To be safe, set the hook when you feel anything out of the ordinary. The fine-wire trebles penetrate easily, so you don't need a powerful hook set. "Crank-set" the hook by reeling faster while making a smooth sweep with your rod.

A bass can throw a crankbait more easily than a single-hook lure like a jig or spinnerbait. But you can minimize the chances of losing the fish by playing it properly. After setting the hook, pull horizontally to get the

TYPE OF WATER: weedy natural lakes and reservoirs
SEASON: post-spawn through fall
WATER TEMPERATURE: effective until water temperature drops below 45°F (7°C) in fall
COVER TYPE: edges of dense submerged weedbeds
WEATHER: warm, overcast, moderate wind
WATER STAGE: normal
WATER DEPTH: 20 feet (6 m) or less
WATER CLARITY: at least 3 feet (0.9 m)
TIME OF DAY: anytime there is a moderate wind

EQUIPMENT

ROD: 6½- to 7-foot (2 to 2.3 m) medium-action, medium-power baitcaster, either graphite or fiberglass
REEL: low-gear-ratio (5:1) baitcaster with longer than normal reel handle for extra cranking power
LINE: 10- to 12-pound (4.5 to 5.4 kg) line
LURES: medium- to deep-running crankbaits

Land a crankbait-hooked fish like this.

fish away from the weeds. If you hold the rod high and pull vertically, you'll bring the fish to the surface where it can easily throw the lure. If you see the line start to move up rapidly, plunge your rod into the water while keeping pressure on the fish. This reduces the chances it will jump and the angle of pull keeps the hooks buried. A word of caution: don't set your drag too tight or attempt to horse a crankbait-hooked bass. The trebles tear out easily, especially when a fish makes a last-minute run.

Don't try to lip-land a bass with a crankbait in its mouth. Instead, keep the line taut, put your hand under its belly, and quickly lift it into the boat.

Principles of Crankbait Design

With thousands of crankbait models on the market, it helps to be able to look at one and have a pretty good idea of how it will perform. On the next page are the major considerations:

LIP. The length, width, and angle of the lip determine a bait's running depth. The longer and wider the lip, and the straighter it extends off the nose, the deeper the lure will track.

The lip also affects side-to-side action. The wider the lip, the more wobble; the more angle, the more roll.

A crankbait with a large, straight lip is the best choice in snag-filled cover. The lip runs interference for the hooks and the straight angle causes the lure to run nose-down, so the hooks aren't as likely to bump the cover.

A bait's action depends on the position of the line-attachment eye on the lip, as well. The closer to the nose, the more the bait tends to roll.

WEIGHTING. Most crankbaits have little or no added weight, so they float at rest. But some have lead inserts, so they sink or are neutrally buoyant. Sinking baits can be counted down to any depth; while neutrally buoyant ones can be retrieved very slowly, without floating up, so they're a good choice when fish are sluggish.

BODY MATERIAL. The type of body material affects a crankbait's action and flotation. Common materials include:

Plastic. Most crankbaits are made of hard or foamed plastic. Hard-plastic models, the most common type, are much more durable. The hard, hollow shell makes them best suited for rattles. Foamed-plastic models are lighter and more "responsive." Assuming a foamed-plastic bait is identical in shape and weighted the same as a hard-plastic, it would ride higher in the water, have livelier action, respond better to a twitching-style retrieve, and be easier to fish above weedtops or float off of snags.

Wood. Balsa and cedar are the most common types of wood used for crankbaits. Balsa is the lightest and most responsive, but cedar is much more durable. Wooden crankbaits are usually more costly than plastic ones.

SHAPE. The body shape of a crankbait also affects its action. Thin-bodied models generally have a tight, rapid wiggle; fat-bodied types, a wider, slower wobble. Deep-diving models usually have a fat body; a thin one does not run as true and is more difficult to keep in tune.

In a general sense, no matter what type of plant or "weed" you are fishing, you can classify them as "short weed" or "tall weed." The crankbait you choose lies solely on which of these two types you are fishing.

Techniques for Short Weeds

Select a crankbait that tracks at about the same depth as the weedtops. Experiment with different casting angles, lures, retrieve speeds, and

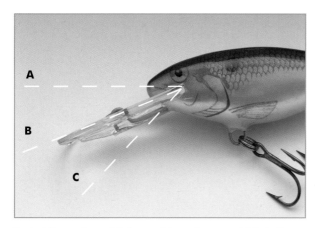

Typical lip angle on (a) deep-, (b) medium-, and (c) shallow-running crankbaits.

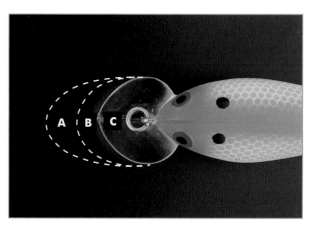

Typical lip size on (a) deep-, (b) medium-, and (c) shallow-running crankbaits.

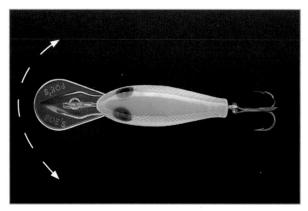

Wobble is movement sideways to the lengthwise axis.

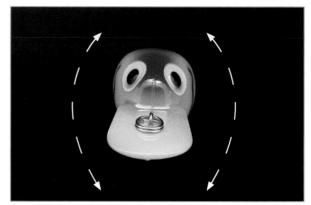

Roll is pivoting movement around the lengthwise axis.

rod positions until you find the combination that keeps the lure barely tickling the weedtops.

If the weeds taper gradually, for instance, position your boat in deep water, cast perpendicular to the break so the lure lands in shallower water, and retrieve so it follows the weedtops. But if the weeds slope sharply into deep water, cast parallel to the break; this way, your lure will have more time to dive to the level of the fish.

For each crankbait, there is an optimum speed at which it tracks deepest. Faster or slower and the lure will run shallower. If possible, keep your retrieve on the slow side in early and late season, when the water temperature is cool.

During each retrieve, carefully note when you start to feel weeds. When you feel the first tick, stop reeling, give the lure slack so it can float up a few inches, then reel again. This stop-and-go retrieve usually works better than a steady one, especially in early season.

Subsequent casts at slightly different angles will reveal relative water depth and weed height. If you start bumping weeds earlier in your retrieve, the water is shallower; if you feel them later, it's deeper.

Techniques for Tall Weeds

With the weeds growing to or just beneath the surface, it's nearly impossible to retrieve a crankbait over the weedtops without fouling. In this situation, you must run the lure nearly parallel to the outside weedline and get it close to the bottom. The technique is sometimes called "crankin' the wall" and is best done by using deep- or super-deep-diving crankbaits.

The key to catching bass along a wall of weeds is finding the perfect casting angle. Instead of holding your boat over deep water and casting toward the weeds, hold it right over the deep edge of the weeds, angle your cast slightly away from the weedline, and retrieve so the bait just bumps the weed edge at its maximum running depth. This way, you'll catch bass holding at the base of the weedline or on any clean point extending from the weeds.

If you cast exactly parallel to the weedline, the lure will bump weeds too soon and probably foul. If you angle your cast too far out from the weedline, you won't bump weeds until too late in the retrieve.

Reel rapidly as soon as the lure hits the water; this way, it will get down in a hurry. Once you feel it tick the weeds, slow down. The lure will stay at the same depth and the slower speed will usually draw more strikes. Under ideal feeding conditions, however, you may get more strikes with a faster retrieve.

The water resistance from a super-deep-diving crankbait can wear you out in a hurry. But a reel with a low gear ratio (5:1) and a long handle minimizes the effort required, enabling you to fish for extended periods with little fatigue.

You can adjust your bait's running depth by changing the distance you hold your rod tip above the water. If you're having trouble getting the lure to run deep enough, push the rod tip into the water. This will give you as much as 3 feet (0.9 m) more depth. If you still aren't bumping weeds, select a deeper-running lure or use thinner-diameter line.

The best way to learn how to crank the weeds is to go out and try it. Don't give up because you're dragging in lots of weeds and few fish. Bass in these lakes seldom see crankbaits and once you learn how to use them, they can be your ace in the hole.

SUSPENDING JERKBAITS: RX FOR COLDWATER BASS

Stickbaits, jerkbaits, minnow baits—it makes no difference what you call them. These lifelike minnow imitations have long been standard items in the tackle boxes of most freshwater anglers.

The first minnow plug was imported to the United States from Finland in 1959 by Ron Weber, former President of the Normark Corporation. "At first, I couldn't get the tackle industry to take the Rapala seriously," Weber recalled. "A store owner would pick one up and hand it right back. 'Too light to cast,' he'd say. That was probably true with the heavy line they used back in those days. But as lighter tackle and lines became popular, the lures began to catch on. It soon became obvious they were terrific baits for practically any kind of gamefish."

When fished with a slow, steady retrieve, the original minnow baits would ride on the surface with a unique wobble that closely mimics a swimming shiner. After these lures became more available, bass fishermen quickly added a retrieve variation. They found that the plug's high buoyancy made it possible to use an erratic twitch-and-pause surface retrieve that worked magic on shallow-water bass. When given a sharp twitch, the lure dives a few inches, then quickly pops back to the surface, where bass strike it at rest. This retrieve has now become a standard bass-fishing technique.

Innovative mid-South anglers added yet another effective twist. They discovered that the twitch-and-pause retrieve worked considerably better with the lure weighted to make it neutrally buoyant. This way, it would "suspend" in front of the fish rather than immediately floating up, a major advantage in tempting uninterested bass to strike. This suspending jerkbait technique is the focus of this section.

This technique is believed to have its roots in Missouri, where tournament anglers were weighting their own jerkbaits to get them to suspend and fishing them in nearby mountain lakes, such as Table Rock and Bull Shoals. Back in the early days, they just drilled a hole in the bait and let it fill with water.

Fishing suspending jerkbaits is definitely a big-bass technique. When the water's cold, big bass just don't want to chase and sometimes you've got to put the bait right in its face. That's when a weighted stickbait really shines. The idea is to make it look like an injured baitfish like a shad struggling to right itself.

When & Where to Use Suspending Jerkbaits

Suspending jerkbaits are most effective at water temperatures from 40 to 60°F (4 to 15.5°C), particularly from late winter through the prespawn period. In winter, however, it takes sunny weather to activate the bass and draw them up into jerkbait range, which is generally a depth of 12 feet (3.7 m) or less. In winter, bass don't move horizontally to reach shallow water, they simply rise vertically to feed on baitfish drawn to the sun-warmed surface layer.

Because the suspending jerkbait technique relies on visual attraction, it's most productive in waters where visibility is at least 2 feet (60 cm). Although jerkbait fishing originated in deep, clear reservoirs, the technique can be used in any man-made or natural lake with adequate clarity.

The exact locations of the bass depend on the type of water you're fishing. In Ozark Mountain lakes, for instance, most bass spend the winter relating to sharp-breaking structure along the main river channel or

TYPE OF WATER: any lake or reservoir with fairly clear water
SEASON: winter through pre-spawn
WATER TEMPERATURE: 40 to 60°F (4 to 15.5°C)
WEATHER: winter: sunny days; pre-spawn: cloudy, windy days
WATER STAGE: any stage
WATER DEPTH: bass must be within 12 feet (3.7 m) of the surface
WATER CLARITY: at least 2 feet (60 cm)
TIME OF DAY: afternoon

major creek channels. They move vertically along the steep breaks, rising to depths of 5 to 15 feet (1.5 to 4.5 m) on warm days and dropping into 25 feet (7.6 m) or more on cold days.

Structure with flooded timber is most likely to hold largemouth. The fish suspend high in the branches in warm, stable weather and use deep branches under cold-front conditions.

As the water starts to warm in spring, bass move up more on the structure, feeding on shallow flats adjacent to the steep breaks where they spent the winter. Cold fronts may push them back to the steep breaks. As spring progresses, they begin working their way toward the small coves and shoreline pockets where they will spawn.

Cloudy, windy weather is better once the fish begin moving shallower in the vicinity of their spawning areas. Choppy water makes them less wary, and they feed aggressively along windswept shorelines, where windblown plankton draws and collects baitfish.

The technique's effectiveness fades by the onset of spawning, which usually begins a few weeks earlier in the creek arms than in main lake coves.

Suspending jerkbaits work well not only for largemouth, but also for smallmouth and spotted bass. But the locational patterns vary somewhat for the three species. Largemouth can be found on suitable structure throughout the lake, even ranging into the back ends of small creek arms. But smallmouth generally inhabit only the main basin and large creek arms. Spots have intermediate locational tendencies.

Weighted stickbaits produce a mixed bag of largemouth (left), smallmouth (center), and spotted (right) bass.

Pea-Gravel Points (shown). Pre-spawn bass seek out a pea-gravel bottom for spawning. They stage on gradual points with this type of bottom, then move into nearby shoreline pockets with the same type of bottom to spawn.

Underwater Extentions. Gradually sloping points often have long underwater extensions or large flats projecting from their tips. The most productive extensions or flats have plenty of 5- to 20-foot-deep (1.5 to 6 m) water.

Channel Swings. Places where the main-river or creek channel but up to a steep shoreline concentrates bass in winter. The fish prefer staying close to the break when making their vertical movements.

Chunk Rock Points. Points with plenty of large broken rocks usually indicate a sharp-sloping breakline. They attract bass, particularly largemouth and spots, during the winter months.

Saddles. Underwater connections, or saddles, between structural elements, such as a point and island, draw all three bass species. The most productive saddles level off at 10 to 20 feet (3 to 6 m).

Techniques for Fishing Suspending Jerkbaits

Many anglers don't realize that water temperature changes a bait's buoyancy. The colder the water, the more weight you need to keep the bait neutrally buoyant. If you're going to be fishing in cold water, test your bait in cold water. You may need to add weight to your bait to get it to perform as it does in warmer water.

Water temperature is also important when selecting plug size. As a rule, top anglers prefer 5-inch (12.7 cm) baits in water of 50°F (10°C) or less; 5½- to 7-inchers (14 to 18 cm) in water warmer than 50°F.

Using a long-handled rod for extra casting distance and keeping the wind at your back, make a long cast. Reel quickly to get the plug down to, or just above, the level of the fish. You may have to experiment to find the presentation that best suits the mood of the fish. Try starting with a basic stop-and-go retrieve. With your rod tip low, twitch the bait sharply to make it dart and flash, then hesitate a few seconds. That's when most fish will strike. Vary the hesitation length; you may have to wait as long as 30 seconds between twitches, but sometimes a series of steady twitches works best. If sharp twitches aren't working, try 3- to 5-foot (0.9 to 1.5 m) sweeps. Or combine sweeps with twitches.

Bass may hit the lure hard or you may just feel a subtle tick or a little extra weight. Set the hook with a crank-set by making a firm, sideways sweep while reeling faster.

Suspending jerkbaits are no longer the secret they once were and pre-weighted models that work very well are now available from most manufacturers.

EQUIPMENT

ROD: 6½-foot (2 m) medium- to medium-heavy power, fast-action, long-handled baitcaster
REEL: high-speed baitcaster
LINE FOR LIGHT COVER: 8- to 10-pound (3.6 to 5.4 kg) low-visibility, abrasion-resistant line
LINE FOR HEAVY COVER: 12- to 17-pound (5.4 to 7.6 kg) low-visibility, abrasion-resistant line
LURES: shallow or deep-running suspending jerkbaits

SWIMBAITS: CALIFORNIA DREAMS FOR TROPHY LARGEMOUTH

Much of what we read about trophy-bass fishing these days involves some kind of live bait. In Florida, for instance, anglers traditionally use foot-long (0.3 m) golden shiners to pull the big females off their spawning beds. In Texas, trophy hunters catch the spawners on water-dogs. In California, now the nation's top giant-bass producer, trophy specialists have learned to entice finicky biters with live crayfish.

Not only are some of these live-bait tactics controversial from a conservation standpoint, many bass anglers simply don't like fishing this way. While you could argue that nothing else catches trophy bass like live bait, California anglers are using artificial bait techniques that aren't far behind.

"Swimbaits" are the general classification for these baits, but they come in numerous styles and sizes. These baits evolved from giant wooden trout-imitating plugs that anglers crafted to mimic the trout that were being stocked in California reservoirs. The most popular are now made of soft plastic, which gives them an enticing swimming action and many different models are available throughout the country.

Swimbaits for Trophy California Bass

California's biggest bass come from deep, clear lakes that have been stocked with Florida-strain largemouth. Of the state's fifty-plus Florida-bass stocked lakes, the very best trophy producers are primarily in the southern one-third of the state, where the growing season is considerably longer than in northern California. Another requirement for production of super-trophy bass: the lake must be stocked with rainbow trout.

In California, bass are classified as trophies, meaning more than 10 pounds (4.5 kg), or super-trophies, meaning more than 15 (6.75 kg). Good fishing for trophies begins about 8 years after the initial trout stocking; for super-trophies, 12 years. Production of super-trophies drops off sharply as the word spreads and numbers of them are removed. Good reproduction and diminished fishing pressure, however, may result in another big-fish boom many years later on a given lake.

Successful anglers pay close attention to big-bass cycles in different lakes. They also know the times of year when the fish are most vulnerable, exactly where to find them, and the techniques most likely to entice them to bite.

In most of these lakes, threadfin shad are also an important part of the forage base. The shad, which are pelagic, spend the summer cruising open water, usually in or above the thermocline. This means big bass are difficult to find and catch consistently in summer.

But the shad go deep in late fall and stay deep through winter. Small bass follow shad into the depths, but big ones seem reluctant to go deep. They're generally linked to some type of structure, usually at depths of 25 feet (7.6 m) or less. Their locations are much more predictable and because they are fattening up in preparation for spawning, they're feeding heavily and are more willing to bite.

Once the shad move to deeper water, the predominant fall and winter big-bass foods are rainbow trout, explaining why the swimbait technique is so effective.

Any type of structure including long points, humps, rock bluffs, riprap banks, dug-out holes, and old roadbeds may hold bass, if it has the right kind of bottom and deep water nearby. Bass will usually concentrate around something different on the structure, like a small rubble pile, an area of broken rock, or a brush pile.

Learning to quickly eliminate unproductive habitat and focus your efforts on prime water is a valuable skill no matter what you're fishing for. But it's especially important when you're looking for trophy fish, because there aren't many of them. It pays to have good electronics so you can pinpoint individual bass, schools of baitfish, and key cover elements.

Bass feed most aggressively early and late in the day, but there's also a feeding peak in midday. However, heavy boating and fishing activity will slow the midday action, explaining why fishing tends to be better on weekdays than on weekends. Once the fish are disturbed, they often move away from structure and don't feed.

When fishing pressure is heavy, it's important to get out early and stake out a spot. If you sleep in, you'll probably have to fish water that's already been combed by other anglers.

California's Trophy Bass Program

Many of the country's biggest largemouth swim in the man-made lakes that supply water to southern Californians. But these lakes have not always held such huge bass. The trophy bass program was born in 1959, when the San Diego County Fish and Game Commission stocked Florida-strain largemouth in Upper Otay Reservoir. Fish from that

Tagging studies enable biologists to check growth rates.

initial plant served as brood stock to supply Florida bass for many other California lakes.

The program has been incredibly successful, producing hundreds of largemouth over 14 pounds (6.3 kg) and seven over 20 (9 kg) since its inception. No other 20-pounders have been caught anywhere else in the world since 1932, when the current world-record bass, weighing 22.25 pounds (10.01 kg), was caught in Montgomery Lake, Georgia. To date, the largest California bass weighed in at 22.01 pounds (9.91 kg). It was taken in Castaic Lake in 1991. Most trophy bass enthusiasts agree it's only a matter of time before a California lake yields a new world record.

The reason California bass reach such mammoth size is explained by the following factors:

During the coldwater months, the lakes are stocked with rainbow trout, which provide high-fat forage for fast growth. Most freshly stocked hatchery trout are about 9 to 11 inches (23 to 28 cm) long, just the right size for a good-sized bass to eat. They have little fear of predators, so they're easy for the bass to catch. These lakes also have healthy populations of crayfish and shad.

The southern California climate allows a long growing season. The water temperature rarely drops below 50°F (10°C), so the fish grow all year long.

The lakes producing the big bass have been stocked with the Florida-strain largemouth, whose inborn growth potential is considerably higher than that of the northern largemouth, the strain originally stocked in California. Not only does the Florida strain grow faster, they're more difficult to catch, so they tend to live longer.

AGE AND GROWTH OF THE 1961 YEAR CLASSES*

	Northern Bass			Florida Bass	
Age	Length (in.)	Weight (lb.)	Age	Length (in.)	Weight (lb.)
1	6.07	.20	1	5.92	.15
2	11.62	1.10	2	12.75	1.50
3	14.73	2.15	3	15.69	2.84
4	16.37	2.91	4	17.65	4.15
5	17.94	3.80	5	20.39	6.44
6	19.11	4.57	6	22.05	8.32
7	20.28	5.39	7	23.08	9.61
8	20.35	5.53	8	23.36	10.05
9	no data	no data	9	24.80	12.15
10	no data	no data	10	25.63	13.32

*Northern and Florida largemouth Bass in El Capitan Reservoir, California

ROD: 7½-foot (2.3 m) heavy
power, fast-action flippin' stick
REEL: baitcaster with gear ratio of
at least 6:1
LINE: 15- to 20-pound-test (6.75
to 9 kg) low-visibility line
LURES: 5½- to 12-inch (14 to 30
cm) swimbaits

Swimbait Techniques

When the bass are zeroing in on stocked trout, it's tough to beat a swimbait. Fish home in on swimbaits because of their size and vibration. They have a heavy, deep, thumping sound underwater that trophy bass probably associate with big prey. An ordinary crankbait has a higher-pitched sound similar to that of smaller prey.

Most trophy seekers prefer the 9½- to 12-inch (24 to 30 cm) size in a rainbow trout color. Casting these big lures is easiest with a heavy flippin' stick. They work best when retrieved at a steady pace, so a high-speed reel will make things easier. Set the drag tight, so it does not slip on a hard hook set. Don't use line heavier than 20-pound test, because it will cut down the lure's running depth. Check the line often for nicks or frays and retie as needed.

The best time to fish these baits is in the windiest, choppiest weather possible. It disguises your approach, so you won't spook as many fish and they can't get a good enough look at the plug to recognize it as a fake.

Another good time to fish big swimbaits is right after they stock the trout. The big bass just move in and gorge on the disoriented new arrivals. It's been described like cattle coming in to eat hay. The bass may hang around the trout-stocking area a few days, but then you'll have to look for them on more traditional structure.

Typical bass structure includes areas such as flats, long points, isolated humps, or any steep shoreline adjacent to deep water. But on these spots, try to focus on very subtle differences such as a change in rock type or any brushy cover. Top anglers have also found that bass on a specific piece of cover may only strike with a certain retrieve angle, so it pays to experiment.

Start fishing with a 9-inch (23 cm) swimbait and use a sidearm lob-cast to toss it as far as you can. This way, the plug can reach its maximum running depth to tempt less aggressive bass and it gives followers more time to grab it. Followers are a common issue with these big baits at times.

Even in cool water, a steady retrieve is usually best. Increase the speed if the bait bumps a rock or stick or you see a follower; this seems to trigger strikes. If a follower strikes short or doesn't strike at all, grab a rod rigged with a smaller or different color swimbait and cast well beyond the spot where you saw the fish.

Bass may smash the bait or just nip at it. If you think a bass has grabbed it, reel rapidly to tighten the line, then set the hook hard to drive in the thick hooks. With such large bait, a big bass can easily shake the hook, especially if you let it reach the surface and jump. If you see your line coming up, push your rod tip under the water to keep the fish down.

Try fishing any underwater extensions. Cast to the deep water and retrieve the plug along the extension into shallower water.

Look for small points along the bank and cast beyond their tips. When you retrieve, the plug will bump the point, often triggering a strike.

Work any shoreline where wave action has discolored the water. The dirty water makes it hard for a bass to distinguish the plug from a real trout.

Estimating Weight of a Trophy Bass

If you want to release a trophy bass, but don't have an accurate scale, here's a handy formula that will give you a close approximation of its weight:

LENGTH x LENGTH x GIRTH Divided by 1200 = WEIGHT

Length means total length in inches, from the tip of the jaw to the longest part of the tail. Girth is measured in inches around the thickest part of the body (left). The formula gives weight in pounds.

TIP: Here's an example of how it would work, assuming you've caught a 25-inch (63.5 cm) bass with a 20-inch (51 cm) girth: 25 (63.5) x 25 (63.5) x 20 (51) Divided by 1200 = 10.42 POUNDS.

BLADES 'N' GRUBS: THE RIGHT COMBINATION FOR MUDDY WATER BASS

Heavy rains in early spring mean big trouble for many anglers on normally clear bodies of water. Huge quantities of silt flushed in from a main river or from tributaries can muddy up large portions of a lake or reservoir.

Creeks swollen by early season rain pour into upper ends of creek arms at a time when they're holding lots of bass looking to spawn or finishing up their spawn. The bass will not leave these areas even when water clarity is reduced to a few inches, but they can be very difficult to catch.

Most anglers will tell you not to even try catching these muddy water bass. It's too tough when every creek is belching out water that looks like heavily creamed coffee. The secret in this situation is to find the creeks that clear quickest. The fish there are often much more cooperative.

One method for quickly finding and catching bass around these clearing creeks is to scour the area with a spinnerbait, trying to find active fish. If you get enough action, just stick with the spinnerbait. Otherwise, switch to a slower presentation, such as using a Texas-rigged grub to coax strikes from less-aggressive fish in heavy cover. Many pro anglers think this is a tough combination to beat; one method or the other will usually do the job.

OPTIMAL CONDITIONS

TYPE OF WATER: any lake or reservoir that muddies up after a heavy rain

SEASON: pre-spawn and post-spawn

WATER TEMPERATURE: areas warmer than main lake

WEATHER: warm, sunny

WATER STAGE: stable to high

WATER DEPTH: 10 feet (3 m) or less

WATER CLARITY: beginning to clear after being muddy

TIME OF DAY: afternoon and evening

When & Where to Find Bass in Muddied Waters

Differences in the makeup of the tributaries leading into a lake or reservoir determine which ones will clear first. A creek flowing through a rocky gorge, for instance, clears much sooner than one draining highly erodible agricultural land. And creeks draining through small tributaries tend to clear sooner than those draining large ones.

In spring, a creek's water temperature is also very important. If the inflow is warmer than the water in the rest of the creek arm, baitfish (particularly shad) will congregate around the inflow area and attract bass. If there are shad around, you'll often see lots of bird and fish activity.

In general, if there are two creeks that both have the right makeup to draw bass, the larger one will draw the most fish, simply because it influences a larger portion of the lake. And a creek arm with a well-defined channel leading well into the back end will probably draw more bass than one with a flat basin. The channel serves as a roadway for bass moving up the creek arm and once the water starts to fall, it offers a deeper-water retreat.

Changes in water level can further complicate the bass location puzzle. If the level remains stable as the creek is clearing, bass may move into flooded brush in the extreme back ends of the creek arms. You'll normally find them at depths of 3 feet (0.9 m) or less, holding tight to the cover. But the pattern changes when the level is falling, as it normally is when the water starts to clear. Instead of holding tight to the cover, they pull away from the bank and seek steeper structure, such as the creek channel.

Or they may suspend over the first significant ledge out from shore. Instinct tells the bass to pull away from the bank when the water level is falling; otherwise, they could become stranded in an isolated pocket with no escape route to open water.

Although bass continue to feed when the water level is falling, fishing is not as good as when the level is stable. The bass are cruising about much more and are not as predictable.

Spinnerbait & Grub-Fishing Techniques

Once you find a likely looking creek, start fishing with a spinnerbait. This is a great search bait, especially in discolored water, and it's versatile enough to let you quickly scout an area to find fish. You can slow-roll it over stick-ups or brush piles, helicopter it alongside a submerged stump, or work it at a controlled depth to catch bass suspended over a creek-channel break.

Spinnerbait selection depends on the mood of the bass and their position in the cover. When they're inactive, as they often are in the morning before the water has warmed, they sit low in the cover. That's the time for slowly retrieving a deeper-running spinnerbait, such as a ½-ounce (14 g) version, with a single willow-leaf blade. But if the water is below 50°F (10°C), a bait with a single Colorado blade is a better choice, because the blade turns more easily with an ultraslow retrieve. When the afternoon sun has warmed the water, try a lighter high-riding model, such as a ¼-ounce (7 g) tandem-spin for active bass.

To maximize the amount of water you can cover, move rapidly with your trolling motor. How you work the cover depends mainly on the water level. When the water is stable, for instance, bass usually hold tight to woody cover on flats adjacent to the creek channel. Make short casts to specific objects and be sure to work the thickest part of the cover. If your casts are too long, a hooked fish could easily wrap itself in the tangle. When the water is falling, bass often suspend over or near the creek channel break, still relating to cover, but not as close to it. Then make longer casts to cover more water and get the bait a little deeper.

Pay close attention to the way a bass strikes. An active fish hits hard enough to throw slack into your line. A sluggish one just feels like extra weight. When you hook a fish, keep firm, steady pressure on it, letting the rod act as a shock absorber. Try to direct it away from the cover. You'll lose too many fish if you try to rip them through it.

If you think there are bass in the area, but they won't hit a spinnerbait, try a slower presentation using a 5-inch (12.7 cm) Texas-rigged curlytail grub. A curlytail often draws more strikes than other soft plastics in dingy water. The wide tail creates tremendous vibration, even with a slow retrieve.

A grub is generally a better producer at water temperatures less than 50°F (10°C), when the fish aren't "chasing." But grubs will also outproduce other baits even at warmer temperatures. So whenever you finish working an area with a spinnerbait, always go back through with a grub.

Rig the grub with a size 4/0 worm hook and a ⅛- to ¼-ounce (3.2 to 7 g) bullet sinker that pegs to your grub to keep it from sliding on the line. Flip or pitch the bait into visible cover, such as flooded brush, keeping your casts short.

Because you're often so close to the fish, it's important to keep boat noise to a minimum. Instead of constantly changing speeds with your trolling motor or stepping on and off the control button, try to keep it

EQUIPMENT: SPINNERBAITS

ROD: 6½-foot (2 m) medium-heavy power, fast-action graphite baitcaster
REEL: high-speed baitcaster
LINE: 14- to 20-pound (6.3 to 9 kg) line
LURE: ¼- to ½-ounce (7 to 14 g) spinnerbait

EQUIPMENT: GRUB-FISHING

ROD: 7½-foot (2.3 m) medium power, fast-action graphite flippin' stick
REEL: narrow-spool baitcaster
LINE: 14- to 20-pound (6.3 to 9 kg) low-visibility line
LURE: ⅛ to ¼-ounce (3.2 to 7 g) Texas-rigged curlytail grub

at a steady speed. This way, there's less creaking and squeaking from the bracket and the fish aren't as likely to spook from the changing rhythm of the prop.

After flipping the grub it will hit the bottom. Vertically jig it in place using a branch as a fulcrum. Shake the grub occasionally for a different look. If the water is falling, try swimming the grub through sparser cover close to the creek-channel break. With so little line out, strikes should be easy to feel and you'll often see the fish strike.

Set the hook with a sharp wrist snap powerful enough to drive the hook through the grub and into the bass's jaw. Then try to pull the fish away from the cover before it has a chance to tangle. The long medium-heavy power rod and narrow-spool reel match up well with the light grub and the rod flexes enough on the hook set to prevent breaking the line.

When the water gets muddy in early spring, many fishermen throw in the towel, but top-anglers see it as an opportunity. You've got a lot less water to cover and with this spinnerbait/grub combination, you can usually coax some fish to bite.

LOCATION TIPS

Note the precise location of exposed structure, such as a rock pile, when the water is low. Then, when the structure is submerged, you'll know right where to fish.

Look for fish-eating birds, such as grebes and gulls, around the mouth of a tributary. The birds are drawn by baitfish, which also draw bass.

SPINNERBAITING THE WOOD

Many of pro bass fishing's top "blade men" rely on spinnerbaits in a wide variety of bass fishing situations. These anglers believe spinnerbaits are like crescent wrenches, because you can adjust them to suit many different conditions.

When asked, they mention their favorite place to use spinnerbaits is in shallow timber and brush. You can put the bait where the fish are and draw strikes with little risk of snagging. This method works best in spring, when spawning bass move into creek arms with plenty of woody cover, but it can also be effective in fall, when bass follow shad migrations back into the same creek arms.

The sound of a spinnerbait often triggers reflex strikes and in profile, they look like a small school of baitfish. But they probably hit it because of its abnormal vibrations, not because it looks like anything they feed on.

Spinnerbaits are considered high-percentage lures because it's tough for bass to shake the big single hook, so you won't lose many of the fish that strike and some days you catch every one that hits.

OPTIMAL CONDITIONS

TYPE OF WATER: reservoirs with lots of timber and brush
SEASON: pre- and post-spawn
WATER TEMPERATURE: at least 50°F (10°C)
WEATHER: overcast
WATER STAGE: stable
WATER DEPTH: less than 12 feet (3.6 m)
WATER CLARITY: less than 3 feet (0.9 m)
TIME OF DAY: warm mornings; late in the day

When & Where to Fish Spinnerbaits in Woody Cover

You can start using spinnerbaits during the pre-spawn period, as soon as the water temperature tops the 50°F (10°C) mark and the bass are feeding actively. But when they're actually spawning, most anglers prefer slower moving baits, something that stays in their face for a longer time. The usual choices are a tube jig, jerkbait, weightless lizard, or soft stickbait.

You can catch bass on a spinnerbait all day and under any weather conditions, but you'll have to fish tighter to the cover in high sun. Early and late in the day or under cloudy skies, the fish roam more and may be shallower and not as tight to the trees.

Spinnerbaits are an excellent choice in water of lower than normal clarity, where sound plays an important role. They excel in newer reservoirs with lots of standing timber, but they're also effective in older reservoirs with many fallen trees and in rivers or reservoirs with an abundance of stumps and brush.

Creek arms with a deep, well-defined creek channel hold lots of bass from the pre-spawn through the post-spawn period and again in fall, when they're following the shad. The best arms have a line of standing timber adjacent to the deep water and a firm bottom for spawning. Other bass hangouts in good creek arms include ditches along old road beds, fencelines bordering old fields, or any kind of tree row.

Another consideration in selecting a good creek arm is water clarity. Creeks arms that are permanently discolored make prime fishing areas. But those that are temporarily discolored due to heavy runoff are seldom productive. The sudden drop in clarity causes the fish to stop feeding.

Early in the pre-spawn, you'll find the most bass near the mouths of creek arms. But as the water warms and spawning time approaches, they move farther into the arms, eventually settling into the back ends of secondary creek arms and coves that receive lots of sunlight and warm early. After spawning, the fish hold in deeper water just outside these bedding areas, gradually working their way toward the main lake.

Remember that not all bass are in the same stage of spawning or in the same areas at the same time. As a rule, creek arms at the upper end of a reservoir warm earliest and draw the first spawners.

Shoreline erosion and wind cause trees to topple into the water (shown). The best ones are those that fall in along steep banks, where a creek channel abuts the shore. You may find bass in the treetops or in shallower water near the trunk.

Old creek channels (shown) make ideal bass habitat because of the deep water adjacent to rows of cover.

Old roadbeds (shown) draw bass because of their firm surface and adjacent deep water in the ditches.

In many cases, trees were cut before the reservoir filled, leaving large stump fields. In others, the treetops rotted off. The stumps make ideal bass cover, especially if they're near deep water, and are sometimes used as spawning substrate.

Firm bottom areas draw spawning bass and often hold good numbers of fish later in the season, as well.

A major cover type in most rivers and reservoirs, brush and small trees develops along shorelines and on humps during low water. When flooded, they draw bass that normally hold in deeper water, where they are difficult to find.

Old fencerows are often the only cover remaining on flooded farm fields. Bass are more likely to follow the fencerows in their daily movements than roam over featureless flats.

Stock tanks draw bass because of the flooded trees, deep water and firm bottom on the dikes.

ROD: 6½- to 7-foot (2 to 2.1 m) long-handled, medium-heavy power, fast-action graphite baitcaster
REEL: high-speed, durable baitcaster with a reliable drag
LINE: 20-pound (kg) clear, abrasion-resistant line
LURES: single- and tandem-spin spinnerbaits

How to Spinnerbait the Wood

A spinnerbait simplifies the job of finding fish in timber and brush, because it can work the cover quickly. But a spinnerbait must suit the type of water and cover you're fishing.

Pro-anglers prefer single-bladed spinnerbaits most of the time in these conditions because they make the most vibration and are best suited for a stop-and-go retrieve. But when fishing over shallow weeds or in clear water, you can switch to a tandem-blade model. They have more lift and the counter-rotating blades dampen the vibration, for a more subtle presentation. Other considerations are as follows:

WEIGHT. The head must be heavy enough to offset the torque of the blade. If the head is too light for the blade, the whole lure will spin or track through the water in a tilted position. You can start with a ⅜- or ½-ounce (10.6 or 14 g) model most of the time, although a ¼-ounce (7 g) is a good choice in very shallow water and a ¾-ounce (21 g) for deeper water. Wind, current, or deep water require a heavier than normal spinnerbait.

BLADE SIZE. A big blade has more lift, so it is a good choice for shallow presentations and, because it makes more vibration, is effective in muddy water. But a bigger blade also has more torque. If you switch blades, be sure it doesn't throw the bait out of balance. You can switch to a smaller blade, which is a good option in clear water or when you want the bait to run deeper, without affecting the balance. When bass are feeding on shad, choose a blade about the same size as the shad that are present.

BLADE STYLE. A willow-leaf blade is the best choice for fishing in clear water and tends to shed weeds better than other blade styles. Because it produces the least vibration, your presentation will be more natural. A Colorado blade generates more vibration, so it's best in murky water. It's also the most effective for helicoptering and, because it has more lift, it works well for fishing over weedtops.

HEAD SHAPE. In woody cover, use a wide head; it helps deflect branches from the hook and tends to ride up in the "Y" of a branch. But if the head is too wide, it may wedge rather than ride up. A narrow, cone-shaped head is a better choice in heavy weeds.

COLOR. The most popular all-around color pattern includes a metal-flake skirt with a combination of white, a contrasting color for a natural look, and a few strands of chartreuse for visibility. In very clear water choose natural-looking patterns, in stained waters, fluorescents are a good choice.

Pros seldom use a spinnerbait without a plastic trailer, preferably one made of harder-than-normal plastic so it doesn't slip off the collar. White or pearl-white work well in most conditions; chartreuse is a good option for extra visibility in muddy water. The trailer not only adds color and wiggle, it also provides bulk, which makes it easier for fish to inhale the bait. A bulky trailer may also decrease the number of missed strikes because it gives the bass something to suck in.

When beginning your search for bass, move the boat faster than normal and cast only to the targets that seem most likely to hold fish. When you get a strike, slow down and work the area more thoroughly, casting to all likely targets.

As you fish, a locational pattern is apt to emerge; you're catching bass only on the shady side of big trees near the creek channel or around brush piles on shallow flats. As the pattern becomes more definite, you can increase your efficiency by keying on a particular cover type.

Spinnerbait-Casting Techniques

Casting accuracy and versatility are crucial when fishing woody cover. It may be necessary to place the bait in a pocket no more than a few inches in diameter or cast beneath a limb that's only inches (cm) above the water. If you're not proficient with the casting techniques highlighted, you'll spend most of your time untangling baits from branches.

BOLO CAST. From a forehand or backhand position with the rod tip low, use a short, circular wrist motion to whip the bait around the rod tip. The lure travels in a low trajectory and makes little splash. This is the best technique when branches restrict your casting motion.

PITCHIN'. With the lure in your free hand and the rod angled slightly downward, sweep the rod in a short upward arc so the lure travels in a low trajectory. This cast is very accurate, gets your lure under low branches, and creates minimal splash.

FOREHAND. When there is an open casting lane and no branches to restrict rod movement on your forehand side, cast with a sweeping sidearm motion. The lure will splash down hard; cast well past the spot to avoid spooking fish. This technique gives good distance, but is not recommended for precise accuracy or a low trajectory.

BACKHAND. Used for much the same purposes as forehand casting, this technique works well where there is an open casting lane and no branches to restrict rod movement on your backhand side. As in forehand casting, be sure to cast well past your target so the splashdown doesn't scare the fish.

Top Spinnerbait Retrieves

There's really no right or wrong way to work a spinnerbait; it will catch fish on a wide variety of retrieves. The saying goes: "If your spinnerbait is wet, you can catch a fish on it."

But more often than not, bass prefer a specific type of retrieve. You must experiment to find the proper speed, depth, and tempo, or you risk fishing through bass that may respond to a different retrieve variation. The types of retrieves used most often are shown on these pages.

It's very important to be in contact with the blade (feel it thumping) at all times to detect strikes. If you feel the blade stop turning, set the hook.

When you hook a fish, keep its head up so it can't dive and tangle around a branch. If a fish does wrap you up, don't try to rip it out. Use your trolling motor, go to the fish, and try to unwrap it. It's typically fishermen, not fish, that break the line in many situations.

The following are the most common retrieve methods:

STOP-AND-GO. Just as a bass is more likely to grab an injured baitfish than one swimming normally, it's more likely to hit an erratically moving bait. You should use some sort of stop-and-go retrieve 50 percent of the time because it is more likely to draw a reflex strike. Experiment with different stop-and-go tempos to find the combination largemouth prefer on a given day. A stop-and-go retrieve is ideal for fishing around woody cover. You can bump the bait off the wood, allow it to flutter a little, then resume your retrieve, drawing the attention of any bass using the cover.

HELICOPTERING. This retrieve, an extreme variation of the stop-and-go, is most effective when fish are holding at the base of cover or feeding on the bottom. When your bait comes to a target that could hold fish, stop reeling; the blade will spin as the bait sinks and that's when fish usually hit. The silt kicked up when the bait hits bottom also helps trigger strikes.

BULGING. This retrieve draws explosive surface strikes, especially when the water temperature exceeds 60°F (15.5°C) and the surface is glassy calm. Keep your rod tip high and reel fast enough so the blade almost, but not quite, breaks the surface.

SHAKING. When there is no visible cover, such as a stump or stick-up, to deflect the bait and give it an erratic action, shake the rod tip rapidly as you reel. You don't need to shake as much in heavy timber or brush; the bait gets action from bouncing off the branches.

For spinnerbait fishermen, short strikes can be a common problem. If the fish are consistently nudging the bait but you're not hooking them, or you're losing too many hooked fish, you'll have to make some adjustments. You could solve the problem by adding a trailer hook, but the trailer will snag too much in heavy cover. The best options are to shorten the skirt by trimming it, remove your grub trailer, or switch to a smaller blade.

Shorten the skirt or thin it out so the bait has a smaller profile. This way, a bass is more likely to grab the hook.

Shorten the skirt or thin it out so the bait has a smaller profile. This way, a bass is more likely to grab the hook.

The Boom-Bust Phenomenon

Have you ever wondered why new reservoirs provide such fantastic fishing in their first few years of life? Or why fishing in old ones is not so good?

As a reservoir fills, trees, brush, and other terrestrial vegetation is flooded and soon dies. The nutrients released by decomposition of this organic matter and leaching from the soil trigger an explosion of plankton and bottom organisms, fueling a concurrent rise in the baitfish population. The rising water also kills a tremendous quantity of terrestrial animals, such as worms, slugs, and insects, providing instant fish food. With such a profusion of food and an abundance of flooded timber and brush for cover, high growth and survival rates produce a gamefish "boom."

Another reason for the boom is the open niche created by the rising water. Although some fish were present in the river before it was impounded or in farm ponds within the reservoir basin, the water is relatively empty. With few large predator fish, the survival rate of stocked fish and naturally produced fry is much higher than in an older lake.

But as the decomposition and leaching processes wind down, cover disappears, and predators become established, the picture changes. There are fewer nutrients to produce the plankton needed to keep baitfish populations high, more predators to eat the baitfish and young gamefish, and less cover to protect them. In addition, siltation covers spawning areas and reduces production of bottom organisms needed by gamefish and baitfish. As gamefish populations wane, roughfish start to take over.

The duration of the boom period is highly variable, ranging from as little as 3 to as much as 20 years, depending mainly on the amount of terrestrial vegetation present when the reservoir starts to fill, and the rate of filling. A slow fill rate may extend nutrient release over several years and the new vegetation flooded each year makes good spawning habitat.

When the "bust" begins, often only a few years after the boom's peak, the sportfishing catch diminishes to one-third or less of that during the boom and stays that way for the remainder of the reservoir's life. Some reservoirs, however, have been rejuvenated when aquatic plants, such as milfoil and hydrilla, became established. The plants provide habitat for young gamefish and food organisms and add to the water fertility when they decompose.

CALLING UP CLEARWATER SMALLMOUTH

Ask most any smallmouth expert to outline his strategy for catching the fish in ultra-clear lakes and here's what he's likely to say:

- use smaller than normal baits

- select natural or drab colors

- use lighter than normal line

- fish deep

But guides and tournament anglers from the northeastern United States learned of a technique that violates every one of the usual fishing clearwater smallmouth rules.

Pioneered in the early 80s by Keith Kline of the Fleck Lure Company and Danny Correia, a B.A.S.S. touring pro, the technique involves "calling up" smallmouth over water as deep as 40 feet (12 m) by retrieving big, often bright-colored spinnerbaits just beneath the surface.

Since then, pros have been using it "under the radar" for decades dating as far back as when pro angler Rick Clunn used big spinnerbaits to call up enough smallmouth to win the 1992 New York BASSMASTER Invitational on Lake Ontario. The technique was also one of the early favorites of top pro Kevin Van Dam, who routinely used it to catch smallmouth in the clear Michigan lakes where he grew up.

Clearwater smallmouth often pursue suspended forage in open water and this technique takes advantage of that behavior. It is easy to figure that the bass are suspended, because they often grab the bait as soon as it hits the water. The main reason the technique works so well is that it doesn't require a pinpoint presentation; all you have to do is cast over an area known to hold fish and they'll come up for the bait.

When & Where to Call Up Smallmouth

You can call up smallmouth over deep water in most any clearwater lake or reservoir, but the technique works best in those with high smallmouth populations and pelagic baitfish that roam open water in large schools.

In the Northeast, for instance, smallmouth have plenty of pelagic forage in the form of smelt and small white perch, which scour open water for zooplankton and small minnows. The bass also eat yellow perch, which have pelagic tendencies in these lakes. In clear Canadian-shield lakes, smallmouth patrol open water to find ciscoes.

OPTIMAL CONDITIONS

TYPE OF WATER: very clear lakes
SEASON: summer and fall
WATER TEMPERATURE: 50°F (10°C) or higher
WEATHER: windy or rainy
WATER STAGE: any stage
WATER DEPTH: as deep as 40 feet (12 m)
WATER CLARITY: at least 10 feet (3 m)
TIME OF DAY: anytime, if weather is favorable

The technique is effective in waters of this type because smallmouth that feed on pelagic baitfish tend to be highly aggressive and willing to chase baits they've spotted from a considerable distance.

After smallmouth finish spawning, look for them around big boulders or beds of cabbage or sandgrass just outside the shoal areas where they spawned. Others lie suspended in open water, but still relating to the breakline or deeper sandgrass beds. Once the fish set up in these locations, they'll remain there until cooling water drives them deeper in mid-fall and makes them less aggressive.

Many anglers have their best success calling up bass relating to points and weed flats connected to shoreline breaks, but it's also possible to call up bass relating to isolated structure, such as a sunken island.

As summer progresses, young baitfish grow large enough to interest smallmouth and draw them from the breakline. The bass spend more and more of their time relating to deep water, either holding on the bottom or suspending. But some smallmouth remain on points and weed flats until mid-fall.

In shield lakes or other clear waters with a lot of exposed bedrock, smallmouth are strongly drawn to sandy structure because it offers the only available weed growth. You'll find the fish on sandy humps and points, along sandy shoreline breaks, and even in sandy bays. An exposed sandy shoreline provides a visual clue on where you're likely to find sandy structure in the lake.

Calling up smallmouth is easiest when it's windy. You need to get out where there's wave action. It's easier to fish in calm water, but you'll catch more fish along the windy shores. Another good time for calling them up is in rainy weather; raindrops break up the calm surface.

Another good area to check is along mudlines that sometimes form along windy shorelines where a sand or clay bottom may get stirred up due to high winds. In these areas, the stirred up, darker water will meet clear water and form a "line." Smallmouth will cruise up and down these edges using the dark water as cover to catch disoriented baitfish. Cast into the darker water and bring the bait to the boat that is positioned in the clear.

NARROWS. A narrows (shown) may be a channel between two islands, an island and shore, or two basins of a lake. Current induced by the wind funneling water through a narrows draws baitfish and smallmouth.

SANDY SHORELINES. Good smallmouth weeds, such as sandgrass and cabbage, grow on sandy bottoms. A sandy shoreline (shown) is a good indicator of a sandy, weedy bottom farther out from shore.

SPAWNING FLATS. Large shallow flats with a sand-rock bottom (shown) are hubs of early season smallmouth activity. Try the top of the flat when they're spawning; otherwise, you'll find them where the flat slopes into deep water.

SADDLES. These subsurface connectors link two pieces of structure, such as two humps, or an island and shore. They serve as underwater highways for bass moving between structures.

BIG BOULDERS. Boulders the size of a car, or even larger, make prime year-round smallmouth cover. The best boulders lie on a break between shallow and deep water. Look for fish along the shady side.

SUNKEN ISLANDS. Large sunken islands that top out at 10 feet (3 m) or less, with a clean, sand-boulder bottom, irregular shape, and variable depth, make excellent summertime smallmouth habitat.

WEEDY FLATS. Sandgrass, a short, stringy weed that grows in water as deep as 25 feet (7.6 m), is a smallmouth magnet from spring through fall. Cabbage does not grow as deep, but is equally attractive to the fish.

EXTENDED LIPS. Look for smallmouth around the ends of underwater extensions of major points from early summer through fall. In many lakes, these extensions are easy to find because of buoys at their tips.

ROD: 6½- to 7½-foot (2 to 2.1 m) long-handled, medium-heavy to heavy power, fast-action, graphite baitcaster
REEL: high-speed baitcaster
LINE: 14- to 17-pound-test (6.3 to 7.6 kg) low-visibility line
LURE: ¾- to 1-ounce (21 to 28 g) tandem Colorado-blade spinnerbait tipped with a curly-tail grub

How to Call Up Clearwater Smallmouth

A smallmouth that will charge to the surface from deep water to grab bait is obviously in a highly aggressive mood. This level of aggression means you can work a likely spot very quickly. If the fish are going to bite, they'll bite right away, so the idea is to move rapidly and keep hitting new water.

The best strategy is first casting to visible shallow-water cover, such as boulders and weed patches, then casting over the deep water adjacent to them. Simply cast a big tandem-blade spinnerbait as far from the boat as you can and retrieve rapidly so it tracks about a foot or so beneath the surface. Long casts not only increase your coverage, they allow you to reach smallmouth that haven't been spooked by the boat.

You'll need a long, powerful rod for distance casting with such a heavy, wind-resistant bait. For two-handed power casting, choose a rod with an extra-long handle. A 6½-foot (2 m) rod is adequate most of the time, but in a strong wind a 7½-footer (2.1 m) works better. It helps you punch your casts into the wind and quickly take up slack for strong hook sets. A high-speed reel starts the bait moving before it can sink and keeps it riding high in the water.

Despite the clear water, pros normally choose bright colors, because high visibility is the key. Many start with an all-chartreuse model (including the blades) most of the time, but if it's calm and sunny, go with a clear/white body and nickel blades.

If the water is calm and spinnerbaits aren't working as well as you'd like, try a surface bait, such as a Zara Spook. Under low-light conditions, try a black one; other times, a minnow or frog pattern may be the best option. A good-sized bait, about 4½ inches (11 cm) long, works well for big smallmouth, but when the fish are fussy, you may do better with a smaller version.

Cast the bait as far as you can, let it rest motionless for 30 seconds or so, then walk it from side to side. After retrieving about 15 feet (4.5 m), reel in and make another cast. The fish usually strike while the bait is at rest or just after you start to reel.

Another option is a jerkbait. Pros often start with a gold or silver plug with a green back. On a rippled surface, retrieve with rapid sharp jerks to give the bait an erratic action. When the surface is calm, let the lure rest for a few seconds, nudge it a few times, then switch to the fast, jerky retrieve. With jerkbaits choose light line, about 10-pound-test (4.5 kg); heavy line may spook fish in the clear water and it affects the action of the bait.

Work the structure by holding your boat well away from the break (shown) and making long casts over the lip using a spinnerbait. This way, you won't spook bass in the shallows. Then turn around and cast over deep water for suspended bass.

Start reeling even before the bait hits the water. Cruising smallmouth are drawn by the frantic action and often strike immediately.

Retrieve your spinnerbait fast enough to keep it running no more than a foot beneath the surface. Cruising smallmouth are looking up for their food. If you don't get a strike within the first 10 feet (3 m), quickly reel in and cast again.

HOW TO CALL UP SMALLMOUTH WITH A JERKBAIT

Softly nudge the bait a few times after casting and letting the ripples subside. On each nudge, the nose of the bait should dip beneath the surface and the tail should come out of the water. Then rip the bait toward you; the change of speed may draw a strike.

Work the bait with a jerk-and-pause retrieve; vary the pause length until you find a cadence that the fish prefer.

Look for followers; smallmouth tend to chase minnow plugs without striking. Should you spot a fish behind your bait in the clear water, try to trigger a strike by slowing down and twitching the bait gently, so it barely moves ahead yet maintains its depth.

HOW TO CALL UP SMALLMOUTH WITH A ZARA SPOOK

Make a long cast (shown) to reach smallmouth that haven't been spooked by the boat; the fish seem drawn by the big splashdown.

Wait for the ripples to subside before starting the retrieve. This gives any smallmouth in the vicinity time to swim over, inspect the bait, and possibly strike it.

Walk the bait by giving it a series of rapid downward twitches. How hard you twitch determines how far the bait will veer to the side.

Switch to a smaller stickbait, such as a Zara Puppy, when smallmouth are making passes at the bait, but not grabbing it.

THINKING LIGHT FOR CLEARWATER SMALLMOUTH

Small lures have long been considered the standard for clearwater smallmouth. Tiny crankbaits, ⅛-ounce (3.2 g) jigs, 4-inch (10 cm) tubes, and small surface lures account for a high percentage of the catch in these waters. In years past, small in-line spinners would have made this list, but their popularity has waned, especially among tournament anglers.

A small number of pros, however, know that spinners are no less effective today than they were decades ago. They have perfected a light-tackle, spinner-fishing method ideal for catching smallmouth in shallow water and have little competition from other anglers.

These anglers found that spinners outfish other lures, particularly during coolwater periods, assuming the water is fairly clear. Small spinners are most effective because they're about the same size as young-of-the-year baitfish and they can be retrieved very slowly to tempt fish that are not feeding aggressively.

Although developed on clear canyon reservoirs, it has wide application. It's effective in any clear body of water with minimal cover, but is not a good choice for fishing heavy cover because of the bait's exposed treble hook.

Where to Find Smallmouth in Clear Lakes & Reservoirs

Smallmouth fishing in clear lakes and reservoirs peaks in coolwater periods. Beginning in early fall, smallmouth gradually move shallower. When surface temperatures dip into the low 60s (teens C) you'll find them actively feeding at depths of 10 feet (3 m) or less. Prime fall fishing continues until the temperature drops to about 50°F (10°C). There may be a midwinter lull, when smallmouth go deep, but the action resumes in late winter, when temperatures begin to edge above the 50°F mark.

Start looking for fish along rocky main-lake banks and points that slope at a moderate rate into deep water. Avoid sheer cliffs at these times of year. The type of rock is also important. Look for rounded baseball- to basketball-size rocks. They seem to hold more crayfish than the crumbly, jagged-edged shale rock.

One of the prime smallmouth fishing areas during coolwater periods is a sun-drenched rocky bank. Many banks in canyon reservoirs never see the sun this time of year, because it doesn't get high enough to reach them.

OPTIMAL CONDITIONS

TYPE OF WATER: any clear lake or reservoir with sparse cover
SEASON: mid-fall through spring
WATER TEMPERATURE: 55 to 65°F (13 to 15.5°C).
WEATHER: warm and sunny
WATER DEPTH: 3 to 10 feet (0.9 to 3 m)
WATER CLARITY: moderately clear to very clear
TIME OF DAY: late afternoon

Smallmouth remain in these areas through spawning time, then gradually retreat to deeper water with steeper structure, particularly bluff walls.

Not all smallmouth are found along rocky banks. A good share of the population remains at depths of 30 feet (10 m) or more. These fish are much less aggressive and more difficult to catch than those in shallow water, but you can take a few by jigging vertically with a jigging spoon.

How to Fish Small Spinners

Many bass anglers consider spinners, like spinnerbaits, to be "no-brainer" baits; all you do is blindly cast and retrieve. But those who specialize in spinner fishing know there's a lot more to it.

You don't just toss your spinner out and reel it in, you must keep your bait in the fish zone and work it the right way to maximize strikes. Slowing it down and speeding it up when needed will draw strikes from neutral fish.

A ¼-ounce (7 g) spinner is ideal for smallmouth fishing because you can retrieve it slowly and the blade will still spin. A heavier spinner has a bigger blade, so you'd have to retrieve faster to keep the blade turning. Color selection depends mainly on cloud cover and water clarity. A good all-around choice is a spinner with a silver blade and a black-and-yellow body. When skies are sunny and the water clear, try a gold blade and black body. When it's overcast and the water is discolored, a fluorescent-orange or chartreuse blade with a black body may work better.

Casting these light baits is easiest with a slower-action rod and light line. The flexible tip lets the rod do the work so you don't have to "throw" the bait. Snags are not much of a problem, so there is really no need for heavy line.

The best way to keep your bait in the fish zone is to position your boat at the depth you expect the fish to be and cast parallel to the bank.

The retrieve is critical. After making a long cast, allow the bait to sink; how far depends on the water depth. You want the bait close to bottom, but not bumping rocks. Then reel slowly, occasionally stopping to let the spinner sink. This often triggers a strike. Resume your retrieve after the spinner sinks a foot (0.3m) or so.

On sunny days, smallmouth often hug the bank, probably because the water there is slightly warmer than the water a few feet (m) deeper. In this situation, position your boat tight to shore and cast parallel to the bank. Don't be afraid to toss the bait within inches (cm) of shore; that's where most of the fish will be.

EQUIPMENT

ROD: 5½ to 6½ -foot (1.7 to 2 m) light power, slower-action graphite spinning rod
REEL: small spinning reel with smooth drag
LINE: 6-pound-test (2.7 kg)
LURE: ¼-ounce (7 g) in-line spinners

Strikes are usually obvious, but there are times, particularly in fall, when smallmouth tend to grab the bait and swim with it; all you feel is a deadening of the blade action. Whenever the blade stops thumping, set the hook. If a fish strikes and misses, stop your retrieve and let the bait flutter down. Many times, the bass will come back and strike again.

With tackle this light, how you set the hook is important. If you jerk too hard, you'll rip the small treble out of the fish's mouth. Instead, when you feel a strike, just raise the rod and start cranking rapidly. Keep steady tension on the fish and allow it to fight against the arched rod until it tires. Make sure your drag is set fairly loose; this way, you can't horse the fish too much and there's little chance it will break your line.

SPINNER-FISHING TIPS

Cast parallel, rather than perpendicular, to the bank when fishing a steep sloping shoreline. A parallel cast keeps the lure in productive water longer.

Make your own anti-twist spinner by bending the spinner shaft as shown. The bend creates a keel effect, which keeps the bait from spinning.

Look for trenches formed by running water. To find the trenches, look for washes along shore and scan adjacent flats with a depth finder.

Apply a spray-on softener to your line to keep it supple. This reduces coiling, so line flows easily off the spool, improving casting distance.

TOURNAMENT FISHING

Most anglers who fish often have seen a group of fisherman gathered at a lakeside weigh-in or witnessed a bass tournament televised on TV and thought; "I could catch more fish than those guys are bringing in." With all of the tournaments available to fish today there is an event nearly every weekend for most of the year. And for the most part if you show up with the entry fee, you can get in and try your luck. You may find out, however, that "luck" has very little to do with the outcome.

Tournament Fishing Basics

The final weigh-in at a major bass tournament such as the Bass Masters Classic is a spectacular show.

Tournament fishing is not for everyone, but if you're the competitive type, you'll probably enjoy it. Not only will you learn a great deal from experienced tournament anglers, you'll meet new friends and may even win a little money.

But don't get into tournament fishing with the idea of making a career of it; only a very few top pros could make a decent living solely from tournament winnings. Much of their income comes from product endorsements, seminars, and other public appearances.

The best way to get started in tournament fishing is to join a bass-fishing club. Most of them conduct low- or no-entry fee tournaments on close-to-home waters. After you develop confidence in your tournament fishing skills, you may want to consider money tournaments and statewide competitions, which sometimes earn you qualifying points for national events.

There's more to tournament fishing than paying your entry fee and showing up. To be competitive, you'll have to do some research, particularly if the event will be held on an unfamiliar body of water. You need to know locations, depths, cover types, and patterns that have worked well in the past. We'll show you how to gather this crucial information.

Everyone you talk to, from bait shop operators, local anglers, guides, and other tournament entrants, will offer you advice on how to proceed. But the only sure way to collect reliable information is to do some pre-tournament scouting and fishing on your own. We'll give you some tips on making the most of your time.

When formulating your tournament strategy, consider the type of event you're fishing. A single-day tournament, for instance, may require a different strategy than a three-day tournament. We'll provide some recommendations for each popular tournament type.

PRE-TOURNAMENT RESEARCH. Tournament fishermen must learn to analyze information collected from many sources and weigh it in light of what they know about bass behavior in a particular body of water. They put the most stock in first-hand accounts, realizing that hearsay from tackle shop operators, resort owners, and weekend anglers could be outdated and are skeptical of information offered by other tournament entrants, which could be intentionally misleading.

When you enter a tournament, it pays to collect the following information before you begin to practice:

TOURNAMENT RULES. Obtain a copy of the tournament rules and study it before doing your on-the-water research. It may limit pre-tournament fishing dates and prohibit use of some techniques, such as trolling. It may also specify certain areas that are off-limits to fishing, such as fish refuges, private waters, tributaries, and release sites from recent tournaments. If you are unsure of a particular rule, consult the tournament director.

LAKE INFORMATION. Information from local fisheries personnel can be helpful in planning your fishing strategy. Request a contour map or get a map chip for your GPS, which may offer different information. Obtain a copy of the latest lake survey, which usually includes information on gamefish and forage fish populations, water quality, and aquatic vegetation types in different sections of the lake. If there is more than one bass species present, get specifics on which sections of the lake are best for each. Knowing what the predominant forage fish is helpful in selecting baits and planning your fishing strategy. If the lake has pelagic forage, such as shad, the bass tend to move and suspend more than in lakes with non-pelagic forage.

NAVIGATION RULES. Collect information on special waterway regulations, such as slow zones. You can save lots of fishing time by avoiding closed-throttle areas. Be sure to ask how water level affects access to various parts of the lake. State fisheries or reservoir personnel should have this information.

PAST TOURNAMENT RESULTS. Check results of past tournaments held on the same body of water at the same time of year. Assuming that conditions are similar this year, those results can help you determine the most productive depths, general locations, cover types, and the most effective techniques. Past results may be available from tournament organizers or from fishing newspapers or magazines.

Tournament results will also give you an idea of what species of bass is most likely to give you a win and what the winning poundage will be. Knowing this will help you formulate an overall tournament strategy, gauge your pre-tournament fishing success, and determine when you need to change locations or techniques.

CURRENT CONDITIONS. Monitoring weather conditions in the weeks before the tournament helps you determine how the season is progressing. For example, if the tournament is scheduled during what is normally the post-spawn period but the weather has been abnormally cold, spawning will probably be delayed. This means you'll find bass farther back in creek arms or bays than you might have thought.

Before you start practicing, check the present water conditions, including temperature, flow, level, and clarity. Monitor these conditions during practice and tournament fishing. Then, should conditions change, you'll have a better idea of what to do. If the water level drops, for instance, the fish will most likely go deeper; if it rises, they'll move shallower.

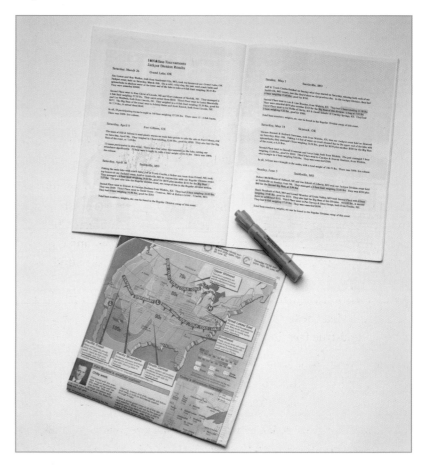

Pre-Tournament Fishing

To have a reasonable chance of cashing a check, you must spend a day or two practice fishing, or "prefishing," as tournament anglers would say. In preparation for major tournaments, some top pros prefish for two weeks or more. You may want to prefish with a friend. This way, you can cover more water in less time and experiment with more presentations.

Prefishing helps you eliminate unproductive water and zero in on the most productive areas. It also helps you determine which techniques are most likely to work in each situation and builds up your confidence so you won't panic and prematurely start switching patterns after the tournament starts.

Another prefishing objective: become familiar enough with the body of water that you can navigate confidently and develop a feel for running times. Begin prefishing in an area known to have a high bass population. It's easiest to establish a successful pattern where there are lots of fish. Later, once you find a good pattern, you can try it in out-of-the-way places that aren't fished as heavily.

When trying to establish a pattern, keep close track of details. If you're fishing submerged timber, for example, note whether most of the fish are holding near the ends of the limbs or close to the trunk and whether they're in the treetops or near the bottom. And try to determine how time of day, water level, and weather, especially cloud cover and wind direction, affect the pattern.

To get a better idea of the exact type of structure and cover the fish are using, note the precise spot where you got a strike, then motor over and examine it. You may find a subtle depth change, a stump, or a clump of weeds that you may not have noticed from a distance. Use this information to help formulate your locational pattern.

It pays to vary your bait choices and retrieve styles when prefishing. Most tournament anglers carry several rods with different baits tied on each. They experiment with different colors, sizes, and types of baits, and different retrieve speeds and tempos, until they find the combination that works best for the location, time of day, and weather conditions. When making bait-choice decisions, do a little research to determine what the locals have been using. It may be hard to improve on tried-and-true favorites.

But don't waste time trying to learn a completely new technique. You won't have enough time to perfect it, so even though it's effective for some anglers, you'll do better by sticking with familiar presentations.

When prefishing, try to identify a number of spots that are likely to produce under different wind and weather conditions. Look for some

"numbers" spots and other big-fish spots. This way, you'll know right where to go should you need several small fish to stay in contention on a slow day or one big one to register a knockout blow.

Never "burn" the fish you want to catch in the tournament. You want to get bites so you know where the fish are and you may want to land a fish or two in each spot so you know how big they are, but you don't want to catch so many fish that you "educate" them. To ensure that you don't catch the fish, bend your hooks closed or cut them off and, instead of setting the hook when you get a strike, just try to jiggle the bait so the fish will drop it.

Keep a notebook describing in detail any productive spots that you find when prefishing. Include sketched maps and landmarks, so you can quickly return to the precise spot at tournament time. It's difficult to re-member all of these details when you're fishing dozens of spots every day.

Tournament Strategies

By the time tournament day arrives, the most difficult part of a tourna-ment fisherman's job is completed. He knows what he has to do—now he must do it.

Your strategy for the day's fishing depends not only on the type of tourna-ment, but also on the overall scope of competition. For instance, you would probably approach a tournament that is part of a total-points annual circuit differently than you would a one-time event. If you're accumulating points, it's important to register a decent weight, even if you don't win, so you should use the numbers philosophy: concentrate on catching as many fish as possible, with the idea that you'll sort out a respectable limit. But in a one-time event, you can go for broke and concentrate on big fish. If you don't catch any, all you've lost is your entry fee.

Another consideration in formulating your strategy is the bass popula-tion itself. If the population is relatively small, the numbers philosophy is best. But if there are lots of bass and most contestants will likely catch a limit, concentrate on big fish. Your strategy will also differ depending on the length of the tournament.

The first thing to do on tournament day is to compare weather and water conditions with those encountered during prefishing. Ideally, conditions will be identical, but this is seldom the case. If conditions are similar, stick with the patterns you found. If not, you'll have to do some adjusting.

Perhaps the most common mistake, particularly among tournament-fishing novices, is to abandon their established patterns too soon. After an hour or so with no fish, they start to panic, so they scrap a proven pattern in favor of an untested one. Had they stuck with the original plan, it probably would have paid off before the day was over.

If the conditions differ from those you faced in practice, use your best judgment to come up with a new pattern. Let's say the weather during prefishing was hot and calm and you were catching bass on topwaters in shallow weedbeds. But on tournament day, you're faced with blustery, cold-front conditions. Don't abandon your pattern completely; make some minor adjustments first. Try slowing down your retrieve a little. Or try fishing with a bait that runs a little deeper.

Pay attention to other tournament boats. If they're moving around a lot, you can bet the bass aren't cooperating. So if you're catching a few fish but are thinking of moving or trying something different, you may want to reconsider.

The most unnerving situation is to find another tournament boat in your prime spot. Should this happen, observe the other anglers closely to determine exactly what cover and structure they're fishing and how they're fishing it. If their pattern is different from yours, you may be able to fish right behind them with good success. Even if it's not, it may be possible to milk a few more fish from the spot by working it more slowly and thoroughly.

Following are descriptions of the most common types of bass tournaments and some specific tips for fishing each type:

TEAM TOURNAMENTS. In this type of tournament, you team up with a partner of your choice. Joint decisions determine tournament strategy, including where to fish and who will run the boat. The combined weight of a team's catch determines its standing.

Here's how you can improve your success in team tournaments:

- Select a partner with whom you're well acquainted; this way, there are no credibility questions and you'll be less hesitant to suggest new strategies. Avoid switching partners for every tournament. If you stick with the same partner, you'll learn to work as a team.

- Assuming both partners are competent anglers, it pays to do your prefishing separately. This way, you can cover more water and improve your team's chances of finding fish.

- The angler running the boat should plan his casts to leave plenty of good casting targets for his partner. Each angler should watch where the other is casting, to avoid covering the same water.

- If there is a shortage of good casting targets, each angler should use a different presentation, including a different retrieve angle.

- When one angler hooks a fish, the other should immediately cast to the same spot in case there's a school in the area.

- When one angler misses a fish, the other should cast to it immediately. The sooner the fish sees another bait, the more likely it is to strike again.

DRAW TOURNAMENTS. Partners are chosen by a drawing. They must make a joint decision on whose boat to use. Each operates the boat for half the day and makes the decision on where to fish during that time. Fish weights are tallied separately for each contestant. Here are some suggestions for fishing draw tournaments:

- Each angler tends to prefer his own spots, but if your spots are far from those of your partner, you'll waste a lot of time running between them. In this case, it pays to compare fishing spots and make a joint determination on whose are most likely to yield a winning weight.

- Don't exaggerate your prefishing success to convince a partner to fish your spots. His may actually be better and you'll both pay the price. You'll also lose the opportunity to learn something from your partner, which is one of the reasons for fishing draw tournaments. If you develop a reputation for embellishing your success, partners will not be truthful with you in future tournaments, making accurate assessment of each other's information impossible.

MULTIPLE-DAY TOURNAMENTS. Both team tournaments and draw tournaments can be multiple-day events. In draw tournaments, you fish with a different partner each day and each angler's weight for each day is tallied for a tournament total. The following hints will boost your success in multiple-day tournaments:

- When prefishing, try to locate a few more spots than you would for a single-day event. The extra fishing days mean that spots are pressured more heavily, so you may not be able to catch as many fish from a single spot.

- Try to develop fall-back patterns when prefishing. With the heavy pressure, anglers soon catch the aggressive fish, but you may be able to take a few more fish from a given spot by using a presentation that's a little different. If most anglers are catching the active fish by bulging spinnerbaits over the weedtops, for instance, try a slightly faster retrieve to make the blade break the surface.

- Work the most popular spots or any small, isolated spots first. By the second day of the tournament, most of the fish in these spots have been caught or at least spooked. Then it helps to have a few less obvious spots as a fall-back.

- Assuming you're in a multiple-day draw tournament, don't hesitate to try your partner's pattern on the first day. You may be able to use it in your own spots on subsequent days.

- Should you catch a quick limit of decent fish on the first day, spend the rest of the day scouting for new spots and bigger fish. This way, other fishermen won't know where you caught your fish and you can use the same strategy the next day without fighting a crowd.

Give your established patterns a chance to work.

ACKNOWLEDGEMENTS

Largemouth Bass:
Cooperating Agencies, Individuals and Manufacturers: Alumacraft Boat Co.; Bagley Bait Company, Inc.; Bass Pro Shops; Blue Fox Tackle Co.; Bomber Bait Co.; Bulldog Lures, Inc.; Bullet Weights, Inc.; Classic Mfg./Culprit Lures; The Coleman Co., Inc.; Larry Dahlberg; Daiwa Corporation; Mister Twister, Inc.; Ditto Products; E-Z Loader Boat Trailers; Gapen's World of Fishing, Inc.; Gray Freshwater Biological Institute; Larry R. Green; R. Douglas Hannon; Hart Tackle Company, Inc.; Hildebrandt Corporation; Hopkins Fishing Lures Company, Inc.; Johnson Fishing, Inc.; Kentucky Dept. of Fish and Wildlife; Bill Lewis Lures; Jim Lindner; Lindy-Little Joe, Inc.; Lowrance Electronics, Inc.; Lucky Strike Mfg., Inc.; Luhr-Jensen & Sons, Inc.; Lunker City; Mann's Bait Co.; Mariner Outboards; Mercury Marine; Jim Moynagh; Normark Corp.; Northland Fishing Tackle; John Oster; Mark Oster; Owner American Corporation; Penn Fishing Tackle Mfg. Co.; Plano Molding Company; Poe's Lure Company; Pradco; Producto Lure Company, Inc.; Ranger Boat Co.; St. Croix Rods; Sheldons', Inc.; Shimano American Corp.; Si-Tex Electronics; Snag Proof Manufacturing, Inc.; Stanley Jigs, Inc.; Strike King Lure Company; Techsonic Industries, Inc.; Tru-Turn, Inc.; Uncle Josh Bait Co.; VMC, Inc.; Yakima Bait Company; Zebco/Motorguide

Smallmouth Bass:
Cooperating Agencies and Individuals: Carter Allen, Arkansas Dept. of Game and Fish; Alumacraft Boat Co. - Bob Hobson, Roger McGregor; Arctic Cat Snowmobiles; B.A.S.S. - Dave Nunley, John Riley, Tommy Thorpe; Larry Belusz, Missouri Dept. of Conservation; Berkley & Company, Inc. - Ben Alspach, Rick Kalsow; Rick Berry; Peter Borque, Main Dept. of Fisheries; Burger Brothers Sporting Goods; California Dept. of Fish and Game - Charles von Geldern, Don Whiteline; Ray Carignan; Glenn Carr, Pro Anglers Inc.; Homer Circle; Dr. Sheryl Coombs, Parmly Hearing Institute; Jack Dallman, Yar-Craft, Inc.; Chuck DeNoto; Lisa Dougherty, Fenwick-Woodstream Corp.; Frankie Dusenka, Frankie's Live Bait; Don Emitt, CarByDon Mfg.; Ferguson-Keller Associates, Inc.; Bill Fletcher, Livingston Boat Dock; Dr. Calvin Fremling, Winona State University; Butch Furtman; Dave Golden, Ontario Outdoors; Mike Grupa, Stearns Manufacturing Co.; Dick Grzywinski; Herrick Enterprises-Wave Wackers; Dave Hughes; Grant and Judy Hughes, Muskego Point Resort; Bill Huntley; The In-Fisherman - Dave Csanda, Doug Stange, Dan Sura; Rick James; Johnson Fishing, Inc.-Minn Kota Trolling Motors; Michael Jones, Stren Fishing Line; Ray Juetten, Michigan Dept. of Natural Resources; Ernie Kilpatrick; Bruce Kirschner, Sage-Winslow Mfg. Corp.; Dr. Weldon Larimore, Illinois Natural History Survey; Fred Leckie, West Virginia Dept. of Natural Resources; Leroy's Minnows; Lindy-Little Joe; Malcolm Lipsey, Morris Ferry Dock; Doug Loehr; Dick McCleskey, New Mexico Dept. of Natural Resources; Mercury Marine/Mariner Outboards - Stan Bular, Jim Kalkofen, Clem Koehler; Dr. Rudolph Miller, Oklahoma State University; Minnesota Dept. of Natural Resources - Gary Barnard, Larry Gates, Gary Grunwald, Mark Heywood, Duane Shodeen; Mister Twister, Inc.; Jim Moore, Lund American, Inc.; Jeff Murray; Tom Neustrom; New York State Dept. of Environmental Conservation - Pat Festa, Bob Lange; Bill Nichols; Terry Niedenfuer, ABW, Inc.; Tony Nigro; Normark Corporation; Ohio Dept. of Natural Resources - Carl Baker, Jim Schoby; Pat Olson; Ontario Ministry of Natural Resources - Terry Hicks, Jim MacLean, Gordon Pyzer, Dr. Richard Ryder, Les Sztramko, Lloyd Thurston; Vaughn Paragamian, Iowa Conservation Commission; Dr. Gile Pauly, University of Washington; Dave Peterson; William Pflieger, Missouri Dept. of Conservation; Floyd Preas; Steve Price; R&R Marine; Mike Radulovich; Nancy Raffeto, University of Wisconsin; Buzz Ramsey, Luhr Jensen and Sons, Inc.; Ed Rezak, Kala Enterprises, Inc.; Jim Rivers; Tom Rodgers, Smallmouth Inc.; Frank Ryck, Missouri Dept. of Conservation; Dan Schuber, Virginia Commission of Game and Inland Fisheries; Bill Scifres, The Indianapolis Star; Si-Tex Marine Electronics, Inc. - Dave Church, Jack Phillips; Thayne Smith, Lowrance Electronics, Inc.; Jack Sokol & Associates, Inc.; Edwin Sox; Howard Steere, Orvis; Stinger Tackle Company; Strike Master, Inc; Suzuki Outboards - Dick Dolan, Frank Wright; Tommy Tenpenny; Texas Parks and Wildlife Dept. - Nick Carter, Phil Durocher; Trilene Fishing Line; Tru-Turn. Inc.; Chuck Tryon, Maxima; Harry Turner, The Outdoorsman; Umpqua Feather Merchants; Dr. James Underhill, University of Minnesota; Vados Live Bait and Tackle; Lou Vogele; Rick Wayne; Billy Westmorland; Bill White; Don Wirth

Advanced Bass:
Contributing Manufacturers: ABU Garcia; Fred Arbogast Company, Inc.; B.A.S.S.; Berkley Inc.; Better Fishing Ways Company; Blakemore Lure Co.; Charlie Brewer's Slider Company, Inc.; Carlson Tackle Company; Daiwa Corporation; Do-It Lure and Sinker Molds; Evinrude Outboards; Fenwick; Fleck Lure Company; Gitzit Inc./Bass'n Man Lures; Granite State Bass Baits; Harrison Hoge Industries, Inc.; Hart Tackle Company, Inc; Hobie Sunglasses; Jerry's Jigs; J-Mac Lures Corp.; Johnson Outboards; Kalin Company; Lake Systems; Luck "E" Strike U.S.A.; Lund Boat Company; Lunker City; Mann's Bait Company; Mercury Marine; Minn Kota Electric Fishing Motors; Mojo Lures; Normark Corporation; Operation Bass; Plano Molding Company; Poe's Lures/Yakima Bait Company; Pradco; Stanley Jigs, Inc.; Storm Manufacturing Company; Stowaway Marine Batteries; Stratos Boats, Inc.; Strike King Lure Company; Uncle Josh Bait Company; VMC Inc.; Gary Yamamoto Custom Baits; Zoomer Products Cooperating Agencies and Individuals: Apache Lake Marina and Resort; Arizona Game and Fish Dept. – Jim Warnecke; Arizona Office of Tourism; British Columbia Ministry of Environment, Lands and Parks – Peter Newroth; California Dept. of Fish and Game – Jim Adams, Dennis Fiedler; Terry Foreman, Dennis Lee, Dwayne Maxwell, Ivan Paulsen, Steve Taylor; Comfort Inn; Dan Foote; John Hale; Homer Humphreys; Robert Jenkins; Keith Kline; David Klossner; Katherine Landing; Los Angeles County Dept. of Parks and Recreation – Brian Roney; Minnesota Dept. of Natural Resources – Chip Welling; Bill Murphy; New Hampshire Fish and Game Dept.; Oak Ridge Resort; Pauls Valley Chamber of Commerce; Rayburn Country Resort; Roosevelt Lake Resort; Bill Ross; City of San Diego Dept. of Water Utilities – Larry Bottroff, Jim Brown; Silver Sands Motel; Texas Parks and Wildlife Dept. – David Campbell, Barry Lyons; Joe Thrun; Western Outdoor News – Bud Neville, Bill Rice

2008 Photography:
Bill Lindner Photography © pages 64, 66, 68, 78, 84, 94, 139, 144, 205, 232, 257, 270, 300, 311, 314, 371
Eric Engbretson Photography © pages 4, 33, 127, 142, 154, 173, 182, 289
Istock Photo © 62, 145, 213
Robert Michelson Photography © page 174 (lower left)

INDEX

Creative Publishing international
Your Complete Source of How-to Information for the Outdoors

HUNTING BOOKS
- 500 Deer Hunting Tips
- Advanced Whitetail Hunting
- Beginner's Guide to Birdwatching
- Black Bear Hunting
- Bowhunting Equipment & Skills
- Bowhunter's Guide to Accurate Shooting
- The Complete Guide to Hunting
- Dog Training
- How to Think Like a Survivor
- Muzzleloading
- Outdoor Guide to Using Your GPS
- Ultimate Elk Hunting
- Waterfowl Hunting
- Whitetail Addicts Manual
- Whitetail Hunting
- Whitetail Techniques & Tactics
- Wild Turkey

FISHING BOOKS
- Advanced Bass Fishing
- The Art of Freshwater Fishing
- The Complete Guide to Freshwater Fishing
- Fishing for Catfish
- Fishing Tips & Tricks
- Fishing with Artificial Lures
- Inshore Salt Water Fishing
- Kids Gone Campin'
- Kids Gone Fishin'
- Kids Gone Paddlin'
- Largemouth Bass
- Live Bait Fishing
- Modern Methods of Ice Fishing
- Northern Pike & Muskie
- Panfish
- Salt Water Fishing Tactics
- Smallmouth Bass
- Striped Bass Fishing: Salt Water Strategies
- Successful Walleye Fishing
- Trout: The Complete Guide
- Ultralight Fishing

FLY FISHING BOOKS
- The Art of Fly Tying (incl. CD-ROM)
- Complete Photo Guide to Fly Fishing
- Complete Photo Guide to Fly Tying
- Fishing Dry Flies
- Fly-Fishing Equipment & Skills
- Fly Fishing for Beginners
- Fly Fishing for Trout in Streams
- Fly-Tying Techniques & Patterns

COOKBOOKS
- All-Time Favorite Game Bird Recipes
- America's Favorite Fish Recipes
- America's Favorite Wild Game Recipes
- Backyard Grilling
- Cooking Wild in Kate's Kitchen
- Dressing & Cooking Wild Game
- The New Cleaning & Cooking Fish
- Preparing Fish & Wild Game
- The Saltwater Cookbook
- Venison Cookery
- The Wild Butcher
- The Wild Fish Cookbook
- The Wild Game Cookbook

To purchase these or other Creative Publishing international titles,
contact your local bookseller, or visit our website at
www.creativepub.com

The Complete
FLY FISHERMAN™